BLACKSTONE'S GUIDE TO

The Mental Capacity Act 2005

Peter Bartlett

*Nottinghamshire Healthcare NHS Trust Professor of Mental Health Law,
School of Law, University of Nottingham*

OXFORD
UNIVERSITY PRESS

OXFORD
UNIVERSITY PRESS

Great Clarendon Street, Oxford OX2 6DP

Oxford University Press is a department of the University of Oxford.
It furthers the University's objective of excellence in research, scholarship,
and education by publishing worldwide in

Oxford New York

Auckland Cape Town Dar es Salaam Hong Kong Karachi
Kuala Lumpur Madrid Melbourne Mexico City Nairobi
New Delhi Shanghai Taipei Toronto

With offices in

Argentina Austria Brazil Chile Czech Republic France Greece
Guatemala Hungary Italy Japan Poland Portugal Singapore
South Korea Switzerland Thailand Turkey Ukraine Vietnam

Oxford is a registered trade mark of Oxford University Press
in the UK and in certain other countries

Published in the United States
by Oxford University Press Inc., New York

First published 2005

British Library Cataloguing in Publication Data
Data available

Library of Congress Cataloging in Publication Data
Data available

Typeset by RefineCatch Limited, Bungay, Suffolk
Printed in Great Britain
on acid-free paper by
Biddles Ltd., King's Lynn

ISBN 0–19–928903–4   978–0–19–928903–5

1 3 5 7 9 10 8 6 4 2

Contents—Summary

Contents

Contents

Preface

After a gestation period of some sixteen years, the Mental Capacity Act 2005 is at last on the statute books. Training sessions are in full swing for doctors, lawyers, patient rights advocates, and others involved professionally with people lacking or of marginal capacity in anticipation of the Act coming into force, probably in 2007. A wide variety of professional and lay carers need to understand how the Act differs from the previous law, what it contains, and the theoretical and practical problems that may arise in its implementation. There is in consequence a clear need for a work that explains the Act, and how it fits into the existing landscape of legal, medical and social care provision. This book is intended to fulfil that role.

At the same time, while the Act is now law, it must be acknowledged that there is a good deal more law and regulation related to the Act to come. This is likely to dribble into the public realm in a piecemeal fashion between now and the Act coming into force. For the information of the reader, a list of pending supplementary material is contained at the end of this preface. The current volume alerts the reader to this pending material as it arises in the text, and suggestions are made as to what issues of relevance it may contain. Nonetheless, we will not know what this material actually contains until it is published. Readers may wish occasionally to check the web sites of the Department of Constitutional Affairs, the Department of Health, the Office of the Public Guardian and other relevant bodies regarding this material.

There have been developments in the few weeks since the text was completed. First, the government has stated that notwithstanding the largely critical report of the Joint Scrutiny Committee of the House of Commons and House of Lords on the Mental Health Bill (see para 2.06), it will press on with mental health reform.[1] A new bill has not yet been published however, so the precise content of the reforms remains a matter of speculation.

At the time this volume was written, three cases were pending appeal: *R (on the application of Munjaz) v Mersey Care NHS Trust and Others*,[2] *R (on the application of MH) v Secretary of State for Health*,[3] and *R (on the application of Burke) v GMC*.[4] The first of these has been heard by the House of Lords, but as of the day this book goes to press, the decision is still pending. Nonetheless, it can be

---

[1] Department of Health, 'Government response to the report of the Joint Committee on the draft Mental Health Bill 2004', sess 2004–5, Cm 6624, HL 79/HC 95.

[2] [2003] EWCA Civ 1036, [2004] QB 395.

[3] [2004] EWCA Civ 1609.

[4] [2004] EWHC 1879, [2005] 2 WLR 431.

expected reasonably soon. *MH* has not yet been argued before the House of Lords, and will therefore not appear imminently.

The Court of Appeal decision in the *Burke* case[5] came down after the bulk of this book was typeset, and indeed the day before the author expected to return the page proofs to the publisher. The practicalities of publishing do not allow for a substantial revision of the text at this stage, but certainly paragraphs 2.101, 3.20, and 3.22 will have to be read with a view to the Court of Appeal decision. More difficult to assess is the broader relevance of the case. The publication schedule for this book and the constraints of space in a preface do not allow for a detailed and considered response, but some comments may assist the reader.

Mr Burke suffers from a degenerative condition. At some point in the future, he is likely to lose the ability to communicate, although not his ability otherwise to experience the world and not his mental faculties at least until very late in the progress of his condition. He was concerned that when he was unable to nourish himself, he would be provided with artificial nutrition and hydration (ANH), and he was concerned that the relevant guidance of the General Medical Council (GMC) might prevent that from occurring as he neared the end of his life. In the order under appeal, the trial court held that the withdrawal of ANH in these circumstances would be a violation of the European Convention on Human Rights (ECHR), and that the GMC guidance was incompatible with the ECHR and domestic law. Usually, as discussed in paragraphs 1.25, 2.101 and 3.20, a patient can decide while capable that a treatment would not be performed on him or her when incapable, but could not insist on the provision of treatment that a doctor was unwilling to perform. After the trial decision in *Burke*, ANH appeared to be an odd case where such a competent patient could insist that the treatment would be performed when he or she had lost capacity.

The Court of Appeal held instead that the whole case was premature, as Mr Burke did not lack capacity and would not lose capacity for some time. It held that the trial court should not have considered the case in what it viewed to be a speculative factual situation, and the appeal was therefore allowed. That would theoretically have been enough to dispose of the appeal. The trial judge had however written a weighty, broad and provocative judgment to which the Court of Appeal felt obliged to respond. There is a resulting paradox. While the Court of Appeal criticised the trial judge for making sweeping legal determinations in the absence of a suitable and defined factual context, their response to those determinations suffers from the same criticism. Indeed, for purposes of the present volume, their decision was in some ways broader than that of the trial judge. A warning is therefore appropriate: it is at best unclear how far the finer points in the Court's judgment were argued specifically before it, and therefore how secure the nuances in the judgment may be in the future.

---

[5] [2005] EWCA 1003.

To begin with what is clear, the Court of Appeal holds that the patient cannot demand ANH or any other treatment. ANH is not an exception to the general rule in this regard. When a duty to provide such treatment exists, it is not based in the patient's demanding the treatment but in some other law.[6] It was however a common law duty on doctors to offer appropriate care to promote the health and life of their patients, and that duty extended to the provision of ANH when it would serve that end. Mr Burke's wishes underscored that duty; they did not create it. ANH had to be provided if a failure to do so would result in a deliberate termination of the patient's life. Such a failure would constitute murder.[7] While not expressly relevant to the discussion in the current volume, the Court of Appeal also found little to fault in the GMC guidance regarding the provision and withdrawal of ANH.

That is the core of the judgment, but other aspects are relevant to the discussion in this volume. In paragraph 29, the Court makes the following statement regarding best interests:

It seems to us that it is best to confine the use of the phrase 'best interests' to an objective test, which is of most use when considering the duty owed to a patient who is not competent and is easiest to apply when confined to a situation where the relevant interests are purely medical.

In this light, the Court notes that best interests may be at odds with the wishes of the patient. It states that the reliance of the trial judge on the 'balance sheet' approach[8] is unhelpful, as that approach 'owes much to cases involving compulsory sterilisation of incompetent patients'.[9]

These views are somewhat startling. The direction of recent jurisprudence in the High Court and the Court of Appeal alike has been to expand the range of factors relevant to determining best interests outside the purely medical, and to apply it to personal care decisions generally.[10] The Court appears to be casting doubt on the appropriateness of those developments. Indeed, the Court may appear to be suggesting a different legal analysis of best interests based on the type of medical treatment—sterilisation versus ANH—and insofar as that is the case, the view is unprecedented.[11] While the discussion below will be critical

---

[6] [2005] EWCA 1003, para 31, 50, 59.

[7] [2005] EWCA 1003, para 34, 53.

[8] This approach is discussed in this volume at para 1.36–40.

[9] [2005] EWCA 1003, para 29.

[10] See paragraphs 1.16–19, 1.37 below.

[11] It is not entirely clear whether this is the distinction the Court wishes to draw. The other possibility is that the distinction is between an individual who lacks capacity at the time of the hearing—the sterilisation cases—and one who has capacity at the time of the hearing—Burke. This is also problematic, however, as the issue is in both cases the best interests when the treatment occurs of an individual who will lack capacity at that time. The thrust of the Court's view of best interests is otherwise to press for an objective approach, limiting the relevance of the patient's views to the best interests determination. It is therefore not obvious why the capacity of the individual at the time of the hearing would fundamentally alter the determination of best interests.

of some of the previous jurisprudential development, it would be astonishing to see it unwound or fundamentally altered without reference to the prior case law.

The *Burke* case was heard under the common law, but in a book devoted to the Mental Capacity Act 2005, it is important to emphasise that the direction of the Court here is not consistent with the statute. As discussed in paragraphs 2.31–48 and *passim*, the Act anticipates that best interests as defined in s 4 will govern all decisions relating to personal care or estate management of persons lacking capacity. The sole exception is advance decisions to refuse medical treatment: see para 2.3 and 2.101–122. Further, consideration of the current incapable and past capable wishes, feelings, beliefs and values are a required part of the determination of best interests under the Act. While the Act does allow other factors in that determination as well, the court's objective view of best interests cannot convincingly be imposed on the statutory language.

The Court of Appeal's overall tone also seems less expansive than is evident in other recent common law relating to the powers of the court in cases of incapacity at common law. The courts had been developing a new jurisdiction to make pronouncements as to what would be in the best interests of persons lacking capacity: see paragraphs 1.11–26 herein, and particularly paragraph 1.19 where the legal status of these orders is questioned. The Court of Appeal in *Burke* appears to offer a more restricted view of these orders than is contained in the recent jurisprudence, pointing out that the court cannot by declaration make something legal or illegal; that is instead a function of other branches of criminal or civil law.[12] However convincing this argument may be, the restrictive view of the court's jurisdiction is in contradiction to a variety of cases in the High Court and Court of Appeal cited below in chapter 1. It would once again be surprising to see these overruled without comment.

For all these reasons, while *Burke* is clearly an important case, it remains to be seen how far it is actually applied.

Pending Legislative Changes

- Mental Health: an entire new Act is expected in this parliament.
- Relating to *HL v UK* (the *Bournewood* case): amendments, probably to the Mental Capacity Act 2005, are required relating to informal admissions to hospitals, care homes and the like of persons lacking capacity to decide to admit themselves. See discussion at paragraphs 1.21–23 below.

Pending Secondary Legislation, Guidance, etc.

- Code of Practice to Mental Capacity Act 2005. To be issued by the Lord Chancellor. A draft has been published, but this was created with reference to

---

[12] [2005] EWCA 1003, para 71.

Bill 120 in parliamentary session 2003–4. While this bill was largely in accord with the Act as eventually passed, there were changes late in the legislative process not reflected in the draft code. The draft is available online at http://www.dca.gov.uk/menincap/mcbdraftcode.pdf.

- Guidance to donors and donees of Lasting Powers of Attorney to be published by the Public Guardian.
- Regulations regarding Lasting Powers of Attorney to be published by the Lord Chancellor.
- Court of Protection Rules to be promulgated by the Court.
- Guidance regarding appointment of individuals to be consulted regarding participation of persons lacking capacity in research to be published by Department of Health.
- Rules regarding advocacy for persons lacking capacity, including the rules defining the precise role of advocates, to be published by Department of Health.
- Regulations regarding use or storage of human tissue of a person lacking capacity, when there is no prior capable consent or refusal to that use or storage, to be published by the Secretary of State for Health.

Peter Bartlett
2 August 2005

Acknowledgements

Inevitably, authors of works such as this benefit by consultations with colleagues. In this regard, I would wish to thank Dr Rob Cryer, with whom I had a spirited discussion of the criminal law as it applies to the destruction or concealment of advance decisions to refuse treatment, and Professor Jean McHale, who provided comments on the section relating to research on people lacking capacity. I also thank Annabel Moss, my editor at OUP, and Kathryn Swift, my copy editor.

My object in writing this guide was to make it accessible to academics, practitioners, and people without legal background. Particularly with the final category of reader in mind, my partner Rick Savage kindly read a draft and provided extensive comments. Those comments were very useful indeed. With his fiftieth birthday pending, it seems right to dedicate this book to him—Happy Birthday.

Table of Abbreviations

D	Person making a decision on behalf of a person lacking capacity
DCOP	Draft Code of Practice to the Mental Capacity Act 2005, published by the Department of Constitutional Affairs (2004)
ECHR	European Convention for the Protection of Human Rights and Fundamental Freedoms
ECtHR	European Court of Human Rights
EPAA	Enduring Powers of Attorney Act 1985
LPOA	Lasting Power of Attorney (see Mental Capacity Act 2005, ss 9–14)
MCA	Mental Capacity Act 2005
P	Person who lacks capacity, or (in some contexts) is thought to lack capacity
REC	Research Ethics Committee, as established by the Department of Health, *Research Governance Framework for Health and Social Care*, 2nd edn (2005)

Table of Cases

References are to Paragraph Numbers

Tables of Legislation

References are to Paragraph Numbers

1

THE LEGISLATIVE HISTORY AND THE ROLE OF THE COMMON LAW

A. THE DEMISE OF *PARENS PATRIAE* AND THE LEGAL LACUNA

For much of English history, the care of persons lacking capacity was governed **1.01**
by the *parens patriae* jurisdiction of the Crown, one of the Royal Prerogative
powers. That was certainly the case by the fourteenth century, when the power
was codified.[1] In modern times, this *parens patriae* power was generally
delegated to Chancery judges. By the end of the mid-twentieth century, it
had become subject to an array of statutes. In 1957, the Percy Commission[2]
recommended placing the entire jurisdiction on a statutory footing, and its
recommendations were implemented by the Mental Health Act 1959. Since
then, the *parens patriae* power as such has ceased to exist for adults lacking
capacity.

1. Estate-related Matters

For matters relating to property and affairs, the 1959 Act created the 'Court of **1.02**
Protection', less a formal court than an office within the Supreme Court under
the jurisdiction of a Master. In substantive terms, the 1959 Act changed little for
estate-related matters. The threshold standards remained flexible, requiring only

---

[1] *De Prerogativa Regis* (1324) 17 Edw II, Stat I, esp c ix, x.
[2] *Report of the Royal Commission on the Law Relating to Mental Illness and Mental Deficiency
1954–1957* (the Percy Report), Cmnd 169 (1957).

that the individual, based on medical evidence, be incapable by reason of mental disorder of managing and administering his property and affairs. If that standard was met, the court took control of the property, depriving the individual of the legal authority to contract.[3] Normally the court appointed a receiver, often a family member, to handle the day-to-day administration of the estate. In law, the court was in control of the estate, and the receiver was required to account to the court.

1.03   These provisions of the 1959 Act were carried over into Part VII the Mental Health Act 1983.

1.04   While this process was considerably less formal than most court applications, it was regarded as unduly intrusive in what was otherwise thought to be a family matter. Furthermore, it had no flexibility: in law, the appointment of the Court of Protection deprived the individual of all powers over his or her estate, even if he or she may still have had some limited areas of capacity. Partly to rectify these difficulties, the Enduring Powers of Attorney Act 1985 (hereinafter EPAA) was passed. Prior to the EPAA, powers of attorney lapsed with the incapacity of the donor.[4] The EPAA allowed powers to continue in effect after the donor became incapable, if the power of attorney so provided. Further, it allowed powers to take effect only upon the individual losing capacity. The holder of an enduring power of attorney was required to register it with the Court of Protection when the individual was losing capacity. This required serving the donor and prescribed family members with notice prior to registration, but providing there was no objection from any of these people, formalities of registration were minimal.

1.05   The enduring power of attorney for the first time allowed people themselves, rather than the court, to designate who would control their affairs. Involvement of the court in overseeing the powers following registration was minimal.[5] Nonetheless, they remained powers of attorney; they did not remove any legal power from the donor, even when that individual lacked capacity. This had the advantage that donors with partial capacity could still exercise their autonomy in the areas of their capacity. Enduring powers of attorney affected estate matters only, however; they could not extend to personal decisions.

2. Personal Decisions

1.06   The provisions of the Mental Health Act 1959 relating to estates were in many ways similar to the provisions of the old *parens patriae* powers. The same cannot be said of personal decision-making, which became subject to an entirely new approach. The 1959 Act superseded not only the statutes relating to the Royal Prerogative, but also the Mental Deficiency Acts 1913, 1926 and 1939, the

---

[3] *Re Walker* [1905] 1 Ch 160; *Re Beaney (deceased)* [1978] 2 All ER 595, 600.
[4] *Drew v Nunn* (1879) 4 QB 661.
[5] *Re R (Enduring Power of Attorney)* [1990] 1 Ch 647.

Lunacy Act 1890, the Mental Treatment Act 1930, and related mental health legislation. No general authority defined in terms similar to incapacity was created relating to personal decisions. The most closely analogous mechanism was guardianship, but that was not phrased in terms of incapacity. Rather, it required the individual to be suffering from one of four specific types of mental disorder: mental illness, 'subnormality', 'severe subnormality' or psychopathy. The last three of these were in turn subject to further definition, with subnormality and severe subnormality requiring 'arrested or incomplete development of mind'. Subnormality further had to be treatable through medicine or 'training', and severe subnormality had to render the individual incapable of independent living or open to exploitation.[6] These definitions would already have been difficult to apply, for example, to adults with intellectual difficulties following a stroke, as their impairment would not stem from arrested or incomplete development. The other substantive criteria were minimal: the individual's disorder had to be of a nature or degree warranting reception into guardianship; and such reception had to be in the interests of the welfare of the individual or the protection of others. The legal status of personal decisions for incapable people not fitting the guardianship criteria under the 1959 Act must have been dubious, although it does not appear to have attracted litigation.

The Mental Health Act 1983 altered guardianship in several ways. First, **1.07** cosmetically, it altered the language from 'subnormality' and 'severe subnormality' to 'mental impairment', and 'severe mental impairment'. Secondly, while maintaining the 1959 Act 'arrested or incomplete development of mind' criteria, it altered the definition of these conditions by requiring 'abnormally aggressive or seriously irresponsible conduct'.[7] Recent case law has taken these new restrictions remarkably seriously, holding, for example, that the desire of an incapable adult to return to the family home did not meet this threshold, even if allegations were true that the standards of hygiene in the home were manifestly inadequate and she suffered sexual exploitation there.[8]

Thirdly, and perhaps most significantly, the 1983 Act limited the powers of a **1.08** guardian. Under the 1959 Act, the guardian had the powers of a parent over a fourteen-year-old child. Under the 1983 Act, these powers were reduced to the power to require the patient to reside at a specific place (but not a power to have the patient returned there, or to confine him or her there); the power to require the patient to attend at a place for treatment (but not to consent to treatment on the patient's behalf); and the power to require access to the patient to be given to various persons such as doctors or social workers. Outside these decisions, it was at best unclear who, if anyone, could make personal decisions on behalf of adults lacking capacity. Such decisions were clearly being made, but in a legal vacuum, and so the common law was called in to fill the lacuna.

---

[6] Mental Health Act 1959, s 4.
[7] Mental Health Act 1983, s 1(2).
[8] *Re F (Mental Health Act: Guardianship)* [2000] 1 FLR 192.

B. THE DEVELOPMENT OF THE COMMON LAW

1.09 The creative use of common law in response to the gap in statutory provision over the last fifteen years has been astonishing. While it is difficult to criticize the motives of those concerned and their desire to craft a pragmatic solution to the statutory difficulties discussed above, the development has been doctrinally unsatisfactory. At issue have been the questions of how incapacity was to be defined, what legal jurisdiction existed to make decisions on behalf of persons lacking capacity and who could exercise it; and how the best interests of the person lacking capacity were to be determined.

1.10 An understanding of these issues is relevant to the Mental Capacity Act 2005 (hereinafter MCA) for two reasons. First, nothing in the 2005 Act expressly overrules the common law. While some must be taken to have been overruled by implication, the remainder will continue in effect. Most of the developments in the common law occurred after the Law Commission had published recommend-ations for codification of the law in this area;[9] at the time, however, legislative reform remained uncertain. It seemed likely that common law remedies would be the only way forward for some time to come. Although that may have appeared necessary at the time, it is now fair to ask whether it is appropriate to continue with these measures. Secondly, the courts will almost certainly look to the common law as they seek for interpretative aids to the new statute. Con-sequently, the question becomes to what extent the common law can serve to guide development of the MCA.

1. A New Jurisdiction?

1.11 The problem of the legislative gap first attracted the court's attention in *Re F (Mental Patient: Sterilization)* in 1989.[10] At issue was a sterilization operation for an adult woman lacking capacity. The immediate practical problems were who, if anyone, could consent to the operation and whether a sterilization for contraceptive purposes would be in the best interests of the woman in question. The legal question was thus whether doctors performing the surgery would be guilty of a crime or liable in tort for battery.

1.12 The House of Lords addressed the issue by expanding the doctrine of necessity. It held that treatment of a person unable to consent owing to incapacity would not incur liability providing the treatment was in the best interests of the incapacitated person. No further consent was required. The procedural mechanism used to reach this result was the court's declaratory

---

[9] Law Com Report No 231, *Mental Incapacity* (February 1995), available at <http://www.lawcom.gov.uk>, accessed 20 June 2005. Previous consultation papers are noted at nn 59–63 below.

[10] *F v West Berkshire Health Authority* sub nom *Re F (Mental Patient: Sterilization)* [1990] 2 AC 1.

jurisdiction, that is, the general authority of the court to make determinations of the rights of parties. Since *Re F*, there has been an expansion to the wording of the scope of the relevant Civil Procedure Rule taking it beyond 'rights' narrowly construed,[11] but the jurisdictional approach is generally the same. The declaratory procedure creates no new substantive jurisdiction for the court; it only allows declarations of law found elsewhere. The declaration in *Re F*, for example, related to the law of tort and crime.

This approach is not without its limitations. In a purely legal sense, the court's **1.13** decision means nothing. The proposed surgery in *Re F* was not made legal by the decision; legality was dependent upon the surgery being in F's best interests. While the House of Lords has stated that an application ought to be made in cases of non-therapeutic sterilization and for the termination of treatment for persons in a permanent vegetative state,[12] it would seem that the court has no mechanism to enforce this, and the judgment itself does nothing *per se* to affect the legality of even these treatments.[13] The judicial decision was in that sense little more than a security blanket.

Even as a security blanket, it has its problems, as it does not bind the patient **1.14** unless the patient is a party.[14] It is now standard practice to make the patient a party,[15] but from a patient rights perspective, this approach is odd. The patient's participation after all may in some cases be merely symbolic. If the patient's incapacity is caused by unconsciousness, to pick a clear example, it is fair to ask what meaningful role the patient will have in a hearing as to whether that decision will be taken. Adults lacking capacity are often represented by the Official Solicitor. Such representation is of course desirable, but in cases of urgency, the ability of the Official Solicitor to assess the situation will be severely limited, circumscribing the meaningfulness of the representation provided. In any event, the logic of the rule that parties will be bound by decisions lies in the notion that they will have had a chance to contest the merits. When the patient's incapacity is such that he or she is unable to engage with the hearing, even if represented by the Official Solicitor, it is difficult to see that this premise is met. This is a problem that hovers over incapacity law. What happens if an individual who regains capacity can point to factors not made known to the court that might well have affected the court's decision? Is the individual precluded from legal action?

More recent cases draw the court's jurisdiction into new territory in two ways. **1.15**

---

[11] See CPR, r 40.20.

[12] See *Re F* [1990] 2 AC 1 for sterilizations; *Airedale NHS Trust v Bland* [1993] AC 789 for permanent vegetative states. See also *Practice Note (Family Div: Incapacitated Adults)* [2002] 1 WLR 325.

[13] *Re F (Mental Patient: Sterilization)* [1990] 2 AC 1, 63–65, 80–83.

[14] *Re F (Mental Patient: Sterilization)* [1990] 2 AC 1, 64, 81–2; *St George's Healthcare NHS Trust v S* [1998] 3 All ER 673, 698.

[15] *St George's Healthcare NHS Trust v S* [1998] 3 All ER 673, 703; *Practice Note (Family Div: Incapacitated Adults)* [2002] 1 WLR 325.

First, as has already been noted, the declaratory jurisdiction proper is parasitic on existing law: it allows, for example, a declaration as to whether a proposed action would be tortious. Recent cases appear to expand this into a new substantive jurisdiction of the court to make declarations in the best interests of an individual lacking capacity without reference to such law: the jurisdiction has apparently ceased to be parasitic, and acquired its own substantive realm. Secondly, courts have begun to involve third parties, typically family members, into the decision-making process in a formal way.

1.16   The first of these flows from a dubious interpretation of *Re S (Hospital Patient: Court's Jurisdiction)*.[16] That case involved a dispute between the estranged wife and the current common law partner of a man who had suffered a stroke. The overarching question was where the man would live, and the specific issue in the hearing was whether the common law partner had sufficient interest in the matter to be accorded standing. The Court of Appeal held that she did, on the basis that 'in cases of controversy and cases involving momentous and irrevocable decisions, the courts have treated as justiciable any genuine question as to what the best interests of a patient require or justify'.[17]

1.17   This was taken in *Re TF (An Adult: Residence)*[18] as authority for the proposition that the courts had a near-unfettered authority to make declarations in the best interests of persons lacking capacity.[19] While Butler-Sloss P acknowledged that *Re S (Hospital Patient: Court's Jurisdiction)* was on its face about standing, she held that 'the underlying issue, recognised by counsel and by this court, was the best interests of S'.[20] She further stated that the substantive question of S's future residence was the focus of the decision when S's case was remitted to the trial court for determination on the merits. This is not clear. In fact, the published version of the case she cited appears to be concerned with conflict of laws questions.[21]

1.18   Such a broad reading goes a long way toward reintroducing a system akin to *parens patriae*. Butler-Sloss P addressed this by asking whether the statutory scheme under the Mental Health Act 1959 was intended to oust the common law of necessity. She held that it did not.[22] The Mental Health Act was not a complete code, and the 1959 Act was held not to be intended to cover all eventualities. Certainly, there is jurisprudential support for the notion that the

---

[16] [1996] Fam 1, CA.

[17] [1996] Fam 1, 18.

[18] [2000] 1 MHLR 120.

[19] See also *Re S (Adult Patient) (Inherent Jurisdiction: Family Life)* [2002] EWHC 2278, [2003] 1 FLR 292, where Munby LJ states at [50], 'The court has jurisdiction to grant whatever relief in declaratory form is necessary to safeguard and promote the incapable adult's welfare and interests.'

[20] [2000] 1 MHLR 120 at [29].

[21] [1996] Fam 23.

[22] [2000] 1 MHLR 120 at [26]–[27]. The concurring judgments of Thorpe LJ and Sedley LJ have similar conceptual problems.

Mental Health Act is not a complete code,[23] but the suggestion that it intended to leave common law remedies for situations such as that of TF is problematic. TF had a developmental disorder, and prior to 1959, she would almost certainly have been under the jurisdiction of the Mental Deficiency Acts. The Percy Commission reported that on 31 December 1954, 76,987 people, of whom 59,221 were over the age of 16, were receiving care in the community under the Mental Deficiency Acts.[24] The number of people who were under voluntary or statutory supervision or guardianship in 1955 was 79,300.[25] Whether or not the Percy Commission would have understood the Mental Health Act as a complete code, it beggars belief to suggest that its intent was to remove these people from statutory provision to the common law, without troubling to mention it.

In any event, the difficulty with expanding the declaratory jurisdiction into **1.19** broad questions of best interests is that it is unclear what power the court is purporting to exercise. If the question is whether specified conduct will be tortious, it is clear what the court is declaring; but what at common law is the legal effect of a decision merely that a course of conduct is in the best interests of a person lacking capacity? If an individual does not abide by the court's decision, where is the illegality? It cannot be that a general decision-making authority has been violated; that authority was provided only under *parens patriae*, and that authority is gone. Is a cause of action created between the incapacitated person and the person not following the court's order? If so, a new tort is created, and there is no suggestion that the court wishes to proceed in that direction. If not, is the individual in contempt of court? If so, a criminal sanction would be being used to enforce a court order enforcing a non-legal norm. If not, then the court order becomes unenforceable.

In *Re S (Adult Patient) (Inherent Jurisdiction: Family Life)*,[26] the court went **1.20** yet another step back towards the *parens patriae* framework by holding that it can appoint a surrogate decision-maker for a person lacking capacity. That decision has its basis from the more specific decision in *Re R (Adult: Medical Treatment)*,[27] where the court held that a decision by a physician to withhold treatment could be made if and only if one of the patient's parents consented. It is difficult to see that this is a coherent position. Under *Re F*, a defence in crime and tort exists if treatment is in the best interests of the patient. Best interests is a question of fact: either the cessation of treatment is in the best interests of the patient, in which case a defence must lie; or it is not, in which case a defence cannot lie. Either way, while the views of the parents may provide relevant

[23] *R v Kirklees MBC, ex p C* [1993] 2 FLR 187.
[24] *Report of the Royal Commission on the Law Relating to Mental Illness and Mental Deficiency 1954–1957* (the Percy Report), Cmnd 169 (1957), table 10a. An additional 58,119 people were receiving institutional care under these Acts.
[25] Percy Report (n 24 above) table 15.
[26] [2002] EWHC 2278, [2003] 1 FLR 292.
[27] [1996] 2 FLR 99; cf. criticism by Ian Kennedy in his note on the case at (1997) 5 *Medical Law Review* 104, 108.

information, their formal consent is not relevant. Indeed, in *Re F*, Lord Goff made it clear that it was merely good practice to consult close family of the patient; it was not a legal necessity.[28] Following the case of *Re S* in 1996, the family could be parties to any subsequent declaration proceedings. There would therefore be nothing objectionable in requiring the family to be given notice prior to the cessation of treatment, allowing them to return to court if they thought it appropriate; but that is quite different to requiring their consent. Expanding the scope of the substitute decision-maker's authority to all personal decisions (as in *Re S*) rather than just consent to treatment (in *Re R*) does not solve this problem: necessity attaches as a defence to the person who would otherwise be civilly or criminally liable.

1.21   In the view of the common law courts, the declaratory jurisdiction can make considerable intrusions into the liberty of the individual. In *Norfolk and Norwich Healthcare (NHS) Trust v W*,[29] it was held that where medical treatment was in the best interests of the adult lacking capacity, reasonable force could be used to effect the treatment. A more expansive view was taken by Sedley LJ in *Re TF (Adult: Residence)*:

> If returning to her mother is in truth a source of danger to her, I agree that, absent any statutory inhibition, the court may, by declaring what is in T's best interests, sanction not only the provision of local authority accommodation (which in any case needs no special permission) but the use of such moral or physical restriction as may be needed to keep T there and out of harm's way.[30]

This expansiveness must now be read in the context of the decision of the European Court of Human Rights in *HL v United Kingdom* (also known as *L v United Kingdom*).[31] This case involved an adult lacking capacity who was admitted informally to a psychiatric facility. Had L tried to leave the facility, he would have been civilly confined under the Mental Health Act. Such recourse was not taken as he never attempted to do so, yet it would seem that his carers were discouraged from visiting him out of a concern that he would have wished to leave with them. At issue was whether in these circumstances his article 5 right to liberty had been infringed. The ECtHR held that it had, and further that such infringement was not justified by law. Specifically, it held that the law in 1997 provided neither sufficient procedural safeguards nor sufficiently well-defined substantive criteria to pass scrutiny under article 5.[32] If a declaratory judgment by the court were to be viewed as a prerequisite to intrusive intervention, it

---

[28] [1990] 2 AC 1, 78.

[29] [1996] 2 FLR 613.

[30] [2000] 1 MHLR 120 at [47].

[31] (2005) 40 EHRR 32. Prior to the application to the ECtHR, this case was reported in the English courts as *R v Bournewood Community and Mental Health NHS Trust, ex p L* [1999] AC 458, HL.

[32] (2005) 40 EHRR 32, paras 118–24.

would presumably solve the first of these difficulties. Under the traditional understanding of the declaratory jurisdiction, however, it is not a prerequisite that makes actions legal, it is a security blanket confirming the legality of actions that are legal in themselves through being in the best interests of the incapable person. There are still no legally defined procedural safeguards admissions of the type in *HL v United Kingdom*, and so they remain in contravention of article 5. Furthermore, the approach of the court to defining best interests has become broader rather than narrower in the last decade: see paras 1.36–40 below. This suggests that the substantive criteria for article 5 compliance have not been met by the common law.

That raises the question of when a deprivation of liberty occurs under article 5. In *HL v United Kingdom* there was such a deprivation, but the apparently enforced admission of a vulnerable individual to a nursing home did not trigger such a violation in *HM v Switzerland*.[33] Distinctions between the cases are difficult, but must revolve around the degree of restraint. Indicators of deprivations of liberty might include locked wards (whether by traditional lock and key or by 'fumble locks'—door hardware designed to require agility to open), a decision that an attempt to leave will be met by civil confinement, and the use of medication that restricts the individual's ability to move or form determinations to leave. Following *HL*, the scope of article 5 protection is broader than that for wrongful confinement in England, and it would seem that the test of whether there is a deprivation of liberty is objective. A realisation by the patient that liberty has been restricted is certainly not required, and it is at best doubtful whether an intent to restrict liberty by the carer is required.   1.22

While certain provisions of the MCA were amended by the Government during the legislative process to take account of some aspects of *HL v United Kingdom*, a considered response is awaited. A consultation document has been published,[34] and it would seem that the Government intends to introduce some form of protective custody relating to people lacking capacity, by bolting a new procedural regime onto the MCA. This may prove problematic, as the substantive criteria of the MCA will not easily adapt to ECHR standards: see further paras 2.46, 3.29, and 3.33 below.   1.23

In a sense, it is difficult to criticize the courts for the jurisdictional developments they have undertaken. The legal exclusion of family members from decisions regarding the loved ones for whom they, at least as much as the doctor, may be caring appears on its face to be callous. A hard-line insistence that decisions regarding best interests be delayed until the law of tort or crime engages would be unlikely to foster considered decision-making with reasonable   1.24

---

[33] (2004) 38 EHRR 17.

[34] Department of Health, *'Bournewood' Consultation: The approach to be taken in response to the judgment of the European Court of Human Rights in the 'Bournewood' case*, DOH #267902 (2005), available at <http//:www.dh.gov.uk/Consultations/ClosedConsultations/fs/en>, accessed 20 June 2005.

standards of evidence. If the issue were intervention into allegedly inadequate social care of an individual, for example, a hearing might well not be held until a *quia timet* injunction would lie.[35] This would result in hearings occurring at times of urgency, and it is difficult to see that this would work to the benefit of anyone in the process. At the same time, the common law's endeavours to move outside the narrow reading of the declaratory jurisdiction have been doctrinally problematic.

1.25   Much less legally problematic are the jurisprudential developments relating to advance directives. It was recognized in *Re T*[36] that the wishes of a competent adult regarding future treatment were binding in a subsequent period of incapacity. In terms of practical enforceability, this was something of a false start in that Butler-Sloss and Staunton LJJ further held that a failure to honour such wishes would give rise to only nominal damages,[37] but the principle was established. In *Re C (Adult: Refusal of Medical Treatment)*,[38] Thorpe J went so far as to issue an injunction precluding future treatment that would conflict with the patient's competent wishes, so providing a remedy in contempt in the event that the wishes were contravened. More than a decade after *Re T*, such advance directives are sufficiently part of the legal consciousness that it is no longer obvious that failure to comply with them would attract only nominal damages.[39] That said, the standards imposed by the courts do suggest considerable hesitancy at enforcement of such advance directives. They may always be revoked by the competent patient, and such revocation may be either express or implied. They do not apply if they appear to be based on a premise or belief which proves unfounded: they must represent the real wish of the competent patient, applicable to the circumstances. The burden of proof is on the individual seeking to establish the continuing validity and applicability of the directive. Where life is at stake, clear and convincing evidence must be presented as to the continuing validity and applicability of the directive, and any doubt falls to the preservation of life.[40]

1.26   There remain practical difficulties with the law as it relates to advance directives. There are no formalities requirements for them, raising difficulties as to what statements meet the threshold of validity. It is also unclear whether a patient now lacking capacity but outwardly consenting to treatment is bound by his or her previous advance directive precluding it.[41]

---

[35] See the judgment of Hale J (as she then was) in *Cambridgeshire County Council v R (An Adult)* [1995] 1 FLR 50.

[36] [1992] 4 All ER 649.

[37] [1992] 4 All ER 649, 665, 669; cf. *Malette v Schulman* (1990) 67 DLR (4th) 321, 72 OR (2d) 417, CA, contra.

[38] [1994] 1 All ER 819.

[39] *Re T* [1992] 4 All ER 649, 665, 669.

[40] See *Re T* (above) and *HE v A Hospital NHS Trust* [2003] EWHC 1017, [2003] 2 FLR 408.

[41] This question is raised, but not decided, by Munby J in *HE v A Hospital NHS Trust* (above).

2. Defining Incapacity

The legal need to define incapacity has as long a history as the legal jurisdiction **1.27** relating to incapable people, so at least as far back as the fourteenth century. Capacity determination has occurred not only in the *parens patriae* context, however, but also in the context of individual disputes: validity of wills, fitness to plead at trial, enforceability of contracts, fitness to serve as trustee, and ability to consent to treatment are obvious examples. The tradition in English law has been that capacity is a functional concept: it is assessed according to the specific decision to be taken. There is no necessary inconsistency, for example, in an individual being competent to execute a will, but incompetent to consent to treatment, or even in being competent to consent to one treatment and not to others. The only recent exception to this concerns Part VII of the Mental Health Act 1983: once the court takes control of individuals' property and affairs under that legislation, they lose the right to conduct all their affairs as defined by Part VII, even if they may have retained capacity over some parts of their affairs.

The result has been a multiplicity of legal approaches to incapacity, with some **1.28** common law tests of incapacity being more similar than others. Space does not permit a systematic canvassing of these tests,[42] but it is fair to note that if diverse strands survive the introduction of the MCA, there may be misalignments. Some of these will be identified in the sections that follow, as context requires.

Certainly, there is a presumption across the common law that an individual **1.29** has capacity, and the onus to demonstrate incapacity falls to the party alleging incapacity. The presumption of capacity is not displaced simply because an individual has a mental disorder.[43] Some cases and academic works are phrased as if capacity must be shown. While this allows these authors to simplify their sentence structures, it should not be allowed to mislead on the presumption of capacity.

Much of the recent academic literature has focused on the capacity to consent **1.30** to medical treatment. The criteria for capacity in this regard were established in *Re C (Adult: Refusal of Treatment)*, where it was held that capacity implied that the patient could comprehend and retain treatment information, believe it, and weigh it in the balance to arrive at a choice as to whether or not to consent.[44] This standard, with its insistence that the individual must have the ability to weigh matters in the balance, may appear to set a high threshold for capacity. Such an approach was not evident on the decision in *Re C*. C had a gangrenous leg. Against medical advice, he refused amputation, but accepted less invasive treatment. He was apparently aware of the risk of death, but was content to run

---

[42] Regarding determination of capacity generally, see P. Bartlett and R. Sandland, *Mental Health Law: Policy and Practice*, 2nd edn (2003) chs 10 and 11.

[43] *Re C (Adult: Refusal of Medical Treatment)* [1994] 1 All ER 819, 824; *Masterman-Lister v Brutton & Co., Jewell and Home Counties Dairies* [2002] EWCA Civ 1889, [2003] 1 WLR 1511.

[44] [1994] 1 All ER 819, 824.

the risk. He had long suffered from schizophrenia and had delusions that he had once been an outstanding surgeon who had never lost a patient. He further identified himself as religious, and believed that he would survive his malady through the aid of God. Nonetheless, it was held that he had capacity to refuse treatment, apparently on the somewhat surprising basis that the delusions did not affect his judgment regarding the treatment. This case supports the proposition that though the threshold of capacity may be relatively high, the presumption of capacity is strong and requires a considerable weight of evidence to rebut.

1.31   Other cases have been more ready to find the patient lacking capacity. This may in part originate from the fact that the reported cases appear to derive from a small number of situations: an inordinate number deal with women in the last stages of pregnancy, and refusals of blood transfusions on religious grounds. Whatever the reason, patients have seldom been held to have capacity when the matter is disputed in court. The tendency is to find that even if the individual is able to understand the information, he or she is unable to 'weigh it in the balance' to arrive at a choice. Thus courts have held that a woman in labour described as having a needle phobia was not competent to decide on whether she should receive an injection: her refusal did not represent a 'real choice.'[45] In theory, if individuals are not incapable, the reasons for their decisions are not relevant; such treatment decisions are to be respected even if 'the reasons for the refusal were rational or irrational, unknown or nonexistent'.[46] While that is certainly true in law, it is equally true that in the rare cases where courts have upheld refusals of treatment, they have also tended to explain that apparently irrational decisions may not be so irrational after all.[47]

1.32   None of this addresses the question of what the patient must understand in order to have capacity. The complication is that a defence to battery exists if the patient has given valid consent based on an understanding 'in broad terms of the nature of the procedure which is intended'.[48] That may be considerably less information than the reasonable doctor is required to give under the law of negligence.[49] Which level of understanding is required for the individual to have capacity? There does not appear to be a satisfactory theoretical answer here. If the battery approach is adopted, a refusal may be honoured of a patient who cannot understand the information that a reasonable doctor is required to provide (the negligence standard). If the negligence approach is adopted, a refusal may not be honoured of a patient who understands the nature of the procedure

---

[45] *Re MB (Medical Treatment)* [1997] 2 FLR 426, 437.
[46] *Re T (Adult: Refusal of Medical Treatment)* [1992] 3 WLR 782, 799.
[47] See, e.g., *Re B (Consent to Treatment: Capacity)* [2002] EWHC 429, [2002] 2 All ER 449.
[48] *Chatterton v Gerson* [1981] QB 432, 443.
[49] *Sidaway v Board of Governors of the Bethlem Royal Hospital* [1985] AC 871; *Pearce v United Bristol Healthcare NHS Trust* [1999] PIQR P53. Regarding conflicting capacities, see M. Gunn, 'The Meaning of Incapacity' (1994) 2 *Medical Law Review* 8, 10–12.

in broad terms and refuses for cogent reasons, but is unable to understand some of the finer points required by negligence law.

At its core, the law of consent is a defence to battery, and if that approach is adopted for determination of capacity, understanding the lower standard of information would be required. That does not appear to be the standard of *Re C* discussed above, however, which is stated in terms of understanding risks and benefits, and weighing information in the balance. Nothing in the law of battery would appear to require that. **1.33**

The courts have increasingly acknowledged in recent years that capacity is not merely a medical question, and when practitioners are in doubt, they have been encouraged to make an application under the court's declaratory jurisdiction.[50] **1.34**

These difficulties invite a practical problem of how the law should approach the situation where the doctor incorrectly considers an individual to be lacking capacity, and treats an individual without consent in purported reliance on the defence of necessity. The legally correct answer must be that a battery is committed in this situation. The defence of necessity can apply only if the individual in fact lacks capacity; there is no obvious way to introduce wiggle room to this. In theory, the answer is for the practitioner to apply to the court, but that is likely to be expensive and time-consuming, and may be impractical if a treatment must be given in haste. While the matter has not been litigated in these terms, the logic of the common law would seem to require a doctor's assessment of capacity to be correct, not merely not negligent in these circumstances. **1.35**

3. Defining Best Interests

The recent jurisprudence regarding the definition of best interests, like the jurisprudence relating to the declaratory jurisdiction, flows from *Re F (Mental Patient: Sterilization)*. As noted in para 1.12 above, that case held that further consent was not required for medical treatment carried out in the 'best interests' of a person lacking capacity. The articulation of best interests in that case was embryonic. Treatment would be in the best interests of patients if it would save their lives or ensure improvement or prevent deterioration of their physical or mental health.[51] Consistent with this medical vision of best interests, the House of Lords adopted the then standard approach to liability:[52] if the view of the treating physician as to best interests was consistent with that of a responsible body of his or her professional colleagues, liability would not attach. This was a decision for the doctor alone. Consultation with close relatives or carers was a matter of good practice, not a legal requirement.[53] **1.36**

Even in a medical context, subsequent cases have moved outside the strictly **1.37**

---

[50] See, e.g., *B* v *Croydon District Health Authority* (1994) 22 BMLR 13.
[51] [1990] 2 AC 1, 66–8, *per* Lord Brandon.
[52] Flowing from *Bolam v Friern Hospital Management Committee* [1957] 2 All ER 118.
[53] *Re F (Mental Patient: Sterilization)* [1990] 2 AC 1, 78, *per* Lord Goff.

13

medical definition of best interests. In *Re MB*, it was specifically held that the concept of best interests was not limited to medical criteria, and that the wishes of the patient prior to losing capacity—in this case wishes mitigating in favour of the treatment—were major factors in determining best interests.[54] The following articulation by Thorpe LJ would suggest that the factors for consideration are exceptionally broad:

> There can be no doubt in my mind that the evaluation of best interests is akin to a welfare appraisal. . . . [T]he first instance judge with the responsibility to make an evaluation of the best interests of a claimant lacking capacity should draw up a balance sheet. The first entry should be of any factor or factors of actual benefit. . . . Then on the other sheet the judge should write any counterbalancing dis-benefits to the applicant. . . . Then the judge should enter on each sheet the potential gains and losses in each instance making some estimate of the extent of the possibility that the gain or loss might accrue. At the end of that exercise the judge should be better placed to strike a balance between the sum of the certain and possible gains against the sum of the certain and possible losses. Obviously, only if the account is in relatively significant credit will the judge conclude that the application is likely to advance the best interests of the claimant.[55]

While these comments were written in the context of medical treatment, the approach has since been applied in the context of other personal decisions, in particular with regard to the removal of incapacitated persons from family care by social service agencies.[56]

1.38   There is no objective threshold to intervention beyond the best interests test. *Newham London Borough Council v S (Adult: Court's Jurisdiction)* involved an adult without capacity in the care of her father. Social services sought to remove her from the father's care, based on the father's alleged problems relating to alcohol and violence. The court found that these problems did not exist, but at the same held that the balance-sheet approach to best interests justified the removal of the adult from family care by social services. Similarly, in *Re S (Adult Patient) (Inherent Jurisdiction: Family Life)*, the uncontested expert evidence was that an adult lacking capacity was given generally satisfactory care by his family; the intervention of social services was nonetheless approved by the court. The court specifically rejected a requirement for a threshold of significant harm, which must be demonstrated in similar cases regarding children, before the local authority could intervene.

1.39   This raises potential difficulties regarding the right to family life under article 8 of the ECHR. If the incapable adult is still understood to be part of the family unit, he or she may have a right to be cared for within the family, and that the

---

[54] *Re MB (Medical Treatment)* [1997] 2 FLR 426, 439. See also *Re A (Male Sterilization)* [2000] 1 FLR 549, 555; *Re S (Adult Patient: Sterilisation)* [2001] Fam 15, 30.

[55] *Re A (Male Sterilization)* [2000] 1 FLR 549, 560.

[56] *Re S (Adult Patient) (Inherent Jurisdiction: Family Life)* [2002] EWHC 2278, [2003] 1 FLR 292 and *Newham London Borough Council v S and Another (Adult: Court's Jurisdiction)* [2003] EWHC 1909, [2003] All ER (D) 550.

family may have a right to care for him or her under article 8. Certainly that cannot be an absolute right—an individual lacking capacity should not be left in an abusive family—but it does suggest the appropriateness of a more substantive threshold than is provided by the existing case law. *Re S (Adult Patient) (Inherent Jurisdiction: Family Life)* acknowledged this difficulty, but held that the best interests of the incapacitated person remained the sole test for intervention. Since the family of a capacitated adult could not enforce family care and contact, so the family of an incapacitated adult's article 8 rights were similarly limited. The court, placing itself in the position of the incapacitated adult, could thus terminate contact or care.[57] This begs too many questions. Understanding how the incapable adult would have exercised his or her article 8 rights if competent may be highly speculative. In the absence of evidence of harm within the family, the threshold denied by the court, the options may be finely balanced. In such a circumstance, is it really convincing that the article 8 rights of the family count for nought? Further, the approach of the court assumes that it has jurisdiction to act as substitute decision-maker for the adult lacking capacity. As discussed regarding the jurisprudence on common law jurisdiction above, this is a tenuous argument: see paras 1.15–21.

1.40   The move to the broad 'balance-sheet' approach has carried with it a move away from a determination of best interests based on the view of the relevant professional. Where under *Re F*, best interests were a matter of professional judgment, to which liability would not attach if the view were consistent with a reasonable body of medical opinion, recent cases have required something more similar to a correctness test. Such an approach is theoretically unproblematic in the context of a court hearing, but cases such as *Re A (Male Sterilization)* now require such a standard of doctors as well:

Doctors charged with the decisions about the future treatment of patients and whether such treatment would, in the cases of those lacking capacity to make their own decisions, be in their best interests, have to act at all times in accordance with a responsible and competent body of relevant professional opinion. That is the professional standard set for those who make such decisions. The doctor, acting to that required standard, has, in my view, a second duty, that is to say, he must act in the best interests of a mentally incapacitated patient. I do not consider that the two duties have been conflated into one requirement.[58]

This significantly reduces the permitted margin of error in the determination of best interests by those charged with the care of adults lacking capacity. The necessity defence would appear to be available only if the care-giver is correct in his or her assessment of best interests. The only legally sound advice at common law to a care-giver in cases of doubt would be to commence court proceedings, with all the inconvenience and expense that would be entailed.

---

[57] *Re S (Adult Patient) (Inherent Jurisdiction: Family Life)* [2002] EWHC 2278, [2003] 1 FLR 292 at [38]–[39], [42].
[58] [2000] 1 FLR 549, 555, *per* Butler-Sloss P.

C. THE LAW COMMISSION PROPOSALS AND THE
ROAD TO LEGISLATIVE REFORM

1.41 The origins of the MCA lie in an investigation, discussion documents, and a final report including a draft Bill by the Law Commission. The impetus for the Law Commission project flowed from a discussion document by the Law Society in 1989.[59] The Law Commission published an initial general consultative document in 1991,[60] followed by more specific papers in 1993 on formalizing, amending and clarifying the rights of carers;[61] medical treatment and research;[62] and public law protection for people lacking capacity.[63] These met with broad academic approval,[64] and a final report was published in 1995.[65] Green and white papers followed in 1997 and 1999.[66] A draft Bill in 2003 received pre-legislative scrutiny,[67] and a further draft Bill with explanatory notes was published in 2004. It was this Bill, in a somewhat amended form, that eventually made its way to

---

[59] *Decision Making and Mental Incapacity: A Discussion Document* (1989).

[60] *Mentally Incapacitated Adults and Decision-Making: An Overview* (Consultation Paper 119) (1991).

[61] *Mentally Incapacitated Adults and Decision-Making: A New Jurisdiction* (Consultation Paper 128) (1993).

[62] *Mentally Incapacitated Adults and Decision-Making: Medical Treatment and Research* (Consultation Paper 129) (1993).

[63] *Mentally Incapacitated and Other Vulnerable Adults: Public Law Protection* (Consultation Paper 130) (1993).

[64] P. Fennell, 'Statutory Authority to Treat, Relatives and Treatment Proxies' (1994) 2 *Medical Law Review* 30; P. Fennell, 'The Law Commission Proposals on Mental Incapacity' [1995] *Family Law* 420; M. Freeman, 'Deciding for the Intellectually Impaired' (1994) 2 *Medical Law Review* 77; M. Gunn, 'The Meaning of Incapacity' (1994) 2 *Medical Law Review* 8; A. Parkin, 'Where Now on Mental Incapacity' [1996] 2 Web JCLI, available at <http://webjcli.ncl.ac.uk/admin/wjclidex.html>, accessed 25 June 2005; P. Wilson, 'The Law Commission's Report on Mental Incapacity: Medically Vulnerable Adults or Politically Vulnerable Law?' (1996) 4 *Medical Law Review* 227. For more critical views, see P. Bartlett, 'The Consequences of Incapacity' [1997] 4 Web JCLI, available at <http://webjcli.ncl.ac.uk/admin/wjclidex.html>, accessed 25 June 2005; D. Carson, 'Disabling Progress: The Law Commission's Proposals on Mentally Incapacitated Adults' Decision-making' (1993) *Journal of Social Welfare and Family Law* 304.

[65] Law Com Report No 231, *Mental Incapacity* (February 1995), available at <http://www.lawcom.gov.uk>, accessed 20 June 2005.

[66] Lord Chancellor's Department, *Who Decides? Making Decisions on Behalf of Mentally Incapacitated Adults*, Cm 3803 (1997); Lord Chancellor's Department, *Making Decisions: The Government's Proposals for Making Decisions on Behalf of Mentally Incapacitated Adults*, Cm 4465 (1999).

[67] See *House of Commons and House of Lords Joint Committee Report on the Draft Mental Incapacity Bill* (HL Paper (2002–3) No 189; HC Paper (2002–3) No 1083). See also government response, February 2004, <http://www.dca.gov.uk/pubs/reports/mental-incapacity.htm>, accessed 30 June 2005. This Bill also received the attention of the Joint Committee of the House of Commons and House of Lords on Human Rights in their 23rd Report, Appendix I (2003–4, HL 210, HC 1282); see also government response <http://www.dca.gov.uk/menincap/response.pdf>, accessed 30 June 2005.

the statute books in the dying hours of parliamentary time before the 2005 election.

The MCA remains in structure and content remarkably similar to the Law 1.42 Commission's draft Bill. The most significant exception is that the public law protections proposed by the Law Commission were not included in the Bills before Parliament, and so have not been implemented. These would have placed a threshold on intervention by local authorities into the lives of vulnerable people in the community. The provisions would have allowed such intervention only in cases of significant harm or serious exploitation. Temporary orders for the protection of such vulnerable persons would have been allowed for up to eight days to allow for the consideration of long-term options.[68] At the end of the eight-day period, resort would have had to have been made to other law, such as the Mental Health Act 1983, for which the Law Commission proposed slightly expanded powers of guardianship. These proposals were directed to 'vulnerable' adults, a group considered to be wider than adults lacking capacity.

Instead of these public law protections, the MCA has provision for the 1.43 establishment of a system of independent advocates who must be consulted at key moments in the intervention of social services and similar organizations. These advocates will have authority to challenge decisions made for adults lacking capacity, but will operate within the substantive framework of the remainder of the MCA.

Notwithstanding the similarity between the Law Commission's proposals and 1.44 the eventual statute, the ten-year delay in its passage onto the statute book cannot solely be attributed to a shortage of parliamentary time. There were several stumbling blocks. First and most significant was the Commission's view that advanced decisions in matters of medical treatment should be enforceable, a view that was taken to be a move to allow euthanasia.[69] Whatever the political relevance of such concerns, it is difficult to see them as having legal merit. By the time of the Commission's proposals, the common law had already accepted the efficacy of advanced directives for medical treatment. Indeed, in *Re C* an injunction precluding apparently life-saving treatment had been granted on the basis of such a competent advanced wish: see para 1.25 above. It is not obvious that the Commission's proposals would have extended this in any way. Advance directives were nonetheless excluded from the green paper, apparently to continue to be governed by common law. Their codification was reintroduced into the Bill, but concerns about euthanasia continued throughout its parliamentary life. Prime Minister Tony Blair was eventually required to provide assurances that the Act would not alter the law relating to murder, manslaughter, and assisted suicide, and at the last moment s 62 was added to that effect.

---

[68] Law Com Report No 231 (n 65 above) Part IX. These provisions would have replaced s 47 of the National Assistance Act 1948 and s 135(1) and (3) of the Mental Health Act 1983.
[69] See Wilson (n 64 above) 228.

1.45   The Law Commission's proposals on medical research involving adults lacking capacity were similarly viewed with some trepidation. Once again the reasons are unconvincing. Prior to the Commission's work, there were no formal legal restrictions relating to research involving people lacking capacity. Such research was taking place on patients unable to consent owing to incapacity, but with no other formal safeguards as to the appropriateness of the research. It is difficult to see how an outright ban of such research could be desirable. Research into conditions such as Alzheimer's disease requires the involvement of people affected by the condition; a ban on their involvement would effectively prohibit research into the condition. The Commission's approach took account of the desirability of appropriate research, but sought to impose certain procedural structures and substantive limitations. The research was already happening in an uncontrolled environment. The Commission's proposals were about providing a structure of appropriate controls, not a research free-for-all. Given this, those who were hesitant about research on adults lacking capacity ought to have favoured them. The proposals were reintroduced prior to the passage of the Bill by Parliament: see further paras 2.123–34 below.

1.46   The Law Commission's proposals and draft Bill were published in the beginning of 1995. The structure and content of most of the MCA dates from that period. The remainder of law however did not stand still in the ensuing decade. The Hague Convention on the International Protection of Adults[70] was signed in 2000, and is implemented by Sch 3 to the MCA. Of more pervasive relevance the Human Rights Act 1998 was passed, and came into effect in 2000. The Strasbourg jurisprudence involving people lacking capacity has been limited, but it is clear (if it could ever have been in doubt) that such people are within the purview of the Convention.[71] The MCA has taken cognizance of the ECHR by precluding people other than courts from restricting an incapacitated person's right to liberty under article 5, but it is not obvious that this will be sufficient for compliance. While both the ECHR and the MCA look to respect for the individual as a core value, they do so in quite different ways. The MCA is designed to provide a flexible regime, allowing carers to act in the best interests of the incapacitated person with minimal interference or red tape. The ECHR tends more to view procedural safeguards as inherent to the protection of rights. In the event that the decisions involved give rise to human rights questions, and many may, it is not obvious that these approaches are easily reconcilable.

1.47   Finally, the growth in the common law described at paras 1.09 onwards above took effect largely after the Law Commission's report. In that time, we have seen the creation of a new jurisdiction to determine (and presumably enforce) actions done in the best interests of an individual lacking capacity, a jurisdiction that apparently allows the appointment of a substitute decision-maker. Best interests

---

[70] Cm 5881 (2000), available at <http://www.opsi.gov.uk/official-publications/command-papers/5800–5899.htm>, accessed 1 July 2005.

[71] See, e.g., *HL v United Kingdom* (2005) 40 EHRR 32 (see text at n 31 above).

has been redefined in a broad and flexible way. Advance directives, recognized prior to the Law Commission's report but still in their infancy, have begun to attract a jurisprudential canon. Even the definition of incapacity itself has become applied much more comfortably by the courts. None of this could have been anticipated by the Commission. It expressly intended its proposals to sit beside the common law, and there is nothing in the MCA to alter this approach. If the new jurisprudential developments continue to exist unaltered, however, many of the approaches of the MCA will be able to be circumvented by appeal to the common law. At the same time, it is difficult to believe that the courts, now increasingly used to dealing with matters of incapacity, will fail to view the new statute in the light of the existing jurisprudence. As the MCA creates a totally new statutory space, how these divergences will be played off against one other is currently a matter of speculation.

2

AN OVERVIEW OF THE STATUTE

A. THE LEGISLATIVE STRUCTURE AND THE CODE OF PRACTICE

The MCA received Royal Assent on 17 April 2005. At the time of writing (June   **2.01**
2005), none of the provisions of the Act had come into force. For the sections of
the Act related to research (ss 30–34) and independent mental health advocates
(ss 35–40), commencement is determined in Wales by the National Assembly
for Wales and in England by the 'Secretary of State', (s 68) presumably the
Secretary of State for Health. Otherwise, commencement is to be determined
by order of the Lord Chancellor. It is currently expected that the MCA will be
brought into force in 2007.

    The statute is buttressed by seven Schedules. Four of these involve the usual   **2.02**
collection of repeals, amendments, and transitional provisions. Schedule 5 to the
MCA repeals all of the Enduring Powers of Attorney Act 1985 and Part VII
of the Mental Health Act 1983 (which concerns property and affairs of
'patients') and Sch 4 contains transitional provisions for those persons under
the jurisdiction of those provisions at the time of their repeal. The three substantive Schedules concern formalities of lasting powers of attorney (LPOAs),

21

supplemental provisions relating to the property and affairs of those lacking capacity, and the international protection of adults lacking capacity.

2.03 In addition, a Code of Practice is to be issued pursuant to the MCA. It will be a statutory code, subject to the provisions of s 42 of the MCA. Section 42 provides that the Code will serve as 'guidance' for virtually all those involved with assessment of or decision-making for persons lacking capacity (s 42(1)). It further provides a separate duty to have regard to the Code on donees of LPOAs, court-appointed deputies, researchers using subjects lacking capacity, mental health advocates under the Act, those acting in a professional capacity, and those acting for remuneration (s 42(4)). Courts are also to take departures from the Code of Practice into account, when relevant to a matter arising before them (s 42(5)).

2.04 Recent jurisprudence has increased the impact of such statutory codes. In *R (on the application of Munjaz) v Mersey Care NHS Trust and Others*[1] the Court of Appeal held that it was incumbent upon those envisaged by a statutory code to follow the code, unless there is good reason to the contrary, and the obligation to do so is particularly strong where the human rights of an individual are at stake.[2] Failure to do so without justification would give rise to remedies in public law and, often, in damages.[3]

2.05 *Munjaz* concerned the Code of Practice under the Mental Health Act 1983, a sufficiently similar context that it must be taken as a strong precedent for the MCA code. The facts of the case related to a psychiatric hospital, which had a policy on seclusion that was at odds with the Code under the 1983 Act, a matter therefore of routine and intentional non-compliance. The case clearly stands for the proposition that such wholesale departures by institutions from the standards of the Code of Practice are not to be permitted. It also seems clear that professionals and similarly placed individuals must follow the Code, in the absence of reason to the contrary. The MCA draws a distinction between those persons relying on the Act and a sub-set of persons who are professionals, holders of LPOAs, court-appointed deputies and so forth (see para 2.03 above) who have special duties to have regard to the Code of Practice. *Munjaz* does not address the question of whether professionals are to be treated in the same way as lay carers, or specific categories of lay carers such as those appointed by the court as distinct from those acting merely in a good neighbourly fashion.

2.06 At the time of the writing, the Code of Practice had been published only in draft form. The version consulted was published in September 2004 (hereinafter DCOP).[3a] Apart from the addition of some due process safeguards to advance decisions to refuse medical treatment, the Act is essentially similar to the Bill

---

[1] [2003] EWCA Civ 1036, [2004] QB 395. The appeal of this case to the House of Lords has been heard, but as of the time of writing, the decision has not been given.

[2] [2003] EWCA Civ 1036, [2004] QB 395 at [71]–[76]. This follows a similar duty already established for social services authorities: *R v Islington London Borough Council, ex p Rixon* (1996) 1 CCLR 119.

[3] [2003] EWCA Civ 1036, [2004] QB 395 at [77].

[3a] <http://www.dca.gov.uk/menincap/mcbdraftcode.pdf, accessed 27 July 05

current at the time the DCOP was drafted, so significant amendments are not expected to the Code overall. Some amendments may be required to take account of the decision in *HL v United Kingdom*,[4] which concerns the deprivation of liberty of people lacking capacity, although the current approach of the MCA is to preclude decision-makers other than courts from making such decisions under its aegis. *HL* is currently the subject of government consultation;[5] the results of that may yet affect the MCA and the DCOP. Further, reform of the Mental Health Act 1983 is also in the air, with a government Bill on the subject dying on the order paper with the dissolution of Parliament in the spring of 2005. Just prior to the dissolution, the Joint Scrutiny Committee of the House of Commons and House of Lords published a highly critical report on this Bill.[6] It is speculation whether the Bill will be revived following the election on 5 May 2005, and if so, in what form. These matters may require amendment to the DCOP or, conceivably, to the MCA itself.

B. THE OVERALL PICTURE

The MCA seeks to introduce flexible and supportive measures to ensure that appropriate decisions are taken in the best interests of adults lacking capacity, with no more procedural difficulty than is required. As the detail can be complex, an overview may be of assistance. **2.07**

In the MCA, and in the discussion that follows, persons lacking capacity or reasonably thought to be lacking capacity are labelled P, and persons caring for them or making decisions for them are labelled D. A set of principles is initially established to colour the overall interpretation of the Act (s 1). Statutory definitions are established for 'people who lack capacity' (s 2), 'inability to make decisions' (s 3), and 'best interests' (s 4). **2.08**

The Act codifies the right to make advance decisions to refuse medical treatment. When such a valid decision exists for a treatment, it is in law as if the individual were competent and making the decision at the time the decision is relied on. In this sole case, issues of best interests or substituted decision-making cease to be relevant: the decision stands (ss 24–26). Unless there is a valid advance directive for health care, the Act is primarily concerned with substitute decision-making, based on the best interests definition. **2.09**

An individual can alternatively execute a lasting power of attorney (LPOA), a power that can withstand or indeed commence upon the incapacity of the **2.10**

---

[4] (2005) 40 EHRR 32.

[5] Department of Health, *'Bournewood' Consultation: The approach to be taken in response to the judgment of the European Court of Human Rights in the 'Bournewood' case*, DOH #267902 (2005), available at <http//:www.dh.gov.uk/Consultations/ClosedConsultations/fs/en>, accessed 20 June 2005.

[6] 2004–5 HL 79, HC 95. Since the completion of this chapter, the government has indicated its intent to press on with the Bill in amended form: see Preface

donor. This allows the holder of the power to make personal or property decisions, as delineated by the power, in those areas where the donor lacks capacity. Unlike the older version, however, LPOAs can be granted for personal decisions as well as for financial decisions (ss 9–14).

2.11 At the most formal level, and generally intended to be as a last resort, a new Court of Protection can make decisions on behalf of P, or can, subject to some restrictions, appoint a deputy to make those decisions (ss 15–21). A deputy cannot be appointed to make decisions inconsistent with the holder of a valid LPOA (s 20(4)), although the court can declare an LPOA void in the event that it was obtained by fraud or undue influence, or that the donee is behaving in contravention of the authority or other than in the best interests of P (s 22(3)–(4)). The structure and administration of the new Court of Protection is contained in Part 2 of the MCA.

2.12 At the least formal level, D can act to provide care or treatment in the best interests of P, and the act will be treated as though P had consented to it. No liability will therefore attach, as long as there is no negligence. There are provisions relating to expenses to ensure that D has access to funds to pay for the care or treatment, and any suppliers of necessaries will be paid (ss 5–8). This 'general defence' does not apply to decisions being taken by a donee of a LPOA, a court, or a court-appointed deputy, or within the scope of a valid and applicable advance decision to refuse medical treatment. While it is expected that this general defence will be the mechanism most frequently relied on in care provision, it is in this sense a default mechanism, taking effect when no more formal authority exists under the MCA.

2.13 The MCA provides some additional procedural safeguards against interventions by public authorities. If there is no person other than a professional carer who would be appropriate to consult regarding P's best interests, an independent mental capacity advocate must be consulted prior to the NHS engaging in serious medical treatment of P, or the NHS or a local authority providing accommodation to P beyond the short term. The advocate's role is to support P as far as possible to be involved in the decision, to obtain further information including additional medical reports if appropriate, to determine P's best interests, and to ascertain alternative courses of action if appropriate. The advocate may be able formally to challenge the proposed course of action, consistent with regulations that have yet to be drafted (ss 35–41).

2.14 The Act further lays down a regulatory structure for the approval of 'intrusive research' involving adults lacking capacity. 'Intrusive' research is defined as research that would otherwise require the consent of the participants. To obtain approval, the MCA requires that such research be into the impairing condition affecting P or the treatment of such a condition, that the proposed protocols are the most effective for gaining the knowledge, and that the risks or inconvenience of participation to research subjects be limited. As part of the recruitment of research subjects, a non-professional carer must be consulted for each participant to determine the appropriateness of the subject's participation in the research, including what his or her views about participation in the research would have been if capable (ss 30–34).

An offence is created for carers, including donees of LPOAs and court-appointed deputies, who ill-treat or wilfully neglect persons without capacity (s 44). **2.15**

The MCA specifically excludes some decisions from its ambit. It does not extend to a variety of decisions related to family relations, including consent to marriage or civil partnership, consent to sexual relations, consent to divorce based on two years' separation, consent to a child's placement for adoption or making of an adoption order, discharging parental responsibilities over a child's property, or giving consent under the Human Fertilization and Embryology Act 1990 (s 27). Further, the MCA does not extend to decisions on behalf of a person lacking capacity regarding voting for any public office or in a referendum (s 29). For all these decisions, if a person lacks capacity to make the decision himself or herself, the decision cannot be made at all. Decisions regarding treatment regulated by the Mental Health Act are also outside the MCA. This will be discussed in more detail below in the overall context of the interface between the Mental Health Act and the MCA (s 28): see further paras 3.35–57. **2.16**

C. THE PRINCIPLES AND THE MEANING OF INCAPACITY

The following five principles are set out in s 1 to guide interpretation of the legislation: **2.17**

(2) A person must be assumed to have capacity unless it is established that he lacks capacity.
(3) A person is not to be treated as unable to make a decision unless all practicable steps to help him to do so have been taken without success.
(4) A person is not to be treated as unable to make a decision merely because he makes an unwise decision.
(5) An act done, or decision made, under this Act for or on behalf of a person who lacks capacity must be done, or made, in his best interests.
(6) Before the act is done, or the decision is made, regard must be had to whether the purpose for which it is needed can be as effectively achieved in a way that is less restrictive of the person's rights and freedom of action.

What is striking about these principles is not how much, but how little new they contain. The principles in subss (2) and (4) flow directly from the common law. The principle in subs (3) grows out of the presumption of capacity. All of these reflect a desire to protect the autonomy of the capable individual. The requirement to provide assistance is not mere window dressing. People who have difficulty communicating their decisions risk being considered unable to make decisions under s 3(1)(d). The requirement to provide assistance should ensure that such persons fall under the MCA only if they really are unable to **2.18** communicate their wishes, not merely because they may require specialist assistance in being understood. Similarly, this principle would suggest that individuals who may have difficulty assimilating information should not be found to lack capacity because it is inconvenient to spend the required time working through the information with them. Moreover, the degree of support an individual receives in his or her overall environment may affect the decisions he or she can make. The presence of carers, professional or lay, may be able to organize the individual's life so that decisions are simplified to a degree where an individual of marginal capacity can make the decision. While it would seem that such support as is 'practicable' must be taken into account, there is no duty in the Act to provide such services. While rights to care may exist under other statutes, they are normally subject to fiscal restraints, a restriction that may well be read by the courts into the word 'practicable'.[7]

2.19 The principle in subs (5) is similar in spirit to the fiduciary duties traditionally governing those charged with the administration of estates of persons lacking capacity, although as will become clear, the definition of best interests is something of a departure from that developed at equity. The principle of least restrictive alternative in subs (6) is common in legal ethics relating to coercion and mental disorder. The precise phrasing of such principles varies. This one directs attention to both the individual's rights and freedom of action. At issue therefore is both protecting the individual's legal autonomy and maximizing his or her practical experience of living.

2.20 Implicit in the Act is also the old common law notion that capacity is a functional concept. Throughout the MCA, reference is made to lacking capacity to make particular decisions. The individual retains legal authority to make those decisions for which he or she continues to have capacity. Previously, the exception had been for people found to lack capacity to administer their property and affairs: at least after 1905, a *parens patriae* determination regarding property resulted in a complete inability to deal with one's property and affairs, even in areas where the individual continued to have capacity.[8] That is no longer the case for court appointments. Section 20(1) states specifically that court-appointed deputies do not have any power where the deputy knows or has reasonable reason to believe that P has capacity to make the decision in question. Once again, this is part of the overall approach of the MCA to ensure that those people with capacity can exercise their autonomy.

2.21 The Act applies to people over the age of sixteen (s 2(5)–(6)). There are several exceptions:

---

[7] Courts have traditionally been notoriously reluctant to enforce the provision of care services when confronted by public authorities crying impecuniousness: see, e.g., *R v Gloucestershire CC, ex p Barry* [1997] 2 All ER 1, HL.

[8] See *Re Walker* [1905] 1 Ch 160. This continued under the codified controls over property and estates of incapable persons under the Mental Health Acts 1959 and 1983: see *Re Beaney (deceased)* [1978] 2 All ER 595, 600.

- An LPOA may be signed only by an individual over the age of eighteen (s 9(2)(c)).
- The court can deal with the property of an incapable minor below the age of sixteen if the court considers it likely that the minor will continue to lack capacity at the age of eighteen (s 18(3)).
- The offence of ill-treatment or wilful neglect of a person lacking capacity has no age limit (s 44).

The situation regarding minors will be discussed in paras 3.07–9 below.

The Act states that a person lacks capacity in relation to a matter if at the material time he is 'unable to make a decision for himself in relation to the matter because of an impairment of, or a disturbance in the functioning of, the mind or brain' (s 2(1)). Such impairment or disturbance may be permanent or temporary (s 2(2)) and is decided on the balance of probabilities (s 2(4)). The presence of a diagnostic threshold, proposed by the Law Commission, was criticized as being stigmatizing.[9] The Commission did not agree that a stigma would follow from this requirement, and viewed it as an important substantive protection against the overuse of the statute. It considered that any violation of liberty under article 5(1) of the ECHR would require justification, and so there was the possibility of needing to ensure that the persons under the aegis of the statute were 'persons of unsound mind' under article 5.[10] As enacted, the MCA has been narrowed, with courts alone able to make decisions restricting article 5 rights,[11] but in this context the concern over consistency with the ECHR remains apposite. The requirement of an impairment to the mind or brain does ignore the possibility of an individual whose purely physical impairment results in incapacity. An individual without brain damage who falls unconscious following an accident, or is immobilized by a severe muscular disease, or is so distracted by physical pain as to be unable meaningfully to consent could be examples where inclusion within the ambit of disorder to the 'mind or brain' might tax language to the breaking point. If such individuals were held to be outside the provisions of the Act decisions about them would still need to be made. In that event, recourse to the common law might still be necessary. **2.22**

The lack of capacity cannot be established 'merely' by reference to age or appearance, or a 'condition' or 'aspect of his behaviour' which would lead to 'unjustified' assumptions about incapacity (s 2(3)). This is presumably intended to ensure that incapacity is not decided by stereotype: extreme age, an unkempt appearance, or an ingrained mistrust of service providers do not of themselves bespeak incapacity. The wording of the provision is nonetheless unfortunate, in **2.23**

---

[9] D. Carson, 'Disabling Progress: The Law Commission's Proposals on Mentally Incapacitated Adults' Decision-making' (1993) *Journal of Social Welfare Law* 304.

[10] Law Com Report No 231, *Mental Incapacity* (February 1995), para 3.8, available at <http://www.lawcom.gov.uk>, accessed 20 June 2005.

[11] MCA, ss 6(5), 11(6).

that 'merely' suggests that these factors can be included in an assessment of capacity, even if they would lead to 'unjustified' assumptions, so long as there is additional evidence corroborating incapacity. This is illogical. If assumptions based on the criteria would be unjustified, the criteria should not be considered at all in an assessment of capacity. In that circumstance, the criterion would be irrelevant, and use of the criterion at all would perpetuate the unfair bias the subsection is intended to challenge.

2.24   The inability to make a decision for oneself is defined in s 3(1) of the MCA. Such inability occurs when the individual is unable:

(a) to understand the information relevant to the decision, even if the information is presented in a culturally appropriate way such as through the use of simple language or visual aids;

(b) to retain that information, even if only for a short period

(c) to use or weigh that information as part of the process of making the decision, or

(d) to communicate his decision (whether by talking, using sign language or any other means).

The similarity with the common law definition of capacity to consent to medical treatment discussed in para 1.30 above is obvious, and there can be little doubt that the courts will use the existing common law jurisprudence as a guide to the interpretation of s 3. The section contains a flexibility similar to the common law approach, particularly in the requirement that the individual be able to 'use or weigh that information as part of the process of making the decision'. When the courts have made controversial findings of incapacity in the past, it has often been as a result of applying this rather amorphous standard.

2.25   The MCA requires that the incapable individual must be unable to understand the reasonably foreseeable consequences of deciding one way or another, and of failing to decide (s 3(4)). This would seem to include reasonably foreseeable risks and benefits flowing from the various decisions possible, or of failing to make a decision. A strand of scholarship in the past claimed that capacity to choose is contingent on the severity of the choice made. Thus an individual might have capacity to consent to a specific treatment, but not to refuse it, because the consequences of having the treatment might be less severe than the consequences of not having the treatment.[12] This is no longer a sustainable argument in England and Wales. Section 3(4) requires an understanding of all possible choices including failure to make a choice; it follows that the standard of capacity is the same, no matter what choice P is to make.

2.26   Through all this, it should be emphasized that the MCA is phrased in terms of ability. Certain academic literature has drawn a distinction between ability

---

[12] See, e.g., B. Dickens, 'Medical Consent Legislation in Ontario' (1994) 2 *Medical Law Review* 283, 287.

to understand and actual understanding.[13] In the legal context of the MCA, where capacity determination is so closely related to specific decisions, the distinction may seem somewhat precious, but in so far as it is an issue, the MCA speaks in terms of ability. It follows from this that people of marginal capacity have the same rights as those of robust capacity to waive information provision. The fact that an individual chooses to hush the warnings of his or her stockbroker regarding equity transactions or doctor regarding adverse effects of treatment may be manifestly unwise, but it does not of itself bespeak incapacity.

Conspicuous by its absence from the definition is any express requirement that **2.27** an individual believes the information provided.[14] What is required is an ability to understand the information and weigh the information. If the information is not believed, inquiries should be made as to the circumstances. If it were the result of a psychotic delusion, the effect of the delusion on the belief of the information would unquestionably be relevant to the assessment of incapacity. However, if the lack of belief flowed, for example, from a view that the person providing the information was not adequately qualified—a house officer rather than a consultant—it would not necessarily bespeak incapacity. In other cases, the failure to believe may come from a refusal to accept that the facts are as presented—for example, a manifestly unrealistic view that P can return to his or her own home and a consequent refusal to move to a nursing home. Once again, it is difficult to see that a failure to be realistic about one's prospects necessarily bespeaks incapacity. The robustly capable may behave in this fashion without any challenge to their right to do so; it does not follow from the fact that an individual has marginal capacity or is in a position of relative vulnerability that this should change.

There is similarly no requirement in the legislation that an individual should **2.28** respect, trust, or even be civil to doctors, local authorities, police officers, carers, family, or other service providers. There may be a wide variety of reasons for such behaviour and responses; they do not all bespeak incapacity by any means. Being difficult, obstreperous, ornery or rude is not the same as being incapable.

In some circumstances ascertaining whether an individual lacks capacity may **2.29** consequently be a difficult question. The individual who must satisfy himself or herself as to the capacity of P is D, the individual who will in the end be liable if the relevant decision is taken wrongly. The incapacity definitions, discussed above, provide guidance on how the decision ought to be addressed. The DCOP provides further useful pointers, encouraging D to consider P at his or her highest level of functioning and noting, for example, that ability can vary

---

[13] See, e.g., the classic paper on capacity, L. Roth, A. Meisel, and C. Lidz, 'Tests of Competency to Consent to Treatment' (1977) 134 *American Journal of Psychiatry* 279, 282. The distinction is made regarding capacity under the Mental Health Act 1983 in *R v MHAC, ex p X* (1988) 9 BMLR 77, 85.

[14] Such a requirement is contained in the common law: see *Re C* [1994] 1 WLR 290, 295.

considerably by time of day.[15] In the event that the decision will interfere with P's rights under article 5 of the ECHR,[16] medical evidence of such incapacity will be necessary, to comply with the requirements of *Winterwerp*.[17] Otherwise such formal evidence is not required, so long as D is satisfied that there is an impairment or disturbance of functioning of the mind or brain leading to the required inability to make decisions. That said, if D is in doubt as to P's ability, medical views should be appropriately obtained. The DCOP suggests that the desirability of medical or other expert involvement will be contingent on factors such as the seriousness of the decision, where P disputes either the allegation of incapacity or the desirability of the decision proposed, where the capacity may be challenged at a later time (the most obvious example being a will, which may be challenged following the death of P), or where P is repeatedly making decisions that put himself or herself at risk.[18] This last factor provides an occasion to remember the distinction between the triggering of a more formalized assessment and the result of the assessment: if P does not lack capacity, he or she remains as entitled as a person of robust capacity to put himself or herself at risk.

2.30   While the responsibility to determine whether P lacks capacity falls on D, the Act is in general sufficiently satisfied if D reasonably believes that P lacks capacity. The DCOP discusses this in a succinct paragraph, noting that D will be required to have reasonable grounds and to be able to point to objective reasons for this view.[19] This is no doubt sound advice. While the DCOP treatment of this point in a single paragraph has the virtue of elegance, it obscures the slightly different wording of the reasonableness provision in the different contexts of the MCA. For that reason, they will be dealt with separately below.

D. BEST INTERESTS

2.31   Decisions made under the MCA must be made in the 'best interests' of P. The sole exception is that a valid and applicable advance treatment directive must be followed whether or not it is in the best interests of P: otherwise, best interests rules. It is of course to be remembered that decision-making under the MCA only occurs when P lacks capacity relative to the decision in question: people who do not lack capacity make their own decisions, in their best interests, or otherwise as they see fit.

2.32   As discussed in para 1.37 above, best interests at common law are determined in a somewhat amorphous fashion, based on a balance sheet of the pros and

---

[15] DCOP, para 3.32.
[16] Such decisions may be taken only by the court: see MCA, ss 6(5), 11(6) and 20(13).
[17] *Winterwerp v The Netherlands* (A/33) (1979–80) 2 EHRR 387.
[18] DCOP, para 3.37.
[19] DCOP, para 3.29.

cons for a proposed course of action. What is to be taken into consideration and how it is to be discovered are largely undefined. The page-long definition of best interests in s 4 of the MCA is therefore an important departure from the common law approach. This section does not purport to be a complete code of what must be considered in determining P's best interests. Indeed, it expressly instructs the decision-maker to take into account all relevant circumstances in assessing best interests (s 4(2)). Instead, it provides a list of factors that must always be considered and a set of consultations and inquiries that must be pursued in each case.

The enumerated substantive criteria combine three different broad sets of **2.33** factors into the best interests determination, which may be summarized as follows:

- Protecting P's position, in the event that P is likely to regain capacity.

- Considering the wishes, feelings, values, and beliefs P had when competent, or would have now if P were competent.

- Considering P's current, incompetent, wishes and feelings, and notwithstanding the incapacity, involving P in the decision-making.

These approaches may be in conflict, and the section establishes no priority between them. Best interests will in this sense be a balancing act based on the facts of the individual situation. The above general themes are embodied in the following way in the statute.

Section 4(3) requires that D consider whether P is likely to regain capacity, **2.34** and if so, when. This is in part a practical set of questions, allowing D to organize his or her decision-making in the context of the period D will be making decisions. If P is unlikely ever to regain capacity, long-term care strategies are appropriate. If P is expected to regain capacity, the object should be to ensure that decisions are not taken during P's incapacity that will continue to bind P long into his or her capacity. Failure to protect P's position in this way would result in P being effectively precluded from decision-making after capacity is regained, a clear violation of the spirit of the MCA.

The substantive criteria that must be considered in determining best interests **2.35** are contained in s. 4(6):

(6) He must consider, so far as is reasonably ascertainable—
   (a) the person's past and present wishes and feelings (and, in particular, any relevant written statement made by him when he had capacity),
   (b) the beliefs and values that would be likely to influence his decision if he had capacity, and
   (c) the other factors that he would be likely to consider if he were able to do so.

The explanatory notes to the 2003 draft Bill state that 'best interests is not a test of "substituted judgement" (what the person would have wanted), but rather it requires a determination made by applying an objective test as to what would be in the person's best interests'.[20] At least in this unqualified form, this statement is not in conformity with s 4(6). The focus on P's wishes, feelings, beliefs and values makes it clear that that the test has an important and express subjective component. These are the classic features of a 'substituted judgement' approach. In this it is to be distinguished from the common law best interests assessment, which is markedly more objective. To put it somewhat crassly, what matters under subs (6) is what P now thinks, thought in the past when competent, or would think now if competent, not how much good a course of action would objectively do him or her. Most people in P's situation, of course, would if capable consider how much good would come from a course of action. As such, an element of objectivity is likely to be introduced in subs (6)(c), but only indirectly.

2.36   The provision makes it clear that account is to be taken not merely of past competent views, but also of P's current wishes and feelings. On one level, this just reflects common humanity. People without capacity experience fear and joy as much as the rest of us do, and it would be inhuman to ignore those factors in determining best interests. It is also one of the ways the statute takes into account the fact that while in law responsibility for decisions must be clearly defined with capacity as a dividing line, in practice abilities vary in an infinite number of ways. The fact that P loses the right to make a decision through incapacity does not therefore mean that P is excluded from the decision, as he or she may have much to contribute notwithstanding legal incapacity. This approach is also reflected in s 4(4), which requires D as far as reasonably practicable to 'permit and encourage' P to 'participate, or to improve his ability to participate, as fully as possible in any act done for him and any decision affecting him'. In the approach of the Act, the loss of capacity is not meant necessarily to entail a complete loss of autonomy.

2.37   The criteria require particular regard to be had to statements written by P when he or she had capacity. It does not follow from this that non-written views expressed by P when competent are irrelevant. Such views, depending on the context in which they were expressed, may retain considerable force. Similarly, the context of written statements will be significant. There is a world of difference between a casual view expressed in an informal letter to a friend and a formal statement in express anticipation of incapacity made following professional advice. The relevance and weight of any view expressed while competent, be it in writing or oral, will depend on the circumstances.

2.38   Unless the view constitutes a valid and applicable advance decision to refuse treatment, it will not be the sole controlling factor in the determination of best interests. The other factors in the section remain relevant. That said, the philosophy of the MCA places considerable weight on advance planning by P and the autonomy of P. It is therefore to be hoped that competent statements

---

[20] Explanatory Notes to HL Bill 13 (2004), para 25.

providing clear indications of P's wishes will be accorded considerable weight in the determination of best interests.

Special considerations apply to best interests determinations relating to the **2.39** provision or withholding of life-sustaining treatment. The issues surrounding this situation under the MCA will be discussed in paras 3.10–27 below. Suffice it here to say that s 4(6) requires that this decision cannot be motivated by a desire to bring about the death of P. It does not follow from this that medically appropriate treatment which is otherwise in the best interests of P cannot be given because it may shorten P's life. Similarly, if treatment has ceased to be effective, there is nothing in the section that requires its continuation, assuming its termination would otherwise be in the best interests of P. Cases involving persons in a permanent vegetative state, where the courts have previously been prepared to countenance withdrawal of artificial feeding, are more complicated and will be discussed in paras 3.19–20 below. Clients who want to ensure that they are allowed to die in such circumstances would be well advised to execute advanced decisions rather than to rely on other decision-making structures in the MCA or at common law.

Section 4(7) requires D, in so far as it is practicable and appropriate, to **2.40** consult the following people as to what would be in P's best interests:

(a) anyone named by the person as someone to be consulted on the matter in question or on matters of that kind,
(b) anyone engaged in caring for the person or interested in his welfare,
(c) any donee of a lasting power of attorney granted by the person, and
(d) any deputy appointed for the person by the court.

The DCOP encourages D to consult with a wide variety of people who are close to P,[21] including, but not limited to, those specifically listed in the subsection. The purpose of this consultation is specific. It is not to ask what the consultee thinks ought to happen; it is to ask the consultee for information about P's best interests as defined by the statute, and in particular the views, feelings, beliefs, and values of P as defined in s 4(6). In the common law, it is unclear whether the best interests of third parties such as carers are relevant to the determination of best interests.[22] Such third party interests are not mentioned in the substantive criteria in s 4, and this subsection does nothing to include them. Once again, of course, many people in P's position would have the interests of those around them in their consideration if making the relevant decision at a time when they were competent. These views will therefore often be relevant under s 4(6)(c). If the evidence is to the contrary, however, there is nothing in the section to make relevant the views of carers as to their own best interests.

---

[21] DCOP, para 4.23.

[22] In support of the relevance of such factors, see *Airedale NHS Trust v Bland* [1993] AC 789, 869, *per* Lord Goff, *Re S (Medical Treatment: Adult Sterilization)* [1998] 1 FLR 944, 946–7. In support of the irrelevance of such factors, see *Airedale NHS Trust v Bland* above at 896, *per* Lord Mustill; *Re A (Male Sterilization)* [2000] 1 FLR 549, 556.

2.41 The requirements to consult apply when such consultation is 'practicable and appropriate'. There are two obvious questions arising from this provision: how hard must D try to have a consultation with a relevant person; and when is a consultation inappropriate? Regarding the former, reasonable and bona fide efforts ought to be made to consult with the individuals named in the provision. These might include:

- ringing the most recent telephone numbers of which D is aware;
- if necessary, checking the telephone directory in the jurisdiction in which the individuals were last known to reside to see if there is a more recent telephone number;
- if time permits, writing to the individuals at their last known address;
- asking P's other friends and family for more recent contact details for the individuals.

Real attempts should be made to contact at least the enumerated people, along with others close to P, but if some, for example, appear to have disappeared, to be unreachable, to have lost capacity themselves, or refuse to speak with D, D should satisfy himself or herself that adequate consultation has occurred to get a good and rounded sense of the views, feelings, beliefs, and values of P as defined in s 4(6).

2.42 The requirement of consultation should not be read as destroying P's right to privacy. Just as P may have nominated a person to be consulted in these matters, there may be cogent reasons why he or she would not want other individuals consulted. The requirement in the Mental Health Act to consult with a specific 'nearest relative' has been found in violation of article 8 of the ECHR on this basis, when the nearest relative was alleged to have a history of sexually abusing the person who was the subject of the consultation.[23] This is a particularly extreme example; more generally, particularly outside the range of enumerated people, D should consider whether P would wish the potential consultee to be made privy to his or her private affairs.[24]

2.43 Laudable though the criteria in s 4 may be, they do become problematic in cases where the individual has never had capacity and has minimal abilities to engage with the decision. This latter point should not be overstated: even people with very minimal abilities are likely to have emotional responses that the criteria require to be taken into account. Nonetheless, determination of the beliefs, values, and other factors that would have influenced P had he had capacity is bound to be highly speculative when P has never had capacity, and where there is consequently little upon which to base the analysis. Such an approach has been used by the common law in the drafting of wills for people

---

[23] See *JT v United Kingdom* [2000] 1 FLR 909; *R (on the application of M) v Secretary of State for Health* [2003] EWHC 1094, [2003] UKHRR 746.

[24] On matters of confidentiality generally, see DCOP, ch 13.

without capacity, with results that are not entirely convincing.[25] The Law Commission seems to anticipate that the test will become more objective for such persons,[26] but there is little in the statutory criteria to support such a reinterpretation. The alternative is equally problematic, however. Does it follow, for example, that the adult child of Jehovah's Witnesses ought to be deemed to be a member of that faith and subject to its restrictions on use of blood products, or that the adult child of socialists would never invest her money in large corporations? Resort to 'objective' criteria does not escape these problems, since an 'objective' decision that a blood transfusion is in the best interests of P would by implication be a finding that P would not have been a Jehovah's Witness. It is difficult to escape the view that this would be making a religious decision about P as much as the reverse finding would be. In the event that individuals providing some aspects of P's care have strong views about the values in question, failure to take those views into account may put those exercising the legal framework on a collision course with the individuals providing aspects of P's care. In this situation, there is a risk that the carers' views as decision-makers on behalf of P as to his or her best interests merge with their own personal views and value systems. There is nothing in the statute to suggest that this is the intent of the legislation.

The best interests criteria limit the use of age, appearance, conditions and aspects of behaviour in the same way as the criteria regarding incapacity, and are subject to the same criticisms as those in para 2.23 above. The restrictions are nonetheless important, and perhaps never more so than for the individual who has always lacked capacity. In the absence of a basis of information regarding competent wishes in the past, decision-makers will be forced to use more speculative information. The risk is that such speculative factors may cross the line into stereotype or unwarranted paternalism. The use of such unjustified assumptions is exactly what s 4(1) is there to protect against. **2.44**

As noted at para 2.32 above, the statute does not purport to create a complete code for the determination of best interests. Other factors may be taken into account in appropriate circumstances.[27] While the flexibility of this approach can work to the considerable advantage of persons lacking capacity, there are difficulties with such an open-ended approach. First, how is D to determine what other factors ought to be taken into consideration? Often it will seem obvious, but some of these apparently obvious factors may serve to undercut the statutory approach. The prescribed statutory criteria are already quite broad. Section 4 allows consideration of any factor P would consider if competent; by definition, therefore, expansion into new territory means considering things which P would not have considered if competent. Unfettered inclusion of such factors risks **2.45**

---

[25] See, e.g., *Re C* [1991] 3 All ER 866, and comment in P. Bartlett and R. Sandland, *Mental Health Law: Policy and Practice*, 2nd edn (2003) 605–8.

[26] Law Com Report No 231 (n 10 above) para 3.25.

[27] See DCOP, paras 4.8–9.

undercutting the overarching ethos of the best interests test as discussed above. The carefully defined approach of the statute would risk being reduced to the crude balance sheet of the common law. At the same time, the statute is designed to establish practical regimes of care for adults lacking capacity. The criteria must function in the real world, and that may in practice require the inclusion of factors not articulated in s 4. The difficulty to be faced by decision-makers, and ultimately by the courts, is how to ensure respect for the statutory structure while ensuring the system can actually function. Inevitably, that will be decided on a case-by-case basis, but decision-makers moving outside the statutory criteria ought to be prepared to explain the appropriateness of their decision.

2.46   The criteria and their open-endedness raise particular problems when rights under the ECHR are at issue. Under the MCA, only the court will be permitted to infringe the rights to liberty under the ECHR, limiting the difficulties of the best interests approach here, but nonetheless the problem remains for the judicial level of decision-makers. When the article 5 right to liberty is infringed, the infringement will only be permitted if, *inter alia*, the deprivation is 'prescribed by law'. The decision of the European Court of Human Rights in *Kawka v Poland* establishes a standard:

> It is therefore essential that the conditions for deprivation of liberty under domestic law should be clearly defined, and that the law itself be foreseeable in its application, so that it meets the standard of 'lawfulness' set by the Convention, a standard which requires that all law should be sufficiently precise to allow the person—if needed, to obtain the appropriate advice—to foresee, to a degree that is reasonable in the circumstances, the consequences which a given action may entail.[28]

Of concern is whether the best interests criteria are sufficiently defined to satisfy this requirement. The statutory criteria may themselves give rise to problems in this regard. They provide a framework for the determination of best interests, but it is a deliberately open-ended framework based on flexible concepts such as values and presumed wishes, not a clear set of criteria such as is usual for article 5 detentions. It is fair to ask whether this set of flexible and subjective criteria will be such that an individual could foresee the consequences of his or her actions. The open-endedness of the criteria extends this problem. The court in *HL v United Kingdom* was concerned that there were no substantive criteria for the deprivation of liberty.[29] It is not clear that an open-ended set of criteria will convince the ECtHR of the clarity of English law any more than the absence of criteria. How, after all, can the individual foresee the consequences of his or her actions, when the criteria on which those actions will be judged are limited only by relevance?

2.47   It is for the decision-maker, D, to satisfy himself or herself that the proposed course of action is in the best interests of P. As discussed in para 1.35 above, at

---

[28] (258774/94) [2001] ECHR 4 (9 January 2001), para 49.
[29] *HL v United Kingdom* (2005) 40 EHRR 32, paras 119–24.

common law such a determination apparently now needs to be correct in order for the decision to be protected from liability. The MCA is much less harsh. The best interests test will be taken to be satisfied by decision-makers (other than courts) if the requirements of s 4 discussed above have been met, and if D 'reasonably believes' the course of action is in the best interests of P. D may sometimes be faced with conflicting views among those with whom he or she is required to consult. The DCOP encourages D to seek consensus in this situation.[30] This is of course desirable, but decision-makers should remain alive to the provisions of the Act, and in particular that the issue is what is in the best interests of P, not the broader realm of family politics and interests except in so far as P would have considered that relevant.

In the event that D is unable to make a clear determination of best interests, **2.48** it may be desirable to seek the advice of the independent advocacy service: see further paras 2.53–4 below. While this is not defined as one of the service's core functions under the Act, the DCOP does suggest this as a possible way forward.[31] In the event of real doubt in the context of a significant decision, it may well be appropriate to seek the advice of the court.

E. A GENERAL DEFENCE IN CIVIL AND CRIMINAL LAW, AND CONTRACTS FOR NECESSARY GOODS AND SERVICES

The 'general defence' is the least formalistic and most innovative of the legal **2.49** devices in the MCA. The essential thrust of the provision is that people who care for people without capacity should be protected from liability for so doing, provided that such care is in the best interests of P and is performed without negligence. The phrasing of this provision has changed between the Law Commission draft and the final statute, although the overall intent has remained the same. The Law Commission provision stated that 'it shall be lawful to do anything for the personal welfare or health care . . . [of P] if it is in all the circumstances reasonable for it to be done by the person who does it'.[32] This would have created a legal power or positive authority for persons engaging in welfare or health care of P. The MCA provision (s 5) is instead structured as a defence:

(1) If a person ('D') does an act in connection with the care or treatment of another person ('P'), the act is one to which this section applies if—
    (a) before doing the act, D takes reasonable steps to establish whether P lacks capacity in relation to the matter in question, and
    (b) when doing the act, D reasonably believes—
        (i) that P lacks capacity in relation to the matter, and
        (ii) that it will be in P's best interests for the act to be done.

---

[30] DCOP, paras 4.31–3.
[31] DCOP, para 4.35.
[32] Law Com Report No 231 (n 10 above), draft Bill cl 4(1).

(2) D does not incur any liability in relation to the act that he would not have incurred if P—

(a) had had capacity to consent in relation to the matter, and

(b) had consented to D's doing the act.

The difference between the Law Commission power and the statutory defence is not obviously material. Certainly, both will provide a defence to reasonable care provided directly to P, so long as the care is in P's best interests. Appropriate surgery provided to P is an obvious example: the surgeon can rely on s 5, as it would similarly have been possible to rely on the Law Commission's positive authority. The Law Commission also had third party relationships in mind, however. Their general authority was to be available for carers acting effectively as agents to arrange contractual care provided by third parties, from the delivery of milk to the replacement of P's roof.[33] These agency arrangements would also appear to be within the scope of s 5 as competent consent of P to such arrangements would be sufficient to establish them, so they would be established under the terms of s 5(2). This applies only to arrangements that require minimal legal formality. The word 'consent' could not be stretched, for example, to include transactions that need to be in writing such as the sale of land.

2.50 The statutory provision therefore places care on a legal, albeit informal, footing. 'Care' is not defined by the Act, and 'treatment' is defined merely as including 'a diagnostic or other procedure',[34] but it is reasonable to surmise that the courts will accord both a wide ambit. The DCOP provides an illustrative list of routine physical care, routine shopping or purchase of services, healthcare procedures, and similar duties.[35] While such routine duties are no doubt within the scope of s 5, there is nothing in the section to limit its ambit to the routine. If the larger expenditures such as roof repairs, an example envisaged by the Law Commission, were in the best interests of P, there is no reason they would be excluded from s 5.

2.51 Section 6 provides particular constraints in reliance on the general defence regarding the 'restraint' of P. Restraint occurs when D 'uses, or threatens to use, force to secure the doing of an act which P resists' or 'restricts P's liberty of movement, whether or not P resists' (s 6(5)). However, restraint does not include the deprivation of P's liberty under article 5 of the ECHR (s 6(5)). Such deprivations of liberty under the MCA can be sanctioned only by the court.[36] Otherwise, restraint is permitted only if two conditions are met:

(2) The first condition is that D reasonably believes that it is necessary to do the act in order to prevent harm to P.

---

[33] Law Com Report No 231 (n 10 above) para 4.7.

[34] MCA, s 64(1).

[35] DCOP, para 5.5.

[36] This is by implication, since all other decision-makers are expressly precluded from depriving P of article 5 rights: see ss 6(5), 11(6), and 20(13).

(3) The second is that the act is a proportionate response to—
   (a) the likelihood of P's suffering harm, and
   (b) the seriousness of that harm.

The first condition speaks to the necessity of the intervention to prevent harm, the second acknowledges that, in some instances, the proposed response may be more invasive than the harm that is set out to be prevented, especially if the harm is relatively unlikely to occur. Harm is not defined in the Act, although the DCOP provides an expansive set of illustrative examples of physical and financial harm.[37] The statutory provisions can be invoked of course only if the person is also incapable of making the specific decision in question. Vulnerability without incapacity does not justify the use of the MCA.

The focus of the definition of restraint is on the response of P to D's actions, **2.52** or the restriction of P. Restrictions placed on a third party in the best interests of P are not within the definition, unless P objects or unless restriction of P's movement is required. For example, if P lives in D's house and D takes the view that association with a third party is not in P's best interests, the exclusion of the third party from D's property would not be restraint within the meaning of the section unless P objects.

Special provisions are provided when 'serious treatment' is to be provided by **2.53** an NHS body, or where defined accommodation is to be provided by an NHS body or local authority (ss 35–40). If no appropriate individual is available to be consulted about P's best interests except a professional who provides care of P for remuneration, the accommodation or serious treatment can only be provided after an 'independent mental health advocate' has been appointed to represent P. Under s 35, independent mental health advocates are to be appointed in Wales by the National Assembly for Wales and in England by the responsible Secretary of State, again expected to be the Secretary of State for Health. The specific role of these advocates is to be subject to regulations by those authorities, as yet unpublished, but it appears likely that it will extend to supporting P's own involvement as far as possible in the decision in question; obtaining and evaluating relevant information, including calling for further medical opinions if appropriate; ascertaining alternative courses of action if any; and ascertaining what P's wishes, feelings, beliefs, and values would be and where P's best interests would lie. The MCA envisages that the regulations will allow the advocate to act on P's behalf to challenge the decision in prescribed circumstances (s 36). The specific breadth of this authority is as yet unclear, as the regulations have not been published.

These provisions apply only for 'serious medical treatment' and defined **2.54** accommodation of persons lacking capacity. 'Serious medical treatment' is to be defined by regulations, as yet unpublished (s 37(6)). Accommodation, when provided by the NHS, means admission to hospital that is expected to exceed

---

[37] DCOP, para 5.31.

28 days or to a care home for a period expected to be longer than eight weeks (s 38). These provisions are meant to include aftercare provided under s 117 of the Mental Health Act 1983.[38] Accommodation when provided by a local authority means residential accommodation for a period expected to exceed eight weeks (s 39(4)(a)). In any of these circumstances, the prior involvement of the advocate may be waived in cases of urgency (undefined), but in cases concerning accommodation, the advocate must nonetheless be involved following the reception of P into the accommodation. The provisions do not apply when another person is appropriate to be consulted regarding P's best interests, and in particular, s 40 of the MCA precludes the application of these provisions if there is a person nominated by P to be consulted in matters affecting his or her interests, a donee of an LPOA created by P, a deputy appointed by the Court for P, or a donee of an enduring power of attorney created by P.

2.55   Section 5 takes effect if prior to taking the action in question D has taken reasonable steps to determine P's capacity and if, while doing the act, D reasonably believes that P lacks capacity and that the act is in P's best interests. While the section provides protection for D in cases of reasonable belief, the section does provide an express requirement for D to have taken 'reasonable steps' to determine P's capacity. Belief alone is therefore insufficient for the section; it must be a belief founded on a reasonable investigation. The belief in P's incapacity must also itself be reasonable. D's determination that the action is in the best interests of P is not expressly subject to the requirement that reasonable steps be taken, but need only be a reasonable belief. That said, the statutory definition of best interests contains a variety of procedural requirements and substantive criteria, including the likelihood that P will regain capacity, maximizing the involvement of P in the decision, the view P would have taken if competent, and consulting with other carers and similar figures: see paras 2.33–45. It is difficult to see that D could arrive at a 'reasonable belief' that an act would be in P's best interests as defined without taking the appropriate procedural steps.

2.56   The MCA anticipates that a variety of individuals may be involved in making decisions about P's care. This raises the possibility of dispute among decision-makers or carers as to the appropriate course of action. The DCOP counsels that attempts should be made to reach consensus in these situations,[39] and this is no doubt desirable, provided that the consensus is consistent with the statutory criteria. In the end, it is the person who will be relying on the general defence who must be satisfied that P's best interests are met by the actions he or she is taking, and the defence will apply so long as that belief is reasonable. That said, where contradictory views are entrenched concerning significant decisions and litigation appears likely at some point, it will usually be preferable to seek a court opinion before embarking on the controversial course of action.

---

[38] Explanatory notes to Mental Capacity Bill (2004–5 HL Bill 13-EN) para 113.
[39] DCOP, para 4.31.

The DCOP suggests that in determinations of capacity and best interests, **2.57** professionals will be held to a higher standard than lay persons.[40] This makes some sense if the determination is viewed according to standards analogous to the law of negligence, where professionals are expected to exercise a higher standard of care than non-professionals in their field of expertise.[41] Such a differential standard is not, however, obvious on the face of the statute. Indeed, as discussed in para 1.40 above, the common law tendency has been to view the capacity determination as a multi-disciplinary matter. The statutory test is consistent with that change, requiring consultation with non-professionals in the determination of best interests. As the law becomes less focused on these determinations as within the competence of specific professionals, the argument for a higher standard of care for those professionals becomes less convincing. If these determinations are not just a medical matter, why should the courts expect doctors to be better at them than other people?

Professionals can of course be expected to know about the statutory pro- **2.58** visions, and their failure to comply with them should meet with little judicial sympathy. Should the same apply to lay persons? Should the protection of the general defence be afforded to a D who honestly thinks he or she is doing right by P even if his or her actions are outside the statutory definition of best interests? There would seem to be three possibilities here: stretch the statutory definition of best interests to include D's actions; deny the statutory protection but allow a defence under the common law jurisdiction; or fail to provide a defence at all. None of these possibilities is attractive. The first would go a considerable way to gutting the statutory definition that has been so carefully developed by the Law Commission and is one of the real strengths of the statute. The second would have a similar effect, because it would allow the substantive and procedural statutory safeguards to be circumvented by an appeal to the common law. The third could result in well-intentioned carers, intending to act to the benefit of P, being subjected to legal sanction. How this will play out in court remains to be seen. One would suspect that case-specific facts such as the manner and personality of individual protagonists may figure significantly in the making of precedent-setting decisions.

The informality of these procedures is their great strength, yet that very **2.59** informality raises potential difficulties. The application of s 5 can result in P's loss of civil rights. Obvious examples include the right to control one's own money, as the MCA allows for P's money to be pledged or otherwise used in payment for services P did not request; and the loss of one's bodily integrity, through the loss of the right to consent to medical treatment. Under article 6 of the ECHR, the loss of civil rights is meant to follow a hearing. Routine hearings under the MCA are not held prior to D's assumption of P's rights. The fact that

---

[40] DCOP, para 5.14.
[41] *Wilsher v Essex Area Health Authority* [1986] 3 All ER 801, CA.

41

D may not actually be correct in his or her belief that P lacks capacity makes this violation appear less savoury. At the same time, the imposition of hearings prior to routine decisions would be manifestly impractical. The insistence on the legal niceties of the ECHR would risk the collapse of the structures of the Act, which are intended to work to the benefit of people lacking capacity.

2.60   The general defence does not affect the operation of an advance decision to refuse medical treatment (s 5(4)). Treatments refused by P in advance cannot then be given by reliance on the general defence. It also does not authorize any individual acting in conflict with decisions made by a donee of an LPOA or a court-appointed deputies acting within the scope of their respective authorities (s 6(6)). The general defence is still available for decisions outside the respective authorities of these individuals. This raises the potentially difficult question as to how an informal carer, the sort that is intended to be assisted by the general defence, is meant to know of these individuals and the scope of their authorities. The MCA provides no answer, leaving the possibility that a person acting in good faith in reliance on the general defence may find that it does not apply in his or her case. If the act in question is otherwise tortious, or if significant financial commitments are made that cannot be avoided, the result could be unfortunate for D. In the event of legal uncertainty flowing from apparent conflicting authorities, however, the Act is clear that life-sustaining treatment may be given and any act done to prevent the deterioration of P's condition, pending a decision of the court (s 6(7)).

2.61   The MCA acknowledges that payment may be required for the provision of care to P. This is primarily covered in s 7, under which P must pay a 'reasonable price' for 'necessary goods and services' supplied to him or her. While this will most frequently be applicable to care provided under the general defence, nothing in s 7 restricts it to such care. If an individual with a valid LPOA for personal decisions did not have a valid LPOA for financial decisions, for example, s 7 would apply to ensure payment for the financial ramifications of the personal decisions, as long as the goods and services provided were 'necessary'. In practice reliance on s 7 may sometimes be unwieldy, so it should not be viewed as a substitute for a well-drawn LPOA with included financial powers.

2.62   The provision contained in the MCA is a consolidation of the common law regarding services and the provision of the Sale of Goods Acts Act 1979 regarding goods. The relevant jurisprudence relating to this other law will therefore apply to the MCA provision.[42] 'Necessary' is in a sense a misleading term, as it implies a restrictive ambit of what must be paid for. In fact, the MCA reflects the existing jurisprudence that takes a broader approach. 'Necessary' under the MCA means 'suitable to a person's condition in life and to his actual requirements at the time when the goods or services are supplied' (s 7(2)). The term

---

[42] For an overview, see P. Matthews, 'Contracts for Necessaries and Mental Incapacity' (1982) 33 *Northern Ireland Legal Quarterly* 149.

therefore extends not merely to minimal food and shelter, but assuming they are appropriate to P's requirements and condition in life, also for example to home repairs, a new television, holidays, and restaurant meals. A particularly expansive example can be found in *Re Bevan*[43] where the person lacking capacity made a living letting property. Necessaries in that case were taken to include all expenses related to rent audit of the properties and the expenses for renovation of one of the rental properties.[44]

While s 7 creates a liability on P to pay for necessaries, it does not create a **2.63** new process to ensure actual payment for expenditures. Section 8 goes part of the way to doing this for acts permitted under the general defence in s 5, by allowing D to pledge P's credit or to apply money in P's possession toward the expenditure. These mechanisms may be used whether the payment is actually owed to D or to a third party: there are no express provisions regarding conflicts of interests and no requirement that such expenditure be reported to any public body. However, the DCOP makes it clear that s 8 does nothing to give D signing authority over P's bank accounts or investments,[45] so D's actual access to funds to disburse may be limited. If P's incapacity is likely to be of some duration, creditors may lack patience and press for more formal steps to be made to the court in order to effect payment.

Other mechanisms may be of more assistance. The social security regulations **2.64** allow a carer to act as an 'appointee' of a person lacking capacity, and so to claim benefits on their behalf. This may be of practical importance, as it provides a steady (albeit modest) stream of income into a carer's hands, with which payment for necessaries may be made.

F. LASTING POWERS OF ATTORNEY

At common law, powers of attorney were deemed to be terminated upon the **2.65** incapacity of the donor.[46] The statutory provisions of the Enduring Powers of Attorney Act 1985 (EPAA) allowed the power to continue in these circumstances if it was clear on its face that this was intended by the donor and provided that the statutory criteria were met, most significantly that the enduring power of attorney was registered with the Court of Protection consistent with the procedures in the EPAA. However, these powers of attorney could extend only to matters of property and affairs—the traditional realm of powers of attorney. They could not extend to purely personal decisions regarding social care or medical treatment.

The MCA provides a new statutory framework for powers of attorney **2.66**

---

[43] [1912] 1 Ch 196.
[44] [1912] 1 Ch 196.
[45] DCOP, para 5.38.
[46] *Drew v Nunn* (1879) 4 QB 661.

intended to survive the incapacity of the donor (now called 'lasting' powers of attorney, hereinafter LPOAs). This framework is broadly similar to the one provided under the EPAA, except that the MCA allows them to extend beyond decisions relating to P's property and affairs to personal decisions (s 9(1)). The DCOP indicates that the Office of the Official Guardian will be publishing guidance on LPOAs both for donors and donees. As yet it has not done so, but reference should be made to that document when it appears. Unlike the code of practice, however, it is not given a special legal status by the MCA. The *Munjaz*[47] decision will therefore not apply to it, and it will have no formal legal force beyond a regular government guidance.[48]

2.67   The MCA revokes the EPAA (s 66). While all new powers of attorney must be executed pursuant to the MCA if they are to survive the incapacity of the donor, the salient provisions of the EPAA regarding registration and legal effect of enduring powers of attorney are contained in Sch 4 to the MCA.[49] Enduring powers of attorney that were validly executed under the statutory framework at the time of their execution need not therefore be re-executed under the new legislation. Some clients may nonetheless wish to execute a new LPOA, for example to include the personal decisions now permitted by the MCA or to take advantage of somewhat different registration procedures.

2.68   The case of *Re K; Re F*[50] held that a donor could have the capacity to execute an enduring power of attorney even if he or she did not have capacity to manage his or her property and affairs. This may appear to be a somewhat surprising result, as it allows the donor to appoint an agent to do things that the donor as principal is incapable of doing,[51] but it seems entrenched in the current law. It seems likely that a similar approach will be adopted under the MCA.

2.69   In *Re K; Re F* the following standard of capacity was adopted:

What degree of understanding is involved? Plainly one cannot expect that the donor should have been able to pass an examination on the provisions of the 1985 Act. At the other extreme, I do not think that it would be sufficient if he realised only that it gave cousin William power to look after his property. Counsel as amicus curiae [for the Official Solicitor] helpfully summarised the matters which the donor should have understood in order that he can be said to have understood the nature and effect of the power: first, if such be the terms of the power, that the attorney will be able to assume complete control over the donor's affairs; second, if such be the terms of the power, that the attorney will in general be able to do anything with the donor's property which the donor could have

---

[47] *R (on the application of Munjaz) v Mersey Care NHS Trust and Others* [2003] EWCA Civ 1036, [2004] QB 395.

[48] See *R v Department of Health, ex p Source Informatics Ltd* [2001] QB 424, CA.

[49] There are a few minor variations between the EPAA and Sch 4 in the procedures applicable. For example, where the EPAA accorded a variety of duties to the Court of Protection, most of these are now given to the Office of the Public Guardian.

[50] [1988] 1 All ER 358.

[51] For a critical analysis of this decision, see P. Bartlett and R. Sandland, *Mental Health Law: Policy and Practice*, 2nd edn (2003) 668–70.

done; third, that the authority will continue if the donor should be or become mentally incapable; fourth, that if he should be or become mentally incapable, the power will be irrevocable without the confirmation of the court.[52]

While the capacity to execute an LPOA is governed by the general definitions of persons lacking capacity in ss 2 and 3 of the MCA, the language in *Re K; Re F* may serve as a guide, in particular to the breadth of the 'information relevant to the decision' in s 3(1)(a). References to 'property' and 'affairs' will of course have to be varied to reflect the terms of the LPOA in question.

While the MCA makes it clear that LPOAs may give authority to make decisions related to P's 'personal welfare' or 'property and affairs' or both (see s 9), it does little further to define these terms. 'Property' is defined in s 64(1) as including any thing in action and any interest in real or personal property. In so far as the provisions relate to property and affairs, it seems reasonable to conclude that the range of powers granted can be as broad as is otherwise permitted by the general law relating to powers of attorney.[53] The scope as it relates to personal welfare lacks this established precedent, but is likely to be read broadly by the courts. A non-exhaustive and illustrative list in the DCOP refers to decisions as to where P should live, decisions regarding medical consent and accessing medical treatment, and applying for access to confidential documents and personal information relating to P.[54]   **2.70**

Section 9(4) of the MCA provides that the authority conferred by the LPOA is subject to: **2.71**

(a) the provisions of this Act and, in particular, sections 1 (the principles) and 4 (best interests), and

(b) any conditions or restrictions specified in the instrument.

These provisions will generally work to the considerable advantage of P, the donor of the power. Subsection (b) allows specific instructions to be provided to D, the attorney. The DCOP uses the example of a person with ethical concerns, who would be able to require the attorney to invest only in ethical investments.[55] Similarly, P might wish to provide his or her views as to future accommodation such as a preference for or against a specific nursing home, or views regarding treatment (although these can also be expressed in an advance decisions to refuse treatment, discussed in paras 2.103–24 below). It should however be recalled that the document is, in the end, only a power of attorney, which can give D no powers beyond those possessed by P when capable. In particular, it cannot require third parties to comply with P's wishes. Thus P may prefer a

---

[52] [1988] 1 All ER 358, 363.

[53] The EPAA was express on this point: see s 3(2). While the language has disappeared from the MCA, it is difficult to see how else the potential breadth of the LPOA relating to property and affairs would be construed.

[54] DCOP, para 6.7. cf. s 17, which defines 'personal welfare' but only for purposes of court-appointed deputies.

[55] DCOP, para 6.14.

specific nursing home, but the LPOA cannot require the home to make that accommodation available.

2.72   Section 9(4)(a) engages decisions under the LPOA with the overall philosophy of the MCA. As a consequence, it will be necessary for D, when making decisions about P, to consider P's current (incapable) views and feelings on the matter and the likelihood that P will regain capacity, the requirement that P be involved as far as possible in the decision-making process, and the other substantive conditions and processes in the best interests definition.

2.73   There is the possibility that paras (a) and (b) of subs (4) will conflict, however. As discussed above in para 2.32 above, the best interests test in the MCA is open-ended. While care in adopting too broad an approach was advocated above (see para 2.45), in theory anything of relevance may influence the best interests determination. It is possible for a clause purporting to provide conditions under (b) not to be in accord with P's best interests under (a). For example, a clause consistent with (b) requiring that decisions be taken to ensure that P reside in her current residence until her death might well at some point cease to be in P's best interests under (a). Similarly, ethical investments required by (b) may not be in P's best financial interests under (a). The two paragraphs have equal status in the section, so the matter would presumably come down to a choice between honouring P's autonomy and measured paternalist intervention. How this is approached by a court may well depend on the facts of individual precedent-setting cases. While the importance of the overarching principles and the best interests criteria in the MCA are not to be underestimated, the courts in the past have shown themselves to be hesitant at intervening when an EPOA is in effect.[56]

2.74   The MCA provides further express restrictions on the use of LPOAs in the context of personal welfare decision-making. First, even when the LPOA has been registered, it extends only to making decisions in areas where P actually lacks capacity or where D reasonably believes that P lacks capacity (s 11(7)(a)). The express inclusion of this restriction in respect of personal welfare decisions suggests that the reverse may be true in matters of property and affairs: upon registration, D apparently receives the full range of authorities relating to property and affairs contained in the LPOA.[57] That does not, of course, remove any authority from P. An LPOA is in the end a power of attorney, and although it gives authority to the attorney, it does not remove any from the donor. Contracts signed by P would therefore remain enforceable if P had capacity to sign them, and in the event that he or she did not have capacity, would be dealt with by the contractual law relating to contracts by people lacking capacity.

2.75   Secondly, LPOAs are subject to the same restrictions regarding restraint, and the same definition of restraint, as persons who act in reliance on the general

---

[56] See, e.g., *Re R (Enduring Power of Attorney)* [1990] 1 Ch 647.

[57] This reflects current practice regarding enduring powers of attorney: see *Re F; Re K* [1988] 1 All ER 358; D. Lush, *Cretney and Lush on Enduring Powers of Attorney*, 5th edn (2001) para 4.2.2.

defence: see paras 2.51–2 above. LPOAs are subject to advance decisions to refuse (ss 11(7)(b), 25(7)). Some caution is appropriate here, however, as s 25(2)(b) holds that an advance decision to refuse treatment is invalid if a subsequent LPOA appears to include authority to give or refuse consent to the treatment. As a matter of caution, a well-drafted LPOA should state that the advance treatment refusal remains in effect, if that is P's wish. Finally, while the LPOA may extend to making treatment decisions for P, it does not authorize the giving or refusing of consent to life-sustaining treatment unless the instrument contains express provisions to that effect (s 11(7)(c), (8)). As treatment decisions in an end-of-life context will be one of the situations where many clients will want the LPOA to be effective, this presumption should be drawn to clients' attention and specific instructions obtained as to whether the LPOA should have effect in these circumstances.

2.76 Special provisions are also made regarding the attorney's power to make gifts. Subject to any conditions or restrictions in the instrument, the attorney with authority over P's property and affairs may make gifts on customary occasions (as defined in s 12(3)) to those related to or connected with P, and may donate to any charity to which P might be expected to make donations. In any event, such gifts and donations must always be reasonable, having regard to all the circumstances and in particular the size of P's estate (s 12(2)).

2.77 The mechanics of making, registering, and revoking LPOAs are contained in ss 10 and 13, and in Sch 1. Both donor and attorney must be over the age of eighteen. The instrument must be in writing, on the prescribed form in Sch 1, with the duly witnessed signatures of the donor and the donee. For personal decisions, the attorney must be an individual, although for property and affairs, it may also be a trust corporation (s 10(1)). In general, the mechanics are similar to those previously in effect for enduring powers of attorney, with a few exceptions. Where there is more than one attorney, it is now assumed that the attorneys will act jointly, unless the instrument specifies otherwise (s 10(5)). Where attorneys are to act jointly, the failure of either one of them to meet the criteria of the Act prevents an LPOA from being created (s 10(6)). While the instrument cannot give the donee the power to appoint a substitute or successor attorney, the instrument itself may appoint such a substitute (s 10(8)). The rather complex provisions regarding notification prior to registration which applied to enduring powers of attorney have been removed. In their stead, the instrument itself is now required to indicate such person or persons as must be notified prior to registration (Sch 1, para 2(1)(c)). The LPOA is registered at first instance with the Public Guardian (Sch 1, para 11). The Public Guardian cannot register an LPOA if it appears to have powers trespassing on those of a court-appointed deputy (Sch 1, para 12). The court has increased jurisdiction to sever provisions in conflict with the Act (Sch 1, para 11). Registration remains a largely administrative affair. No formal evidence of P's incapacity is routinely required, although P may of course object to the registration. In that event, the LPOA cannot be registered without an order of the court (Sch 1, para 14).

2.78   Section 13 of the Act concerns revocation of LPOAs. While packaged somewhat differently to the EPOA, its effects are similar. P may revoke the power at
any time he or she has capacity (s 13(2)). The power is revoked if P becomes
bankrupt and is suspended if P is subject to an interim bankruptcy order. The
power is also revoked if D disclaims the appointment, dies, loses capacity, or,
except in so far as the LPOA gives authority over P's personal welfare, D
becomes bankrupt. Unlike the previous legislation, it does provide that dissolution or annulment of a marriage or civil partnership between donor and
donee will terminate the power, unless the power specifically provides to the
contrary (s 13(6)(c), (10)).

2.79   The provisions of the Act and Sch 1 are to be supplemented by regulations
from the Lord Chancellor, not yet published. In particular, statements signed by
donees will need to be attached to the LPOA at the time, acknowledging understanding of the principles in s 1 of the MCA and of the best interests test, along
with information prescribed in the regulations. A certificate must also be
included confirming that the donor is capable of executing the LPOA and that
no fraud or undue pressure has induced the donor to create the LPOA. The
persons eligible to sign such certificates are also to be prescribed in the
regulations. Conditions and procedures for D to disclaim the power will also be
included. Further provisions regarding execution, registration, and revocation
are likely to be included in the regulations, when they are published.

2.80   The LPOA creates a fiduciary relationship between P and D. The DCOP
provides a good overview of how a donee ought to approach his or her duties.[58]

2.81   The powers of the court over LPOAs are set out primarily in ss 22–23.[59] The
court has a general power to determine points of law relating to an LPOA. It can
revoke or refuse to register the power if there has been undue influence or fraud,
or if the donee is not acting in the best interests of P or in contravention of
authority. Pending a court determination on these matters, the general defence
allows life-sustaining treatment to be given to P, and for care-givers to do such
acts as are reasonably believed to be necessary to prevent a serious deterioration
in P's condition (s 6(7)). The court can also give directions to D as to how to
exercise the powers contained in the LPOA and provide consents the donee
would need to get from P. It can insist on rendering of accounts or production of
information, and allow remuneration or payment of expenses to the donee. The
court may also relieve the donee from liability. In the past, the courts have been
reluctant to intervene to any considerable extent in the implementation of
enduring powers of attorney, holding that their role extended to administrative
matters only and not to the core of the power.[60] The wording of the sections
relating to the court's powers in the MCA is not particularly more expansive

---

[58] DCOP, paras 6.17–34.

[59] See also DCOP, paras 7.18–21.

[60] See *Re R (Enduring Power of Attorney)* [1990] 1 Ch 647. For a critical view of this approach,
see P. Bartlett and R. Sandland, *Mental Health Law: Policy and Practice*, 2nd edn (2003) 666–7.

than that of the previous legislation, but the overall context of the Act itself does point towards a more interventionist role for the courts. It remains to be seen how the courts will approach their role in overseeing these instruments.

LPOAs are no doubt a welcome development. They are flexible—a donor P **2.82** may give different people different powers of decision relating to all or part of P's personal welfare, estate, or property. They have the tremendous advantage of allowing P to decide whom he or she trusts to make the decisions P would want made. That said, a slight note of caution is appropriate. While the Office of the Public Guardian has authority to investigate allegations of abuse (s 58), it is not obvious how abuses will come to the attention of that Office. Particularly if the courts continue their laissez-faire approach, P may be left vulnerable. There is in any event unlikely to be routine scrutiny to ensure that the system is operating as it ought. It is therefore essential that donors of these powers give serious consideration into whose hands they wish to commit their lives.

G. THE POWERS OF THE COURT AND THE APPOINTMENT OF DEPUTIES

Under the MCA, the Court of Protection is reconstituted and receives a sig- **2.83** nificantly expanded statutory jurisdiction over the personal and financial affairs of persons lacking capacity. The court itself is constituted under ss 45–49 of the Act. Standing to commence applications to the court is considered in s 50, and ss 51–56 provide authority for the usual issuance of rules and practice directions relating to procedures, appeals, costs, and fees. Some additional guidance on the administration of property and affairs is contained in Sch 2 to the MCA, but otherwise the rules and practice directions have not been published as of the time of writing. Part VII of the Mental Health Act 1983 is repealed by the MCA, and transitional arrangements for those currently under its jurisdiction are contained in Part 1 of Sch 5 to the MCA.

The court is assisted in its functions by the Public Guardian and the Court of **2.84** Protection Visitors. The former has a variety of functions set out in s 58 of the Act, related to administrative oversight of LPOAs and court-appointed deputies. Specific duties include maintaining registers of LPOAs and deputies, supervising deputies, and receiving reports from donees of LPOAs and deputies. The Public Guardian can also investigate complaints regarding the exercise of powers by LPOAs and deputies, and can direct a Court of Protection Visitor to visit and report on donees of LPOAs, deputies, and those for whom donees and deputies are making decisions. The Court of Protection Visitors include 'special' visitors who have medical qualifications and are knowledgeable about mental disorder, and 'general' visitors. As their name suggests, their role is to visit donees of LPOAs, deputies, and those for whom they make decisions, in response to requests from the Public Guardian or Court of Protection. In carrying out these duties, the visitors and the Public Guardian may examine and copy health records, social services records held by local authorities, and records held by persons registered under Part II of the Care Standards Act 2000, as far as they relate to the person lacking capacity who is the subject of their inquiries.

2.85   The Court of Protection has three sorts of function. It has a general supervisory jurisdiction to make declarations regarding the care provided under the provisions of the MCA. It is given its own jurisdiction to make orders over the personal welfare and property and affairs of persons lacking capacity. This allows it, for example, to make specific decisions concerning the sale of a major asset or the drafting of a will. Finally, it can appoint receivers for ongoing decision-making.

2.86   The general supervisory jurisdiction includes the authority to determine whether P lacks capacity regarding a specific decision or class of decisions, and whether acts either done or proposed to be done in relation to P are lawful (s 15). The court therefore has jurisdiction to consider any issue which may arise under the general defence, as well as the applicability and effect of any advanced refusal of treatment. The court also has jurisdiction to determine whether a document creates an effective LPOA and whether an LPOA ought to be registered (s 22). It may further provide directions on matters within the scope of an LPOA, require the donee to submit accounts or records, and set remuneration of the donee (s 23). The court therefore has jurisdiction to adjudicate on all relevant matters that may arise under the care provisions of the Act.

2.87   The court's power to make orders over personal welfare and property and affairs of P are defined by the MCA. For personal welfare decisions, the definition is non-exhaustive, but includes (s 17):

(a) deciding where P is to live;
(b) deciding what contact, if any, P is to have with any specified persons;
(c) making an order prohibiting a named person from having contact with P;
(d) giving or refusing consent to the carrying out or continuation of a treatment by a person providing health care for P;
(e) giving a direction that a person responsible for P's health care allow a different person to take over that responsibility.

The powers of the court as regards property and affairs are coextensive with the court's previous powers in this area, which were contained in s 96 of the Mental Health Act 1983. They encompass a wide array of powers, including disposition or acquisition of property, carrying on of a trade or profession, discharge of debts, the execution of a will, and the conduct of legal proceedings (s 18(1)). Where normally the provisions of the Act do not apply to persons under the age of sixteen, for matters relating to property and affairs the court may make decisions on behalf of, and appoint deputies for, persons under that age if it appears that they will continue to lack capacity at the age of eighteen years (s 18(3)).

2.88   The court's powers are, of course, subject to the remainder of the Act, and in particular the principles in s 1 and best interests criteria (s 16(3)). The court is not necessarily bound by the terms of the application before it, and can make whatever order it views as best promoting the best interests of P (s 16(6)).

The Law Commission intended the court to be the decision-maker of last **2.89** resort.[61] The DCOP encourages informal resolution of disputes,[62] but acknowledges there will be times when applications to the court are necessary. It gives as examples disagreements between professionals as to the capacity of P, and situations where disputes are wide-ranging, as when family members disagree about the validity of an LPOA and the best interests of the individual.[63] While it must be ensured that the statutory criteria are followed for decision-making, certainly some care should be given to avoiding court applications. Costs of litigation have in the past often been paid for from the estate of P. As litigation can be expensive, this is not necessarily going to be in the best interests of P.

There are, however, some situations where a court application may be legally **2.90** required. Within the terms of the MCA, if violation of an individual's liberty under article 5 of the ECHR is to be imposed, it may only be done by the court. In the absence of express provision in an LPOA, many legal decisions will require court applications, including the sale of property and access to bank accounts to make funds available for care. Prior to the MCA, the courts held that judicial determinations ought to be sought for decisions regarding the termination of life-sustaining treatments of persons in a persistent vegetative state and the non-therapeutic sterilization of people lacking capacity: see para 1.13 above. This requirement is not contained in the MCA, nor does the Act make any express provision for it in regulations. The DCOP does not require such applications as a matter of routine, and the Act does seem to envisage that decisions to refuse life-sustaining treatment by the donee of an LPOA may be relied upon without court intervention in some circumstances (see s 11(8)(a)). It remains to be seen whether court applications will be required in these situations either by judicial interpretation or in the DCOP.

Only the court can make or amend a will on behalf of P. A will can only be **2.91** made if P has reached the age of eighteen years. The mechanics of the court's jurisdiction to make wills are contained in Sch 2 to the MCA. The relevant portions of that Schedule are coextensive with s 97 of the Mental Health Act 1983. The body of law that has developed under the Mental Health Act in this regard is therefore likely to continue to apply to wills made under the MCA.[64] While the will must conform to the whole of the best interests test in s 4, it is reasonable to surmise that the past and present wishes of P, as well as the beliefs, values, and other factors which would have been likely to influence P if he or she had capacity, should be pivotal in the drafting of the will.

---

[61] Law Com Report No 231 (n 10 above) para 8.2.

[62] DCOP, ch 10.

[63] DCOP, para 7.10.

[64] See, e.g., *Re B (Court of Protection)* [1987] 2 FLR 155 and *Re D (J)* [1982] 1 Ch 237 with regard to drafting generally and *Re C (A Patient)* [1991] 3 All ER 866 regarding bequests to charities.

2.92   The court further has jurisdiction to appoint deputies to make decisions on behalf of P. In coming to its decision, the court must in addition to the best interests criteria in s 4, have regard to the principles that a decision by a court is preferable to the appointment of a deputy, and that the powers conferred on a deputy should be as limited in scope and duration as reasonably possible (s 16(4)). The objective here is to minimize the scope and duration of control: specific decisions of the court are to be preferred to the ongoing appointment of a deputy; and when a deputy must be appointed, it is to be for the narrowest scope and shortest time reasonably practicable. Deputies for personal welfare decisions must be individuals aged eighteen or over. For decisions relating to property and affairs, they may also be public trust corporations. Holders of offices for the time being may be appointed (s 19(2)), so a director of a social services agency could be appointed to make personal decisions regarding a person lacking capacity.[65] Deputies must consent to their appointment, but once appointed have a duty to act.[66]

2.93   Section 20 of the MCA creates restrictions on the powers of deputies. Notwithstanding the terms of his or her appointment, a deputy does not have power to make a decision if he or she has reasonable grounds to believe that P has capacity in relation to the matter. Deputies cannot require a change in the individual responsible for P's health care. They may not settle P's property, or exercise powers vested in P. They may not make decisions which are within the scope of a valid LPOA, and they may not refuse life-sustaining treatment on behalf of P. Their powers regarding restraint are similar to those imposed on donees of LPOAs and persons acting under the general defence: see para 2.51–2 above.

2.94   The overall duties of deputies are described in the DCOP.[67] They will normally be expected to post security and are subject to the supervision of the court. That will normally include periodic reports to the Public Guardian, who also has an authority to investigate complaints regarding the exercise of the authority of a deputy.

2.95   Whether the application is for a declaration, an order, or for the appointment of a deputy, the application process is governed by s 50. The following persons may apply to the court as of right under s 50(1):

(a) a person who lacks, or is alleged to lack, capacity,
(b) if such a person has not reached the age of eighteen, by anyone with parental responsibility for that person,
(c) the donor or donee of an LPOA relating to the application,
(d) a deputy for the person to whom the application relates,
(e) a person named in an order of the court, if the application relates to that order.

---

[65] See DCOP, para 7.29.
[66] DCOP, para 7.28.
[67] DCOP, paras 7.36–51.

Other persons must receive the leave of the court to apply. In deciding whether to grant leave, the following factors are to be considered by the court (s 50(3)):

(a) the applicant's connection with the person to whom the application relates,
(b) the reasons for the application,
(c) the benefit to the person to whom the application relates of a proposed order or directions, and
(d) whether the benefit can be achieved in any other way.

The provisions regarding leave are more systematic than the common law approach to standing in declaration applications. While they do not represent an entirely new direction in this regard, they should serve to clarify the jurisprudence in this area.

In the hearing of the application, the court has all the powers of a superior **2.96** court, as well as the power to call for reports (s 49). This provides the court with investigative resources not generally available to courts in an adversarial system. The court can require investigations and reports to be made by the Public Guardian, a Court of Protection Visitor, or a local authority or NHS body or one of its officers or employees. In complying with such a requirement, the Public Guardian or Court of Protection Visitor may examine and copy any health record, local authority social services record, or record held by a person registered under Part II of the Care Standards Act 2000 relating to P.

The introduction of a statutory court jurisdiction in personal welfare matters **2.97** is to be greeted with enthusiasm. In general, here as in the remainder of the MCA, standards of drafting are refreshingly good. There are however a few places of potential uncertainty.

First, the MCA makes it clear that acts done by an individual acting on the **2.98** general defence or pursuant to an LPOA sufficiently meet the standards of best interests if D reasonably believes them to be in P's best interests (s 4(9)). Certainly, the court on application has the authority to overrule such decisions taken in good faith; the more difficult question is whether it will choose to exercise some deference to ground-level decision-makers, particularly those selected by P through an LPOA. These individuals have after all been entrusted by the donor to make the relevant decisions; if they are making the decisions to the standard anticipated in s 4(9), should the court intervene if its view of best interests is different?

Secondly, the view since 1905 of the *parens patriae* power over property and **2.99** affairs, carried over into the jurisprudence under Part VII of the Mental Health Act 1983, was that it extinguished any authority of P to deal with his or her property. Once P became subject to these powers, any purported contracts with him or her were void, as P was not legally able to contract.[68] This was not the previously traditional view. Earlier nineteenth-century authority held that a

---

[68] See *Re Walker* [1905] 1 Ch 160; *Re Beaney (deceased)* [1978] 2 All ER 595, 600.

contract signed in a so-called 'lucid interval' was valid.[69] This appears to have been restored by the MCA: it is clear that P has authority to make decisions if competent to do so, as notwithstanding the content of an order of appointment, the deputy ceases to have jurisdiction in areas where he knows or reasonably believes P to have capacity (s 20(1)).

2.100   While this works to the advantage of the competent individual, the twentieth-century rule worked to the protection of the individual lacking capacity. When such individuals were subject to the *parens patriae* or statutory scheme, contracts signed by them were void. This saved them from the common law of contract, where the contract was enforceable if the other party contracted without knowledge of the incapacity of P.[70] What is the situation now that the court order may not preclude P's exercising his or her rights in a period of capacity? Contracts signed by P during the period of the court order presumably cannot now be assumed to be void. They would be enforceable in any event if P has capacity; but if he or she does not, it is at least arguable that they will still be enforceable, unless the other party was aware or ought reasonably to have been aware of P's incapacity.

H. ADVANCE DECISIONS TO REFUSE TREATMENT

2.101   The MCA places the common law authority to make advance decisions refusing treatment on a statutory footing. Such advance decisions may be made by any person with capacity, aged eighteen or over. Section 24(1) states that if:

(a) at a later time and in such circumstances as he may specify, a specified treatment is proposed to be carried out or continued by a person providing health care for him, and

(b) at that time he lacks capacity to consent to the carrying out or continuation of the treatment,

the specified treatment is not to be carried out or continued.

This provision contains considerable flexibility, and carries considerable power. The person making the statement, P, may specify the disorder or the treatments at issue, and specify any conditions for its application. It applies not merely to the commencement of treatment, but to the continuation of treatment. P could, for example, decide that treatment should not be continued beyond a specified period, if a particular level of result were not obtained. It is, however, an advance *refusal* of treatment. Under an LPOA, P may state treatment preferences, but such views are not within the scope of an advance decision to refuse treatment. Neither the LPOA nor the advance decision can require a treatment provider to

---

[69] See, e.g., *M'Adam v Walker* (1813) 1 Dow 148, 177–8.
[70] *Imperial Loan Company v Stone* [1892] 1 QB 599.

offer a specific treatment.[71] Nor does an advance decision permit the active intervention of a treatment provider to hasten the death of P: the criminal laws relating to homicide, euthanasia, and assisted suicide are unchanged by the MCA (s 62). It acts instead as equivalent to a competent refusal of consent to treatment. Consistent with that, it will not operate to prevent treatment where consent is not necessary, such as where enforced treatment is provided to civilly confined patients under Part IV of the Mental Health Act 1983.

The advance decision will take effect only if P lacks capacity at the time **2.102** treatment is to be provided or continued; should P have capacity at that time, he or she will be able to consent as any other competent person would. Where P lacks capacity to consent and the advance decision is valid and applicable to the treatment proposed, the advance decision has the same effect as if P had competently refused the treatment (s 26(1)). It thus takes precedence over any consent provided by donees of LPOAs, court-appointed deputies, or pursuant to the general defence in s 5. While the Court of Protection has jurisdiction to determine whether the advance decision is valid and applicable to the proposed treatment, it does not have jurisdiction in any other way to alter or override the decision.

For most treatments, there are no formalities requirements for the advance **2.103** decision: oral refusals will suffice, although as the DCOP suggests, written decisions adopting some formality will be evidentially helpful.[72] This flexibility is somewhat illusory. Advance decisions to refuse life-sustaining treatment, probably the most frequent use of such advance decisions, do have formalities requirements.[73] While there is no statutory form for such advance decisions, the Act does require them to state specifically that they are to apply when life is at risk, and they must be in writing, either signed by P or by another person under P's direction, and witnessed (s 25(6)). These are new requirements: common law had no such requirements in these circumstances. Unlike the provisions for validly executed enduring powers of attorney, there are no transitional provisions for advance refusals of life-sustaining treatment that were valid at the time they were made, but will cease to be valid under the MCA. Individuals who made such decisions in the past must execute a version compliant with the MCA, if their wishes are to be honoured as of right rather than merely to go into the mix of factors to be considered in a best interests determination.

The Law Commission draft would have also included a presumption that **2.104** advance refusals of treatment would not apply if the viability of a foetus were at

---

[71] It may be the case that an advance statement that the provision of artificial feeding and hydration is in the best interests of P can require that this treatment be carried out well into P's incapacity: see *R (on the application of Burke) v General Medical Council* [2004] EWHC 1879, [2005] QB 424, discussed at para 3.20 below. This case is currently under appeal.

[72] DCOP, para 8.15 provides a useful list of information which may be included.

[73] This formalities requirement was inserted late in the legislative process, and the latest version of the DCOP at the time of writing did not anticipate it: see, e.g., para 8.11. The DCOP should be approached with care in this regard.

risk.[74] This presumption is not contained expressly in the MCA, but given the court's reluctance to uphold treatment refusals in this situation,[75] it would be prudent for women of childbearing age to address this contingency expressly in the advance decision.

2.105   An advance decision will only preclude treatment if it is valid and applicable. It will not be valid if P has withdrawn the decision at a time when he or she had capacity; has since the decision executed an LPOA that gives the donee authority to give or refuse consent to the treatment in question; or done anything else 'clearly inconsistent' with the advance decision remaining his or her fixed decision (s 25(2)). While an LPOA which does not overlap with the advance decision does not affect its validity (s 25(7)), it may be prudent in drafting an LPOA that touches on treatment to state expressly that it is subject to the advance decision, if that is P's wish.

2.106   The scope of the final provision, doing something 'clearly inconsistent' with the advance decision, is potentially remarkably expansive. An obvious example would be if P has while competent and since the advance decision, consented to similar treatment in circumstances like those contained in the advance decision. The ambit is however considerably wider than this. In *HE v A Hospital NHS Trust*[76] an advance refusal was held to be invalid because of subsequent inconsistent conduct. The key inconsistency in this advance refusal of a blood transfusion lay in P's religious conversion from Jehovah's Witness to Muslim, coupled with her failure to mention the advance treatment refusal for two days during a previous hospital admission. While one may have sympathy with this result, the inconsistency is not immediately apparent. Certainly, Jehovah's Witnesses do not accept blood transfusions; but is it obvious that a conversion to Islam is inconsistent with a decision to refuse such treatment? The court in that case suggests that advance refusals of life-sustaining treatment will be honoured only in cases of manifest and unambiguous validity. If this approach is followed in the implementation of the MCA provisions, persons making advance treatment refusals will have to be vigilant for their views to be respected.

2.107   The conditions for an advance decision to be held inapplicable are as follows:

(a) that treatment is not the treatment specified in the advance decision,
(b) any circumstances specified in the advance decision are absent, or

---

[74] Law Com Report No 231 (n 10 above) para 5.26.

[75] See, e.g., *Norfolk and Norwich Healthcare (NHS) Trust v W* [1996] 2 FLR 613; *Re MB (An Adult: Medical Treatment)* [1997] 2 FLR 426; *Re T (Adult: Refusal of Medical Treatment)* [1992] 3 WLR 782; *Tameside and Glossop Acute Services Trust v CH* [1996] 1 FLR 762; *A Metropolitan Borough Council v DB* [1997] 1 FLR 767; *Re S (Adult: Refusal of Medical Treatment)* [1994] 2 FLR 671. In *St George's Healthcare NHS Trust v S* [1998] 2 FLR 728, [1998] 3 All ER 673, the patient was permitted to sue following a court application granting the treating professionals the authority to enforce treatment on her, although the situation in this case was highly unusual in that the facts as presented to the court granting the authority to treat her had been materially incorrect.

[76] [2003] EWHC 1017, [2003] 2 FLR 408.

(c) there are reasonable grounds for believing that circumstances exist which P did not anticipate at the time of the advance decision and which would have affected his decision had he anticipated them. (s 25(4))

Once again, considerable elasticity is provided in these provisions. If P wishes his or her wishes to be honoured, clarity of articulation will be significant. The third condition is intended to allow changes of circumstance, most obviously progress in medical science that would have affected P's decision. The aim is to ensure that P does not become a prisoner of prior conditions, unable to take advantage of new developments. While there is merit in such a condition, there are risks that a court reluctant to allow a refusal of treatment to stand could exploit its relatively broad language. The DCOP takes the view that the length of time since the expression of the decision, and 'changes in the patient's personal life' will be relevant.[77] While it is inappropriate to rule these factors out, they should be approached with considerable caution. The fact that an advance refusal was made a considerable length of time ago does not mean it is forgotten. Especially if the decision has been made with some formality, it may be the case that P has not reiterated the decision specifically because he or she believes the previous decision still to be in effect. This might be the case, for example, if the decision is made as part of a package at a lawyer's office, along with a will and an LPOA, as is frequently the case in countries where there is experience of these mechanisms. The insistence that such documents be re-executed periodically to ensure their ongoing validity would create an unjustifiable gravy train for lawyers. Changes in personal circumstances should similarly be approached carefully. It does not follow, for example, that marriage or an increase in religious fervour affects an individual's view regarding consent to life-sustaining treatment. The risk is that the views holding sway become those of the treatment provider, family, or individual judge, rather than those of P himself or herself. That is not the intent of the provision. That said, because of the approach in the DCOP, it would be prudent for persons with advance decisions to reiterate or re-execute them upon significant changes in their life.

In the first instance, it is for the person who would be providing the treatment **2.108** to determine whether an advance decision to refuse treatment is valid and applicable. An individual will not incur liability for providing treatment unless 'satisfied' that a valid and applicable advance decision to refuse the treatment exists; an individual will not incur liability for withholding treatment if he or she 'reasonably believes' that a valid and applicable advance decision to refuse the treatment exists (s 26(2)–(3)). These standards of certainty differ: satisfaction implies a higher level of certainty than reasonable belief. A margin is thus created within the system, serving to protect treatment providers from liability in cases of honest doubt. A valid and applicable advance decision is effective as

---

[77] DCOP, para 8.27.

if P were competent and refusing the treatment at the time the treatment is offered, however, so treatment of P if the provider is satisfied that such a valid and applicable advance decision exists would be a battery and, potentially, a criminal offence. Similarly, failure to treat when there is no reasonable belief that such an advance decision exists is likely to constitute negligence.

2.109   That offers little by way of understanding how the standards are to be understood. The DCOP offers no elaboration on the meaning of 'satisfied'. It offers the following example of what would be reasonable grounds for belief that an advance decision exists:

> Reasonable grounds might arise if a decision is recent, in writing, countersigned by a health professional who certifies that he gave advice about available treatments, and the maker's signature has been witnessed by a family member with no interest in the patient's estate.[78]

While certainly a treatment provider would be justified in honouring such a refusal, it is well above what would be a marginal case. The wording reflects language in the report of the pre-legislative scrutiny committee,[79] but the Act itself does not go so far. Advance decisions do not necessarily need to be in writing; there are no formal requirements as to what if any information must be provided prior to making the decision; and there are no restrictions in the MCA on who can witness such statements when they are in writing (although presumably a witness ought to be an adult). In so far as the example might be viewed as creating a norm, the DCOP raises the bar well above what is contained in the legislation. Treatment providers would be better advised to consider the overall circumstances of the alleged advance decision. Certainly, the formality of the setting in which the decision is made will be relevant: wishes expressed after sober reflection in doctors' or lawyers' offices will have more credence than those expressed informally and with less forethought. The provider should also consult with those well known to P, to determine whether the decision is consistent with P's values and wishes as understood by those people. If a consistent view comes back that the wishes are reliably the wishes of P, and that the decision is in other respects valid and applicable, it is to be hoped that the courts would hold that the provider should be satisfied that the advance decision is in effect.

2.110   The DCOP places particular responsibility on 'the relevant health care professional who is in charge of the patient's care'[80] to determine the validity and applicability of an advance decision. While it may well be appropriate for this individual to have primary responsibility for ensuring appropriate investigation into the matter, it does not follow that others in the treatment team are absolved of their responsibilities. Anyone whose role would require the consent of the

---

[78] DCOP, para 8.41.
[79] See 2003–4 HL 189, HC 1083, para 205.
[80] DCOP, para 8.45.

patient if competent, and who would therefore be relying on the effectiveness or not of an advance directive as a defence under s 26, must bring himself or herself within the terms of the section. Thus anyone treating must not be 'satisfied' that a valid and applicable advance decision exists; and anyone under a duty of care to P who does not treat must 'reasonably believe' that a valid and applicable advance decision does exist. There is no reason why reliance on superior officers will apply here any more than anywhere else in the law of consent.

In the event of doubt, the matter of validity and applicability can be referred to the Court of Protection. The court can rule on whether an advance decision exists, is valid, and is applicable to the treatment proposed (s 26(4)). If the court holds that it is, the decision must be honoured. There is no mechanism for the court to overrule a valid and applicable decision to refuse treatment. Pending such court determination, and notwithstanding any apparent advance decision to the contrary, life-sustaining treatment may be provided to P, and care provided if it is reasonably believed to be necessary to prevent a serious deterioration in P's condition (s 26(5)). **2.111**

Courts in the past have indicated that court determinations *ought* to be made prior to the cessation of or failure to provide life-sustaining treatment.[81] Neither the MCA itself nor the DCOP contains this requirement, and it is not envisaged in the regulatory structure of the Act. It remains to be seen if it will be introduced by judicial interpretation. In any event, because of the seriousness of the situation, treatment providers with honest and reasonable doubts regarding validity or applicability of an advance decision may wish to consider a court application in these circumstances when time allows. If such court applications are not formally required, however, and if the provider is satisfied that the advance decision is valid and applicable, it would be binding (see further paras 3.25–7 below). **2.112**

An advance decision may be distinguished from an LPOA that covers matters relating to medical consent. The LPOA appoints someone to make treatment decisions, subject to the best interests criteria and such restrictions as are contained in the instrument itself. The advance decision makes the decision: there is at least in theory no routine assessment of the wisdom or desirability of the decision. The inclusion of medical decision-making in an LPOA will be appropriate to deal with unforeseen maladies occurring after the onset of incapacity. The advance decision will be appropriate when P has firm and fixed views about refusal of a definable treatment, set of treatments, or course of treatment in definable future situations. **2.113**

The MCA is clear that a person may withdraw or alter his or her advance decision while he or she has capacity to do so (s 24(3)). Withdrawals need not be in writing (s 24(4)). This would appear to apply even when the advance decision **2.114**

---

[81] See *Airedale NHS Trust v Bland* [1993] AC 789. See also *Practice Note (Family Div: Incapacitated Adults)* [2002] 1 WLR 325.

was in writing, and even when the advance decision was required to be in writing.[82] Except for a withdrawal or partial withdrawal, an alteration of the decision does need to be in writing if it concerns life-sustaining treatment (s 24(5)).

2.115   This raises the question as to whether the decision may be varied by the individual after losing capacity: is an individual who appears compliant with and perhaps enthusiastic about treatment following a loss of capacity bound by the advance decision refusing the treatment? The answer is not entirely obvious. On the one hand, the point of the advance refusal is that an individual may make decisions to apply during their subsequent incapacity. These are not matters to be entered lightly, and persons making these decisions must be taken to have adopted a considered view of their wishes. The sections of the statute referring to withdrawal or amendment refer specifically to P having capacity when that occurs. Passive compliance with treatment on its own can surely be insufficient to circumvent this. Otherwise people who were unconscious might not have their decisions respected, and that cannot be the intent of the legislation. On the other hand, the MCA provides that the advance decision will be invalid if the individual 'has done anything . . . clearly inconsistent with the advance decision remaining his fixed decision' (s 25(2)(c)). That provision is not expressly limited to matters arising during the individual's capacity. It may thus at least arguably be broad enough to include decisions made when P has lost capacity.

2.116   Different issues arise if the treatment is life-sustaining, as the termination of such treatment raises questions regarding the right to life in article 2 of the ECHR. Article 2 rights are enjoyed by everyone, including those lacking capacity. In at least some circumstances, most obviously when P indicates an incompetent but clear wish to receive the treatment, failure to provide such treatment could raise questions of article 2 compliance. Alternatively, the right to make advance decisions could be considered an aspect of the right to privacy under article 8. There is no ECHR jurisprudence that assists in ascertaining how the presence of a competent, advance refusal of a treatment should be considered to affect the current and incompetent views of an individual apparently now wishing to have that treatment.

2.117   The Law Commission proposed that concealing or destroying an advance decision ought to be an offence, punishable by imprisonment up to two years.[83] While the Commission took the view that any forgery of such documents was covered under existing law relating to fraud, it considered the existing law to be uncertain as to whether destroying or concealing such a document was a crime. Curiously, this provision was dropped from the final legislation. This is a matter of some concern, as anecdotal evidence suggests that such decisions do sometimes disappear from medical records.

---

[82] See *HE v A NHS Hospital Trust and Another* [2003] EWHC 1017, [2003] 2 FLR 408 at [39].
[83] Law Com Report No 231 (n 10 above) para 5.38.

Notwithstanding the failure to include the specific offence in the Act, legal **2.118** consequences may nonetheless flow from the concealment or destruction of an advance decision. Certainly, when the concealment or destruction is by a member of a medical, legal, or similar profession, it would constitute grounds for professional discipline. Whether destruction of such a document is a property crime depends on the ownership of the document. If the document is owned by the NHS trust, which would be the case for example for hospital records, a doctor, nurse, or other person destroying the document might well be guilty of criminal damage. Further, if the advance decision were signed and witnessed in circumstances where P would own it and then given to someone else, be it doctor or anyone else, P may retain some rights over it. Section 5(3) of the Theft Act 1968 holds that where a person receives property from another, and is under an obligation to the other to retain and deal with that property in a particular way, the property is to be regarded as regards the recipient as belonging to the giver. A credible argument could be made that this provision applies to an advance decision given to a medical professional for placement in a clinical record, and the destruction of the record therefore constitutes theft from P. The legal duty to retain and deal with the property is less clear if the advance decision is instead given to a non-professional such as a friend; the argument for criminal liability here is still coherent, but less convincing.

The above analysis applies whether or not the precluded treatment has **2.119** actually been performed. If that absence were discovered prior to the provision of the treatment, P could of course execute a new decision if he or she continues to have the capacity to do so. If P lacks capacity to execute a new decision, it may be worth considering an application to the Court of Protection for an order precluding the treatment in question. In some circumstances, it may be appropriate to consider whether the person destroying the original decision should be required to pay the costs of such an application.

If the precluded treatment has occurred, other provisions of the criminal law **2.120** may also become relevant. It is not obvious that the destruction of the written evidence of the decision destroys the decision. A decision that was valid when it was signed and witnessed may perhaps remain a valid decision, even if the evidence of the decision is 'misplaced'. A doctor who is satisfied of the existence of such a decision but performs the precluded treatment anyway may thus still be guilty of a criminal assault. The case would be particularly strong if the treating physician had destroyed the decision; it would be more problematic if the decision had been destroyed by another, but the doctor had strong grounds for believing it had existed and had never been withdrawn by P.

It is a more difficult question whether criminal consequences flow if a doctor **2.121** performs the treatment innocently, unaware that the decision has been destroyed or concealed by someone else ('C'). Clearly, the innocent doctor is protected by s 26(2). The situation regarding C is less straightforward. The initial question concerns the scope of s 26(2). If that provision renders the treatment not a criminal act at all, then it is difficult to see that C is guilty of anything related to the treatment. That seems unlikely, however. Medical treatments are assaults, to which consent provides a defence. The scope of s 26(2) would seem to be analogous to the provision of a defence of consent to the treating physician. In that case, the treatment could still constitute a criminal act as regards C, if the precluded treatment is a sufficiently foreseeable result of C's actions. If C actively conceals the existence of the advance decision in the face of an express inquiry from the treating physician, for example, C may well be inciting an assault. Even absent such a direct request, if the provision of the precluded treatment is sufficiently foreseeable from the destruction of the advance decision, C may also be guilty of assault.[84]

2.122   The application of criminal law to the situation where an advance decision is concealed or destroyed is a matter of speculation. It is not a set of facts that the court has been called on to deal with, and the approach of judge and jury may well be dependent on the specific facts before it. Cases of this sort may prove evidentially problematic. All this makes a word of warning appropriate. The person making an advance decision may find it prudent to make several copies, lodging one with his or her medical adviser, and one or more others with friends who can draw the decision to the attention of any successor medical advisers if necessary.

I. RESEARCH RELATING TO PEOPLE LACKING CAPACITY

2.123   The research provisions in the MCA supplement the legal and ethical regulations, governance, and guidance relating to research generally. Of particular relevance in this regard is the *Research Governance Framework for Health and Social Care*,[85] which establishes Research Ethics Committees (RECs) to approve any clinical or non-clinical research to be carried out within the NHS. The Research Governance Framework emphasizes the importance of each research subject providing informed consent.[86] It does not contain specific provisions relating to research subjects who lack capacity. That is provided by the MCA. Where the Research Governance Framework is government guidance, the MCA is primary legislation. In the event of conflict, the MCA therefore takes priority. The MCA provisions are also in some ways broader than the Research Governance Framework. The Framework covers research occurring in the Department of Health and NHS broadly conceived, including social care services.[87] The MCA applies whenever people lacking capacity are involved as

---

[84] The arguments here are by analogy from cases such as *R v Bourne* (1952) 36 Cr App R 125 and *R v Cogan and Leak* [1976] QB 217.

[85] Department of Health, 2nd edn (2005), available at <http://www.dh.gov.uk/PublicationsAnd-Statistics/fs/en>, link to Research and Development Publications, accessed 23 June 2005.

[86] Research Governance Framework, para 2.2.3.

[87] Research Governance Framework, para 1.2.

subjects of research, whether or not the research occurs in the DOH/NHS environment.

The MCA provisions do not affect research governed by the Medicines for **2.124** Human Use (Clinical Trials) Regulations 2004,[88] introduced consequent on the EU Clinical Trials Directive.[89] These regulations apply to 'clinical trials', defined as follows:

'clinical trial' means any investigation in human subjects, other than a non-interventional trial, intended—
(a) to discover or verify the clinical, pharmacological or other pharmacodynamic effects of one or more medicinal products,
(b) to identify any adverse reactions to one or more such products, or
(c) to study absorption, distribution, metabolism and excretion of one or more such products
with the object of ascertaining the safety or efficacy of those products[90]

Schedule 1, Part 5 of the regulations contain provisions relating to incapacitated adults. Consent to participation in clinical trials is provided by the subject's 'legal representative', defined as an individual who 'by virtue of their relationship with that adult . . . is suitable to act as their legal representative for the purposes of that trial' and is available and willing to do so. If there is no such person, the legal representative is the doctor primarily responsible for the adult's treatment, or his or her nominee.[91] A donee of an LPOA covering health-care decisions or a court-appointed deputy with a similar remit would be obvious people to function as legal representatives in this context. While the views of P against participating in such a clinical trial are to be considered, they do not appear to be binding.[92] Instead, informed consent provided by the legal representative 'shall represent that adult's presumed will'.[93]

The MCA provisions apply to 'intrusive' research, defined as research which **2.125** would be unlawful if it were performed on a person with capacity without his or her consent (s 30(2)). Under traditional English law, this would have applied to any research involving the touching of an individual, as without consent this would have constituted a battery. Purely observational research however would probably have been outside the scope of the provision. That was the intent of the Law Commission,[94] but the situation has become more complicated with the introduction of the right to privacy under article 8 of the ECHR. Research on people lacking capacity is likely to occur on a hospital ward, in a doctor's office,

---

[89] SI 2004/1031.

[88] Directive 2001/20/EC [2001] OJ No L121, pp 34–44. See J. McHale, 'Clinical Research' in A. Grubb (ed), *Principles of Medical Law*, 2nd edn (2004).

[90] SI 2004/1031, reg 2(1).

[91] SI 2004/1031, Sch 1, Part 1, para 2.

[92] SI 2004/1031, Sch 1, Part 5, para 7.

[93] SI 2004/1031, Sch 1, Part 5, para 12.

[94] See Law Com Report No 231 (n 10 above) draft Bill, cl 11(4)(d).

in a care home, or in the subject's own home. In all of these situations, the individual would have a reasonable expectation of privacy to some degree or other. In the doctor's office, when the subject is undergoing a medical examination, the expectation of privacy is particularly strong. On a hospital ward where routine visits by other members of the public are permitted, it is more questionable whether mere observation by a researcher on the ward would be a sufficient intrusion to trigger article 8. In either case, it may be relevant if the researcher is already a member of the medical team who already has access to the otherwise privileged environment. If the research protects the anonymity of the research subject, it is less obvious that article 8 will be triggered. If the research infringes the right to privacy under article 8, such research will be within the definition of 'intrusive'.

2.126   Similar concerns might well be raised about researchers using clinical records, if the researcher would not otherwise have been made privy to the information. It does seem however that notwithstanding government guidance, data anonymized by a person who has already had access to the information such as the individual's treating physician may be made available to researchers with no breach of the law of confidentiality occurring.[95] Such use of information would probably not reach the threshold of an article 8 violation, and would therefore be outside the scope of the MCA.

2.127   Intensive research where all or some of the subjects are unable to consent to the research are within the scope of the MCA. That means that such research projects must be approved by the 'appropriate body' (s 30(1)) and comply with the conditions of the Act. The appropriate body is to be specified by regulation in Wales by the National Assembly, and in England by the Secretary of State.[96] The regulation has not yet been published, but the DCOP anticipates that these authorities will in practice be the existing RECs.[97] On that assumption, the MCA provisions can be seen to buttress rather than to cut across current systems of research governance.

2.128   The Act provides substantive limitations on the research that may be carried out on people lacking capacity (s 31) and process requirements regarding the attainment of substitute consent (s 32). The substantive provisions require that the research project in question must be connected with an impairing condition affecting P, or the treatment of that condition. 'Impairing condition' is further defined as a condition which is or may be attributable to, or which does or may cause or contribute to, disturbance in the functioning of the mind or brain. The researcher must further demonstrate that research of comparable effectiveness cannot be carried out using only people who have capacity to consent (s 31(2)–(4)). Historically, people in psychiatric and long-stay institutions, many or most of whom lacked capacity to consent, were sometimes used as captive

---

[95] R v Department of Health, ex p Source Informatics [2001] QB 424, CA.
[96] Secretary of State is again likely to be the Secretary of State for Health.
[97] DCOP, para 12.16.

subjects in research unrelated to the disorder thought to cause their mental impairment. The view expressed through the MCA is that this is unethical: research on people lacking capacity must be related to the causes or effects of their incapacity. People lacking capacity may not simply be used as a matter of convenience.

The research must also either have the potential to benefit P without imposing **2.129** a disproportionate burden on him or her, or be intended to provide knowledge of the causes or treatments of, or care of people affected by, the same or a similar condition. In the latter case, where the treatment is to provide knowledge and will not potentially benefit P directly, there must also be reasonable grounds under s 31(6) for believing the following:

(a) that the risk to P from taking part in the project is likely to be negligible, and
(b) that anything done to, or in relation to, P will not—
   (i) interfere with P's freedom of action or privacy in a significant way, or
   (ii) be unduly invasive or restrictive.

Projects that are for the increase in knowledge of P's condition but which offer no obvious benefit to him or her must therefore carry virtually no burden of participation. Projects that may benefit P must not bear disproportionate burdens. Clinical trials are not subject to these rules, so these restrictions will not serve to limit drug testing. There may be complications, however, in that some of the factors relating to intrusiveness might vary between individual participants. The rules would seem to require that the appropriate level of intrusiveness not be exceeded for each given research participant prior to approval of the project, but in standard research application procedures, it is unethical to recruit for a study prior to receipt of REC approval. The effect of factors applying differently to different individual research participants could not be known at the time of project approval.

For approval, projects must also be shown to comply with the provisions **2.130** regarding consultation with carers and provision of consent. In this regard, for each participant lacking capacity, the researcher is required to identify an individual who is engaged in the participant's care or welfare in a non-professional capacity, and is prepared to advise on whether P should participate in the project (s 32(2)). Donees of LPOAs and court-appointed deputies relating to P are specifically not precluded from fulfilling this role (s 32(7)), and may indeed be the appropriate choice. If no such non-professional carer is available, guidance not yet issued will allow appointment of an individual unconnected to the research project to fulfil this role (s 32(3)). The structure of the Act provides that this person advises the researcher. While the researcher is to consult with this person, it remains the researcher's responsibility to ensure that participation in the research is in the best interests of P. However, the MCA also provides the consultee with concrete controls. If at any time before or during the research the consultee informs the researcher that P if competent would be likely to decline participation, then P must be withdrawn from the research (s 32(5)).

2.131   In determining whether P should participate in the project, the best interests provisions of the Act apply. If there is a prospect that P will receive some direct benefit from the research, some objective factors may enter this determination. If the research relates instead to the general development of knowledge of P's condition and is research from which P is unlikely to benefit directly, the aspects of the best interests test relating to P's current views and the factors he or she would consider if he or she had capacity will be central to the decision of the person consulted. Consistent with this, the MCA specifically requires the consultee to advise on what the wishes and feelings of P would have been if P had had capacity (s 32(4)). In any event, nothing may be done to P in the name of research that is contrary to an advance decision to refuse treatment or 'any other form of statement made by him and not subsequently withdrawn'.

2.132   Further, nothing may be done to P to which he appears to object except where it is to protect P from harm or to reduce or prevent pain or discomfort (s 33(2)). There is no capacity requirement here: an incapable objection will require P's removal from the research. Such objection need not be verbal, but may, for example, be by showing signs of resistance. Specifically, if P indicates in any way that he or she wishes to be withdrawn from the project, he or she must be withdrawn without delay (s 33(4)). In addition, the balance of benefit outweighing risk, which must be shown for approval of the project, continues to apply to each participant lacking capacity. If burdens at any time outweigh benefits, and if there is any burden inherent in a project from which P will not directly benefit, the researcher must withdraw P from the project forthwith (s 33(5)). The sole exception is that treatment may continue if a significant risk to P's health would result from its discontinuance (s 33(6)).

2.133   In general, P may be involved in the research only if the above criteria are satisfied. The exception is when P is about to receive urgent treatment, and where 'having regard to the nature of the research and of the particular circumstances of the case . . . it is also necessary to take action for the purposes of the research as a matter of urgency' and when it is not practicable to engage in the consultation process outlined above (s 32(8)). Nonetheless, such treatment may only be given with the agreement of an independent medical practitioner or, if that is not practicable, the researcher acts 'in accordance with a procedure approved by the appropriate body [the REC] at the time when the research project was approved' (s 32(9)). This 'urgency' exception is presumably intended to allow research into incapacitating injuries, at the time the injury occurs. One does not know in advance who will be injured, so planning is not necessarily possible. The usual criteria are therefore unable to be met.

2.134   Special considerations may be relevant in the event that the research involves the use or storage of human tissue from a person who lacks capacity to consent to that use or storage. That is envisaged by s 6 of the Human Tissue Act 2004, due to come into effect in 2006. If that individual has consented to or refused to consent to the use or storage prior to losing capacity, that decision continues in effect. Otherwise, the section provides that the Secretary of State may publish regulations deeming such consent to have occurred in specific circumstances. These regulations have not yet been published, so these requirements are not yet known.

J. ILL-TREATMENT OR NEGLECT OF PERSONS LACKING CAPACITY

The MCA makes it an offence to ill-treat or neglect people lacking capacity **2.135** (s 44). The offence applies to an individual D who either:

(a) has the care of a person ('P') who lacks, or whom D reasonably believes to lack, capacity, or

(b) is the donee of a lasting power of attorney or an enduring power of attorney created by P, or

(c) is a deputy appointed by the court for P. (s 44(1))

If the relevant relationship is contained under subs (1)(a), P's incapacity or D's **2.136** reasonable belief in P's incapacity must be demonstrated. The subsection is disjunctive: either will suffice. The section can therefore be triggered if P lacks capacity unbeknownst to D, or alternatively when D has a reasonable belief that P lacks capacity that turns out to be incorrect. There is no minimum age for P, although the statutory definition of incapacity applies, requiring an impairment or disturbance in functioning of the mind or brain.

The meaning of incapacity is problematic in s 44(1). As discussed in para 2.20 **2.137** above, the MCA is structured around capacity as a functional concept: it relates to a specific decision or set of decisions. In this context, the scope of the offence is unclear: what is it P is meant to lack capacity to do or decide, to trigger the section? It would seem odd if any incapacity could trigger the section. That would mean, for example, that a prosecution for neglect might lie if D does not address P's malnourishment, even when P's only lack of capacity concerns his ability to care for his property. It is surely not the case that D is guilty of an offence for failing to provide care in a situation where D rightly believes that P retains capacity to make decisions. D would not, after all, have the legal right to intervene in these circumstances. At the same time, requiring too close an association between the abuse and the specific decisions relating to which P lacks capacity incapacity will unduly restrict the offence. As an obvious example, consider a case where D is hitting P, a case that might be expected to fall at the centre of the offence. That abuse does not relate clearly to a type of decision or specific functional incapacity in P. If the abuse must be related to a set of decisions where P lacks capacity, it is not obvious that D would be guilty of the offence here. D would, of course, be guilty of the crime of assault in such circumstances, and P's vulnerability would be an aggravating factor in sentencing. The specific offence in the MCA in no way precludes the application of other provisions of criminal law. Nonetheless, it would seem extremely odd for those facts not to constitute a violation of the MCA offence as well.

2.138   Under s 44(1)(a), there must be a relationship of care between D and P. 'Care' is not defined in the Act, but it is reasonable to suspect that the courts will accord it a broad meaning. The first part of the definition would certainly include people providing care in reliance on the general defence, but it is not restricted to them. It presumably extends to situations where P is in a relationship of reliance on D, and D is either legally required to provide goods, services, or support in response to that need, or voluntarily agrees to do so. Where P lives with D in D's premises, for example, a care relationship is likely to exist whatever the legal structure of the arrangements between P and D. If D goes to P's home to assist with cleaning, a care relationship is also likely to be found to be established. That may be the case even if the assistance is voluntary. If P is heavily reliant on such care, there is perhaps a question as to how D may cease the arrangement, lest simply terminating the arrangement be viewed as neglect. There can be little doubt that D cannot be forced to continue voluntary care indefinitely; but it might nonetheless be prudent to notify another person involved with P's care, the Public Guardian, or social services in cases where withdrawal of the care will have major adverse consequences to P.

2.139   Paragraphs (b) and (c) of s 44(1) lack some of these ambiguities. These paragraphs are based on legal relationships between D and P. Presumably the definition of P in para (a) applies in addition to the other two parts, so that P must lack capacity or reasonably be believed to lack capacity by D. For para (b) to apply, D must be the donee of an LPOA, but there is no requirement that the LPOA be registered. The point is important: ill-treatment, or neglect of P, possibly including an extreme case of failing to register an LPOA when P was losing capacity, might meet the conditions of the offence. There is no express requirement that the abuse be within the legal authority granted to the donee of the LPOA or deputy. As discussed in para 2.137 above, alleged neglect of P relating to acts where D lacks the legal authority to intervene because of P's continuing capacity should not be caught by the provision. If P's capacity in the area is lacking or ambiguous, however, it is perhaps arguable that the donee or deputy cannot turn a blind eye to severe deprivation, but must alert some relevant authority such as social services or the Public Guardian, even if the neglect is outside the scope of D's authority.

2.140   The offence occurs when D 'ill-treats' or 'wilfully neglects' P (s 44(2)). A similarly worded prohibition relating to psychiatric patients is contained in s 127 of the Mental Health Act 1983. This may provide a guide to interpretation of the MCA section. The jurisprudence under the Mental Health Act offence holds that 'ill-treatment' and 'wilfully to neglect' were conceptually different, and warranted separate counts in an indictment.[98] The elements of ill-treatment were articulated by the Court of Appeal in *R v Newington*:

---

[98] *R v Newington* (1990) 91 Cr App R 247.

In our judgment the judge should have told the jury that for there to be a conviction of ill-treatment contrary to the Act of 1983 the Crown would have to prove (1) deliberate conduct by the appellant which could properly be described as ill-treatment irrespective of whether this ill-treatment damaged or threatened to damage the health of the victim and (2) a guilty mind involving either an appreciation by the appellant at the time that she was inexcusably ill-treating a patient or that she was reckless as to whether she was inexcusably acting in that way.[99]

The court further held that the actual occurrence of injury or unnecessary suffering was not pivotal to the offence. This has led Michael Gunn to argue that the judgment is broad enough to include inadequate feeding or heating, the use of harsh words, or bullying.[100] A course of conduct is not necessarily required; a single slapping incident is sufficient to trigger the offence.[101] Under *Newington*, violence was not necessarily evidence of ill-treatment, if it were used, for example, 'for the reasonable control of a patient'.[102] For the purposes of the MCA provisions, that must now be read in light of the provisions on restraining individuals, discussed above in paras 2.51–2, 2.75 and 2.95.

There is little jurisprudential guidance on the meaning of 'neglect'. In *New-ington*, the court suggested that unlike 'ill-treatment', it would be related to a particular state of mind,[103] but it did little to elaborate. Richard Jones suggests instead that it is an objective state, which would 'probably' include the failure to provide medical care to a patient.[104] Such an objective standard may perhaps define the scope of 'neglect', but the actions of D must also be 'wilful', suggesting a level of knowledge of the relevant circumstances and a choosing not to intervene. Certainly, failures to take due care of P in situations where D has and is aware that he or she has a legal obligation to do so might be obvious examples of neglect. A failure to make decisions by the donee of an LPOA or court-appointed deputy might be obvious examples. The failure of these individuals or other carers to act on knowledge coming to their attention, or that ought to have come to their attention, is a less clear case, but may perhaps be within the scope of the section. Acting on such knowledge cannot mean enforcing on D an expanded caring role, because the legal recognition of such roles requires the consent of D, but it might mean notifying relevant social services agencies, other carers, or the Public Guardian. **2.141**

Persons convicted of offences under s. 44 are subject on summary conviction to a maximum of twelve months' imprisonment or a fine not exceeding the statutory maximum; and on indictment to a term of imprisonment not exceeding five years or a fine. **2.142**

---

[99] (1990) 91 Cr App R 247, 254.

[100] M. Gunn, 'Case note on *R v Newington*' (1990) 1 *Journal of Forensic Psychiatry* 360, 361.

[101] *R v Holmes* [1979] Crim LR 52.

[102] (1990) 91 Cr App R 247, 253.

[103] (1990) 91 Cr App R 247, 252.

[104] R. Jones, *Mental Health Act Manual*, 8th edn (2003) para 1–1134.

3

ROUGH EDGES?

A. ENFORCEMENT

The overall approach of the Law Commission report and the MCA is facilita- **3.01** tive. In a legal world of perceived confusion, where decisions taken on behalf of people lacking capacity were of dubious legal validity, the intent was to introduce clarity and to place decisions on a firm legal foundation. The reform process commenced in the late 1980s during a period of particular financial stringency and this may explain why the Law Commission proposed little by way of specific enforcement mechanisms to ensure compliance with its substantive proposals. Its proposals would have given the reformulated Court of Protection jurisdiction to oversee the administration of the Act, but it was unclear what machinery would support the court in its role. The objective of the new scheme was specifically to avoid legal formality, and the Commission proposed no routine hearings to determine whether decisions were being taken properly. Similarly, while deviation from the new law would be within the jurisdiction of professional complaints procedures, there was no suggestion that it would be at the core of the functioning of the relevant professional standards bodies.

There was some increase in the administrative infrastructure between the **3.02** Law Commission proposals and the MCA as enacted. The Office of the Public Guardian is included in the MCA. A considerable part of its role will be administrative: it is to maintain registers of LPOAs and court deputies, and receive any security required by the courts of carers (s 58(1)(a), (b), (e)). However, it also has a substantive role: it is to supervise deputies; it can direct the

Court of Protection Visitors to visit donees of LPOAs, court-appointed deputies, and the individuals for whom they make decisions; it receives reports of donees of LPOAs and deputies as required by the court; it deals with representations including complaints about the exercise of powers by donees of LPOAs and deputies; and provides reports to court as the court requires (s 58(c), (d), (f), (g), (h)). The precise breadth of the Public Guardian's powers will be established by regulations that have not yet been published. If these powers are given real meaning in general by the regulations and in specific cases by the courts, and the Public Guardian is given sufficient staff and resources, the office may be important in ensuring legal compliance among deputies and donees of LPOAs.

3.03   The Lord Chancellor's Visitors, under review at the time the Law Commission reported, are retained and renamed the Court of Protection Visitors (s 61). They will serve as the investigative arm of the Office of the Public Guardian. The so-called 'special' visitors will have professional expertise in cases of mental impairment, and will in the main be medically qualified. 'General' visitors need not have medical qualifications. Both the visitors and the Public Guardian may, as part of their investigations, consult and take copies of health records, social services records held by local authorities, and records held by those registered under Part II of the Care Standards Act 2000. The visitors may also interview the subject of their investigations in private.

3.04   Independent advocacy is also to be provided under the MCA, through the Department of Health in England and National Assembly in Wales (s 35). The role expressly envisaged by the Act for these advocates involves safeguarding P in the event that serious medical treatment is to be provided to P, or long-term accommodation is to be provided by either the NHS or a local authority to P in a hospital, care home, or other local authority facility: see further paras 2.53–4 above. The role of the advocates is essentially to advise on best interests and to ensure the fullest possible involvement of P in the decision-making process. Under the MCA, advocates provide a routine procedural intervention in specific decisions that will be regulated by the general defence. This is unusual and significant because otherwise decisions taken under the general defence are invisible to the system: there is no obligation or process to report the decisions that are being taken under that mechanism, rendering other routine scrutiny impossible. The specific situations in the Act in which an advocate must be involved are a minimum. The MCA provides that the role of advocacy, and the range of situations where an advocate must be consulted, may be expanded by regulation (ss 36, 41). The Act also allows for the possibility that advocates will be empowered to challenge decisions in which they are involved (s 36(3)). If appropriately expanded, the independent advocates could be an important force in ensuring that major decisions taken under the general defence are consistent with the Act.

3.05   While some administrative capacity has been introduced into the MCA, problems remain. There is no suggestion that close monitoring of decisions taken under the general authority, under LPOAs, or even by deputies will be closely scrutinized. This is likely to be an issue particularly for personal welfare decisions. Standard and relatively easy accounting practices make financial decision-making relatively easy to monitor. The same cannot be said for personal decision-making, where there is no reporting mechanism that corresponds to the 'balanced books' of financial accounting. Inevitably, personal decisions cannot be subject to the same level of systematic scrutiny. The enforcement of the standards of the Act is likely therefore to be somewhat haphazard in this area, relying on reports of people who see P. This is of particular concern for care decisions taken under the general defence, which need not be reported to any official. Care-givers under these sections will not necessarily receive any information about the scope of their authority, or the requirements of the Act. No one will routinely receive any routine information about the scope, provision, or quality of care provided under this mechanism of the Act. It is difficult to see in these circumstances how a system of enforcement of the Act's requirements can operate effectively. Similar concerns apply to a somewhat lesser degree for care provided by donees of LPOAs and court-appointed deputies, who will at least be identifiable by the Public Guardian and will receive some information as to the terms of the MCA.

Some of these decisions are serious. The MCA, for example, regulates the **3.06** restraint of people lacking capacity: see further paras 2.51–2, 2.75 and 2.93 above. The resulting acts can be highly intrusive, allowing the use or threat of use of physical force against P and restricting P's liberty of movement. As another example, it is difficult to see that carers will not be tempted to allow their own convenience to weigh unduly heavily in the best interests determination, significantly undermining the intent of the Act. With the best will in the world, it would be naïve to pretend that the administrative capacity in the Act is sufficient to ensure anything approaching universal compliance with the Act.

B. CHILDREN

The MCA applies in general to people aged of sixteen or over (s 2(5)). There are **3.07** several exceptions. Eighteen is the minimum age to execute an LPOA (s 9(2)(c)), to make a binding advance decision to refuse treatment (s 24(1)), and for the court to draft a will on P's behalf (s 18(2)). The courts may also deal with the property of minors lacking capacity if the court considers it likely that the minor will continue to lack capacity at the age of eighteen (ss 2(5)–(6), 18(3)). Finally, there is no lower age limit for the offence of ill-treatment or wilful neglect of a person lacking capacity (s 44), although the statutory definition of capacity in s 2(1) applied to that offence means that the victim must be suffering from an impairment or disturbance of functioning of the mind or brain. Incapacity flowing solely from youth will not trigger the offence.

3.08   The end result is a further complication of an already complex situation regarding children. For property, children are in general restricted from conveying until the age of eighteen. Their affairs are generally dealt with by the Public Guardian. For children who lack capacity as defined by the Act, however, a new possibility has been introduced, not available to non-disabled children. If the child will remain incapable upon attainment of his or her majority, the court may deal with his or her property under the Act. The law relating to contracts for necessaries applies to children in any event, so the fact that it applies for mentally incapable minors aged sixteen or older appears to add little.

3.09   In personal matters, including consent to medical treatment, there is already a range of overlapping jurisdictions and legal authorities. The presumption of capacity takes effect at age sixteen. Below that age, while not presumed competent, a child who is in fact competent can make a variety of personal decisions, including consent to treatment.[1] The attainment of age sixteen, however, does not extinguish the parental authority over the child, which remains until the age of eighteen. The parent can therefore consent to treatment on the child's behalf up to the age of eighteen. One might reasonably expect that this would be the usual course of events for minors lacking capacity. Similarly, the court's jurisdiction over the minors does not cease until the age of eighteen.[2] The criteria for the court making decisions on behalf of minors are much more flexible than those under the MCA. Under the court's jurisdiction over minors, the 'balance-sheet' approach discussed in para 1.37 above is adopted. It is difficult to see that the MCA will be resorted to with any frequency in these circumstances, as applications under the court's power over minors will almost inevitably prove more flexible. In any event, the flexibility of the system is increased by a power awarded by the MCA to the Lord Chancellor to transfer proceedings to courts with jurisdiction under the Children Act 1989 from the Court of Protection, and vice versa (s 21). This might allow the more flexible provisions of the MCA relating to property and affairs to be dealt with by the Court of Protection, and personal matters by a court with jurisdiction under the Children Act 1989.

C. END-OF-LIFE DECISIONS

3.10   Experience from other jurisdictions would suggest that resort may frequently be had to the MCA regarding decisions at the end of life. The MCA contains a variety of provisions regarding such decisions, styled in the Act as relating to 'life-sustaining treatment'. While they are discussed elsewhere in this book, they

---

[1] *Gillick v West Norfolk and Wisbech AHA* [1986] AC 112.

[2] Regarding the continuing rights of parents and courts over *Gillick*-competent minors, see *Re R (A Minor) (Wardship: Medical Treatment)* [1991] 4 All ER 177, 185; *Re W (A Minor) (Medical Treatment)* [1992] 3 WLR 758.

form a particular enough category of decision to warrant consideration as a unit.

The provisions relating to life-sustaining treatment, as is the case for the **3.11** remainder of the Act, apply only if P lacks capacity to make the required decisions himself or herself. If that is not the case, then P may consent to or refuse treatment at his or her pleasure. The principles in s 1 of the MCA further provide that all practicable steps must be taken to help P make the decision, and P is not to be considered incapable merely because he or she makes an unwise decision. In end-of-life decisions, as in other decisions, the policy of the Act is that individuals should be supported to make their own, competent, decisions.

The MCA expressly does not alter the law relating to homicide or assisted **3.12** suicide (s 62). The administration of medication with the object of bringing about the death of an individual, even if it is at that individual's instigation, remains a very serious crime.

'Life-sustaining treatment' is defined in s 4(10) of the Act as 'treatment which **3.13** in a view of a person providing health care for the person concerned is necessary to sustain life'. Notwithstanding its inclusion in s 4, the section defining best interests, this definition applies for purposes of the entire Act (s 64(1)). The definition provides that the decision as to whether the special provisions of the Act related to life-sustaining treatment apply will fall within the expertise of the health-care provider. It does not say that for purposes of determination of best interests in cases of life-sustaining treatment there is any departure from the overall test contained in the section. The full range of procedural and sub-stantive criteria contained in the statutory best interests test must be applied to reach the best interests determination. The views of the doctor as to what is in the best medical interests of P will be relevant; they will not be determinative. It is not yet known whether the cessation of life-sustaining treatment will be brought within the realm of 'serious treatment' for purposes of s 37 and the provision of independent advocacy, as the relevant regulation has not yet been published.

As discussed in paras 2.101–22 above, the MCA codifies the right of a com- **3.14** petent individual to refuse medical treatment in advance, such refusal to take effect during subsequent incapacity. This situation is unique in the care pro-visions of the MCA in that if an advance decision is valid and applicable, there is no place for the statutory best interests test. If an individual is determined that he or she wants their wishes regarding refusal of treatment respected in specific circumstances, he or she should execute an advance decision. This is the only way the decision will be binding in the future. Views can also be expressed, including in conditions or restrictions contained in an LPOA, but such views will merely go into the mix of factors that will be relevant in a best interests determination; they will not be binding. Equally, persons making advance decisions to refuse life-sustaining treatment should exercise due care. Often, the decision will be taken when the individual is unaware of when and in what specific circumstances the incapacity may occur and the advance decision may be relied on. Advance decisions should only be made if P is sure that he or she wants to refuse the treatment in the situation defined in the advance decision, whatever other circumstances may be.

3.15   When an advance decision concerns refusal of life-sustaining treatment, it must be in writing and witnessed. The written advance decision must state expressly that it is to apply to life-sustaining treatment in the event that P's life is at risk (s 25(5)). These requirements concerning formalities are introduced by the MCA. Previously, advance decisions to refuse life-sustaining treatment had no such formalities requirements. People who have made their wishes known in the past would be well advised to check and ensure that their decisions meet these requirements. There is no transitional provision for wishes that were enforceable at the time they were made, but do not meet the requirements of the Act. Any alterations to such decisions also need to meet these requirements, although withdrawals of the decision can be oral (s 24(4)–(5)). An advance decision will further be enforced only if it is 'valid' and 'applicable'.

3.16   Considerable care must be exercised in drafting advance decisions. While the courts have been clear for a number of years that, in the abstract, they are enforceable,[3] the courts have shown a marked reluctance actually to enforce them. Indeed, while there are cases of capable people present in court having orders made either to protect their decisions to refuse life-sustaining treatment during subsequent incapacity[4] or to terminate life-sustaining treatment immediately,[5] there are no reported cases of the English courts upholding a written advance decision to refuse life-sustaining treatment when the person lacked capacity at the time of the court hearing. Instead, the courts in cases such as *HE v A Hospital NHS Trust*[6] have held that the onus of proof lies on an individual seeking to enforce an advance decision to refuse treatment, and the proof of validity and applicability must be clear and convincing.[7] Any doubt as to the validity and applicability of an advance directive to refuse life-sustaining treatment is, according to *HE*, to be resolved in favour of life.[8]

3.17   The DCOP suggests that the length of time since the advance decision was signed may be a factor in determining ongoing applicability.[9] While such a requirement is not contained in the Act, it may be prudent for signatories of such decisions to revisit and review these decisions periodically, and certainly to reiterate at reasonable intervals to those entrusted with them that the decision remains in effect.

---

[3] This is the case since at least 1992. See *Re T (Adult: Refusal of Medical Treatment)* [1992] 3 WLR 782.

[4] *Re C (Adult: Refusal of Medical Treatment)* [1994] 1 All ER 819; *Re AK (Medical Treatment: Consent)* [2001] 1 FLR 129.

[5] *Re B (Consent to Treatment: Capacity)* [2002] EWHC 429.

[6] [2003] EWHC 1017, [2003] 2 FLR 408.

[7] *HE v A NHS Hospital Trust and Another* [2003] EWHC 1017, [2003] 2 FLR 408 at [23]–[24].

[8] *HE v A NHS Hospital Trust and Another* [2003] EWHC 1017, [2003] 2 FLR 408 at [46].

[9] DCOP, para 8.27.

Notwithstanding the recommendation of the Law Commission, the **3.18** destruction or concealment of an advance decision to refuse treatment is not made a specific offence under the Act. As discussed above at paras 2.117–22 above, such destruction or concealment may nonetheless legal consequences.

Unless there is a valid and applicable advance decision to refuse treatment, **3.19** the decision whether to provide life-sustaining treatment is to be made in the 'best interests' of P. Section 4(5) of the MCA makes it clear that conduct is never in the best interests of an individual if it is 'motivated by a desire to bring about his death'. This is consistent with the Act's upholding of the prohibition of homicide and assisted suicide. Treatment that is otherwise medically justified will not necessarily be illegal, however, if an adverse effect of the treatment happens to shorten the individual's life. Moreover, while it may be the case that the failure to treat an individual may result in his or her death, it does not follow at common law that the treatment is necessarily in the best interests of the patient. In *Airedale NHS Trust v Bland*,[10] the leading case on the termination of life-sustaining treatment, the withdrawal of artificial feeding was permitted on the basis that the medical consensus was that its continuation would have no therapeutic benefit. *Bland* must now be read in the light of the statutory test of best interests, and some of its peripheral discussion is now open to question, but its basic principles do not appear to be disturbed by the MCA.

A potential variation has been introduced by the case of *R (on the application* **3.20** *of Burke) v General Medical Council*.[11] In that case the court, relying on articles 2, 3 and 8 of the ECHR, held that a valid and applicable advance directive to require the provision of artificial nutrition and hydration was enforceable in the period between the patient losing capacity and the patient losing all sensation in a coma.[12] This is an unusual situation, where the doctor can be required to provide treatment that he or she might otherwise decline to provide. The court's decision is specific to the facts of the case, and expressly does not concern difficulties of weighing treatment priorities and potentially competing claims to scarce resources when expensive treatments may be at stake.[13] The views of the patient would of course be highly relevant in any event in the best interests determination; what *Burke* provides, if it is upheld on appeal, is that an advance decision to demand provision of artificial nutrition and hydration is enforceable during subsequent incapacity, to the exclusion of the best interests calculus.

There are a variety of other safeguards that affect life-sustaining treatment. **3.21** If the donee of an LPOA is to have the power to refuse such treatment on P's

---

[10] [1993] AC 789.

[11] [2004] EWHC 1879, [2005] QB 424. At the time of writing, the appeal of this case had been heard, but not decided. A discussion of the Court of Appeal decision is contained in the Preface.

[12] [2004] EWHC 1879, [2005] QB 424 at [169]–[175].

[13] [2004] EWHC 1879, [2005] QB 424 at [27].

behalf, the LPOA must say so expressly (s 11(8)). There is no express requirement in the MCA that a court application is required prior to the donee making
such a decision. It remains to be seen whether such a requirement will be introduced in subsidiary legislation. Certainly, if the donee is in any doubt as to P's
best interests, the Court of Protection has jurisdiction to determine the matter
on the donee's application.

3.22   Court-appointed deputies are required to consent to life-sustaining treatment
(s 20(5)). If life-sustaining treatment within the authority of a deputy is to be
refused, it must be done by the court. It does not follow that the deputy has a
right to demand life-sustaining treatment. If a doctor takes the view that further
treatment is not in the best interests of P, the doctor cannot be required to
provide it, subject to *Burke*. The deputy is not permitted to change medical
professionals to obtain this result, as the change of personnel responsible for P's
health care is reserved to the court (s 20(2)(b)).

3.23   The MCA envisages a number of situations where the court may be called on
to make determinations regarding treatment, including life-sustaining treatment. Where there are disputes as to whether treatment may be given under the
general defence, where there is doubt whether the donee of an LPOA who
refuses such treatment is acting in the best interests of P, or where there are
questions as to the validity and applicability of an advance decision, the MCA
provides that life-sustaining treatment may be given to P and any other act may
be done to prevent a serious deterioration of P's condition, pending a court
hearing into the merits of the matter (ss 6(7), 26(5)).

3.24   When a court application will clearly be required as, for example, when the
validity or applicability of an advance decision is contested and is likely to
become relevant, the application should if at all possible be launched in
sufficient time for a considered hearing to occur. The *HE* case[14] provides an
example of the difficulties when this does not occur. In that case, the patient was
unconscious at all relevant times. She was or had been a Jehovah's Witness and
had signed an advance directive to refuse blood products. Since that time, she
had become engaged to a Muslim man, and a condition of the marriage was
that she reconverted to her original Muslim faith. She had been absent from
Jehovah's Witness services for three months at the time of her hospital
admission. During her hospital admission, there were differing views between
her family members as to the veracity of her religious conversion, and the
applicability of the advance directive. It did not arrive in court until eleven days
later, on an urgent application with only the Muslim side of the family present.
The treating physician's evidence was in writing only, faxed to the court. Given
the urgency of the application, it is difficult to criticize the court's handling of
the matter. At the same time, it is fair to wonder whether the Jehovah's Witness
side of the family might have presented a different and relevant perspective on

---

[14] *HE v A NHS Hospital Trust and Another* [2003] EWHC 1017, [2003] 2 FLR 408.

the facts. A more timely application would have permitted a more meaningful assessment of the evidence.

At common law, it was expected that a court application would be made prior **3.25** to the termination of life-sustaining treatment.[15] Under the MCA, there is no formal requirement for such applications, and it remains to be seen whether such a requirement will be introduced by implication by the judiciary or in the code of practice. It is not contained in the DCOP, although it is mentioned as a possibility in the Government's response to the Joint Scrutiny Committee's Report on the Mental Incapacity Bill.[16] Such a requirement has advantages and disadvantages in policy terms. It has the advantage of providing a procedural safeguard to protect against the cessation of life-sustaining treatment in error. In a society that values the sanctity of human life, that is important. At the same time, it makes it effectively impossible to refuse treatment in some circumstances. There will be cases when the judicial system simply cannot act quickly enough. The insistence that a court order is necessary if life-sustaining treatment is to be withheld would mean, for example, that Jehovah's Witnesses may well get blood transfusions immediately following automobile accidents when their lives are in imminent danger, even in situations where there is little if any doubt that they would refuse such transfusions. As cases such as *HE* show, the courts have in the past made every effort to deal expeditiously with cases in urgent situations; but the processes cannot be instantaneous. It is also fair to wonder how far these urgent decisions by the court lead to considered decision-making, and correspondingly how much benefit they actually bring to the calibre of decision-making.

If it turns out that court decisions are not required in these circumstances, **3.26** the question arises as to when they ought to be sought. Certainly, if a health-care provider or other decision-maker is in honest and legitimate doubt as to the proper legal course to follow, then the court's views should be sought. If there is no reasonable doubt, the situation is less clear cut. May a treatment provider seek a court declaration not because of a sincere doubt over the validity and applicability of an advance directive, but instead in order to access the provisions of s 26(5) allowing life-sustaining treatment pending the court decision? How expeditiously is the provider required to press the matter on the court? The use of s 26(5) (or s 6(7), for treatment provided under the general defence) might well be considered ethically dubious in these circumstances. It may also be of dubious legality. Section 26(2) states that a treatment provider does not incur liability unless 'satisfied' that a valid and applicable advance directive exists. It the provider is satisfied that such an advance decision exists without the court order, liability would attach if the treatment were given.

---

[15] See *Airedale NHS Trust v Bland* [1993] AC 789. See also *Practice Note (Family Div: Incapacitated Adults)* [2002] 1 WLR 325.

[16] Government response to recommendation 40 (February 2004), available at <http://www.dca.gov.uk/pubs/reports/mental-incapacity.htm>, accessed 23 June 2005.

3.27   Some doctors may have personal ethical beliefs that oppose the withdrawal or failure to provide life-sustaining treatment to patients, even in situations where patients refuse such treatment. The approach of the DCOP is that patients should be transferred to the care of other treatment providers if the requirements of the Act would otherwise draw a practitioner into a practice that he or she views as morally objectionable.[17] This is no doubt appropriate whenever possible, and all reasonable efforts should be made to ensure such transfers occur in a timely fashion. There may be circumstances however (for example, when only one doctor is on call) that it is not possible. When this occurs, the provisions of the Act must nonetheless be followed. A valid and applicable advance decision to refuse life-sustaining treatment has the same legal status as if a competent patient were refusing the treatment in question. It must be honoured, even if that is morally repugnant to the practitioner. While every effort should be made to avoid that situation, the statement in the DCOP that 'doctors are entitled to have their personal beliefs respected and will not be pressurised to act contrary to those beliefs'[18] must be qualified in this situation.

D. THE HUMAN RIGHTS ACT 1998

3.28   The Law Commission report was completed in early 1995, before the passage of the Human Rights Act 1998 and indeed before it became Labour Party policy to incorporate the ECHR directly into English jurisprudence. While the Law Commission was of course well aware of the ECHR, its direct applicability in domestic law has introduced a new level of immediacy to its substantive and procedural guarantees unforeseen by the Law Commission. This is complicated by the fact that ECHR jurisprudence has not remained static in the last decade. The first case calling on the ECtHR to interpret the scope of article 5 relating to persons of unsound mind was not determined until late 1979,[19] almost thirty years after the ratification of the ECHR. A trickle of cases thereafter has grown considerably in volume more recently, and the sophistication of the ECtHR's jurisprudence has similarly increased markedly. Many of the relevant cases have been framed in a mental health contest rather than one of mental incapacity, and implicitly assume a level of comprehension and will on the part of complainants. The ECtHR is still coming to terms with the nuances of the situation when such conditions may not be present. The jurisprudence is thus very much in a process of development.

3.29   The ECHR jurisprudence has a different ethos to the MCA. The MCA is designed to create a supportive framework in which decisions are taken for the

---

[17] DCOP, paras 8.43–4.
[18] DCOP, para 8.44.
[19] *Winterwerp v The Netherlands* (A/33) (1979–80) 2 EHRR 387.

benefit of people lacking capacity. Procedure is to be kept to a minimum, and criteria are intended to be flexible enough to meet a wide variety of needs. The statutory best interests test at the core of the MCA is a particularly clear example of this. It is not restrictive, but rather requires an approach to decision-making. Matters that must be considered are drawn broadly—the 'beliefs and values' P would have had if competent, for example. Indeed, under s 4(2), anything considered by the decision-maker to be relevant is incorporated into the best interests test. The ECHR by comparison is designed to protect the individual against human rights violations. It therefore tends to favour procedural safeguards and clear criteria. Obvious examples of this approach include article 5, where the deprivation of liberty must be subject to challenge in a court or court-like process, and article 6, which requires tribunal or similar hearings to be available when civil rights are violated. In the event of conflict, it is difficult to see how these divergent approaches can be integrated.

A number of ECHR rights may be relevant to the subject matter already **3.30** discussed in this book, including the right to life (article 2), the right to be free of inhuman or degrading treatment (article 3), the right to liberty (article 5), the rights to legal process established by article 6, the right to respect for private and family life (article 8), the right to freedom of conscience or religion (article 9), the right to peaceful enjoyment of possessions (protocol 1, article 1) and the prohibition of discrimination (article 14) are obvious examples. The ECtHR has made it clear that particular vigilance is to be exercised to ensure that the rights of vulnerable people, such as those lacking capacity or in institutions, are not violated.[20]

Not all decisions made on behalf of a person lacking capacity will potentially **3.31** constitute breaches of human rights under the 1998 Act and the ECHR. The articles of the ECHR have severity thresholds, and unless those thresholds are met there is no violation. Questions surrounding the threshold for the deprivation of liberty were discussed in para 1.22 above, for example. There is further ECHR jurisprudence to the effect that medically approved treatment of an individual lacking capacity will not reach the threshold of severity to trigger article 3,[21] although there was no advance decision at issue in that case.

Potential human rights issues arise from a variety of situations discussed **3.32** elsewhere in this book. As discussed in para 2.55 above, it is possible for an individual to lose his or her rights even though it later transpires that he or she did not actually lack capacity, if the decision-maker has a reasonable belief in his or her incapacity. The routine removal of rights under the general defence, without formal notice and without routine access to a juridical-style decision-maker may raise questions under article 6 or 8. The right to insist on treatment such as the provision of artificial nutrition or hydration, discussed in para 3.20

---

[20] *Herczegfalvy v Austria* (1992) 50 EHRR 437, para 82.
[21] *Herczegfalvy v Austria* (1992) 50 EHRR 437, para 82.

above may raise issues under article 2 or 8 or, if the desire is based on a religious belief, article 9. The balance between state care and family care may generate issues under article 8. The admission of people to psychiatric facilities or social care homes, or their control in other environments, certainly give rise to issues under article 5: see para 1.22 above. The court's approach to advance decisions to refuse treatment, where cases often concern religious objections to treatment, may raise issues under article 9. This is only a taster. No doubt experience of the MCA and its administration will raise a wide variety of unforeseen issues.

3.33   It is easy to spot potential tensions—it is much more difficult to determine how they should be resolved. The process-based jurisprudence of the ECtHR works most convincingly when the rights subject is a competent individual, able to defend his or her rights. This is precisely what cannot be assumed in matters related to the MCA. It is not obvious how it helps L in the *Bournewood* case[22] to gain the right to a hearing. According to the facts of that case, L was unable to express a view as to whether or not he consented to the admission; it is difficult to see how he would have been able to take advantage of his new right to a hearing. Allowing that right instead to be exercised by a family member or other carer does little to solve the problem convincingly. A perusal of a number of the common law cases regarding the right to make personal decisions for P suggests that this right is relevant when there is a row between family carers and social services or medical practitioners.[23] While it may be appropriate to provide a forum for those disputes, at times in these cases, the rights of P seem to be lost in the crossfire. Further, it is not obvious that P's rights are protected unless the other parties are prepared to litigate. P's rights do not seem to be reliably protected through this mechanism. The court in *R (on the application of MH) v Secretary of State for Health*,[24] held that for one of the civil confinement provisions of the Mental Health Act, tribunal hearings should routinely be provided to those lacking the capacity to apply for one. Notwithstanding the resource implications of such routine hearings, and those are considerable, it is unclear how successful this approach would be. The tribunal and the doctor will be present, but who would represent the patient, and on what terms? It cannot be assumed that these patients will be able to instruct counsel, and while a lawyer might be appointed as *amicus*, it is not obvious how such individuals would understand their role in the proceedings.

3.34   Neither the English courts nor the ECtHR have as yet proceeded very far in coming to terms with the complexity of these situations. Unlike most other European countries, the United Kingdom has a significant number of barristers

---

[22] *R v Bournewood Community and Mental Health NHS Trust, ex p L* [1999] 1 AC 458.

[23] See, e.g., *R v Bournewood Community and Mental Health NHS Trust, ex p L* [1999] 1 AC 458, 479F, *per* Lord Goff; *Re S (Adult Patient) (Inherent Jurisdiction: Family Life)* [2002] EWHC 2278, [2003] 1 FLR 292 at [66], [74], [77]; *Newham London Borough Council v S and Another (Adult: Court's Jurisdiction)* [2003] EWHC 1909, [2003] All ER (D) 550 at [26(iii)], [53].

[24] [2004] EWCA Civ 1609, [2005] 1 WLR 1209. At the time of writing, this case is under appeal to the House of Lords.

and solicitors who devote a considerable part of their practice to work relating to mental disorder. There are academic journals devoted to law and mental disorder based in the United Kingdom[25] and a good collection of academics working in the field. The MCA is also an intelligent and reasonably sophisticated statute. There is the potential for the United Kingdom to play an important part in articulating how, at the beginning of the twenty-first century, the rights contained in the ECHR can be made real for individuals lacking capacity.

E. INTERFACE WITH THE MENTAL HEALTH ACT 1983

Mental disorder and mental incapacity are different concepts, and the presumption of capacity continues to apply for individuals with mental health problems.[26] Nonetheless, a significant number of individuals with mental health difficulties will also lack capacity for personal welfare and health-care decisions, raising questions as to the interface with between the MCA and the Mental Health Act 1983. **3.35**

The starting point for the analysis is s 28(1) of the MCA: **3.36**

Nothing in this Act authorises anyone—
(a) to give a patient medical treatment for mental disorder, or
(b) to consent to a patient's being given medical treatment for mental disorder,
if, at the time when it is proposed to treat the patient, his treatment is regulated by Part 4 of the Mental Health Act.

Part IV of the Mental Health Act 1983 regulates treatment in several ways. First, and most straightforwardly, s 57 prohibits some treatments without the competent and informed consent of the patient as well as a second opinion from an independent doctor registered for the purpose by the Secretary of State for Health. This applies to all patients, whether or not they are sectioned.[27] Currently, the treatments in question are psychosurgery and the surgical implantation of hormones to reduce male sex drive.[28] Of these, only the former is of practical relevance, as male sex drive is now controlled through the use of a hormone analogue rather than an actual hormone, ingested orally rather than surgically.[29] Certainly, s 28(1) of the MCA ensures that these safeguards may not

---

[25] In addition to generalist journals devoted to medical law, see *Journal of Forensic Psychiatry* and *Journal of Mental Health Law*.

[26] *Re C (Adult: Refusal of Medical Treatment)* [1994] 1 All ER 819, 824; *Masterman-Lister v Brutton & Co, Jewell and Home Counties Dairies* [2002] EWCA Civ 1889, [2003] 1 WLR 1511.

[27] Mental Health Act 1983, s 56. In theory, patients need not be hospitalized either, although it is difficult to see that psychosurgery would occur outside a hospital setting in any event.

[28] Mental Health Act 1983, s 57(1) and the Mental Health (Hospital, Guardianship and Consent to Treatment) Regulations 1983 (SI 1983/893), reg 16.

[29] Such analogues ingested orally are outside the scope of the section: see *R v MHAC, ex p X* (1988) 9 BMLR 77.

be circumvented for persons lacking capacity. Such treatments cannot be given to an individuals lacking capacity to consent to them.

3.37   The definition of capacity used for the Mental Health Act is contained in its code of practice.[30] It is based on the common law of capacity, which lacks some of the nuances of ss 2 and 3 of the MCA. The Mental Health Act code includes an inability to believe information related to treatment as an indicator of incapacity, a provision not express in the MCA. The MCA by comparison includes a number of factors absent from the Mental Health Act code:

- incapacity cannot be established merely by age, appearance, or unjustified assumption regarding personal behaviour (s 2(3));
- while P will lack capacity if he or she is unable to retain the information necessary to make a decision, such retention need only be for a short period for an individual to have capacity (s 3(3));
- in determining capacity, the information that must be understood relevant to a decision includes the reasonably foreseeable consequences of deciding one way or another, or of failing to make a decision (s 3(4)).

While these factors are not express in the criteria in the Mental Health Act code, they are not in opposition to those criteria. It may well be that practitioners read the Mental Health Act code in light of the MCA criteria, as a categorical clash could prove problematic and unduly confusing with no obvious advantage. However, the MCA does limit its application to those aged sixteen or over. There is no age restriction in the Mental Health Act.

3.38   Part IV of the Mental Health Act also restricts treatment that can be given to involuntarily detained ('sectioned') patients. For electro-convulsive therapy and when any treatment for mental disorder continues beyond three months from the first day the patient was given treatment for mental disorder during this detention, either informed consent must be obtained or an opinion received from an approved independent doctor.[31] Once again, s 28(1) of the MCA makes it clear that this safeguard cannot be circumvented for patients lacking capacity, when those patients are sectioned.

3.39   Under the Mental Health Act, a sectioned patient may be given other treatments for mental disorder for up to three months without consent or the need for a second opinion.[32] As this treatment is authorized within Part IV, it comes within the purview of s 28 of the MCA. Certainly, treatment under the Mental Health Act must be in the best interests of the patient,[33] but the code reflects the

---

[30] Code of Practice to the Mental Health Act 1983 (revised 1999) para 15.10, available at <http://www.dh.gov.uk/PublicationsAndStatistics/fs/en>, accessed 23 June 2005 via search in Publications library link.

[31] Mental Health Act, s 58(1) and SI 1983/893, reg 16.

[32] This is the combined effect of the Mental Health Act 1983, ss 58(1) and 63.

[33] Code of Practice to the Mental Health Act 1983 (revised 1999) para 15.21. As the code was last revised in 1999, it therefore does not reflect developments in the common law since that time: see para 1.37 above.

common law approach rather than the statutory framework of the MCA. It is thus considerably more objective than the MCA definition, lacking express reference to the views and values of P and the consultation requirements of the MCA. Following *Munjaz*,[34] the Mental Health Act code of practice must be followed unless there is good reason to depart from it, but the code offers few relevant concrete safeguards. It does require information about the treatment to be given to the patient,[35] though this information could not be withheld from a patient able to engage with it under the MCA. The code's guidance on treatment of people lacking capacity offers few formal safeguards, apart from the reminder that sterilization procedures require court approval.[36] Section 28 therefore removes the protections of the MCA for this group of patients, where the Mental Health Act provides few safeguards by way of compensation.

Section 28 of the MCA applies only to medical treatments for mental disorder **3.40** regulated by Part IV of the Mental Health Act 1983. It therefore does not apply to civil confinement or Mental Health Act guardianship, both of which are governed by Part II of that Act, or to informal admissions, which are governed by s 131 of the 1983 Act. It further does not extend either to treatment other than for mental disorder[37] for anyone under the jurisdiction of the Mental Health Act, or to any medical treatment of informal patients, be it for mental disorder or not. In these areas, the statutes offer no guidance as to when resort should be had to the Mental Health Act, and when to the MCA. Each offers advantages and disadvantages to P. The Mental Health Act is generally weaker on substantive standards, and lacks the nuanced analysis of incapacity contained in the MCA. The Mental Health Act is however much stronger on formalized process. For example, as noted above, the treatment of patients confined under the Mental Health Act has to be formally reviewed at the end of three months, with an independent second opinion offered. The doctor offering that opinion must consult with two other professionals who have been involved with the patient's care, one of whom must be a nurse, and the other not a medical practitioner (generally a social worker).[38] This may offer an objective, professional review of treatment considerably more robust than anything routinely on offer under the MCA.

'Informal' patients are those in-patients who are not civilly confined. At **3.41** common law, the guardian of a child could admit the child as an informal patient to a psychiatric facility.[39] Similar powers over persons aged sixteen or

---

[34] *R (on the application of Munjaz) v Mersey Care NHS Trust and Others* [2003] EWCA Civ 1036, [2004] QB 395. Currently under appeal.

[35] Code of Practice to the Mental Health Act 1983 (revised 1999) para 14.5.a.

[36] Code of Practice to the Mental Health Act 1983 (revised 1999) paras 15.22–24.

[37] As defined, rather broadly, in the Mental Health Act 1983, s 145. For a summary of relevant jurisprudence regarding this section, see P. Bartlett and R. Sandland, *Mental Health Law: Policy and Practice*, 2nd edn (2003) 349–61.

[38] Mental Health Act 1983, s 58(4).

[39] *R v Hallstrom (No 2)* [1986] 2 All ER 306, 312.

over are within the remit of those with decision-making authority over where P would live under the MCA, subject to the usual rules regarding best interests and the following restrictions. Informal admissions to hospitals and care homes under the jurisdiction of the NHS are subject to special provisions contained in s 38 of the MCA. When such hospital admission is expected to be for a period exceeding twenty-eight days, or care home admission for a period exceeding eight weeks, the provider is required to seek the advice of an independent advocate unless there is a donee of an LPOA or EPOA, an individual named by P to be consulted in matters affecting his interests, or a court-appointed deputy: see paras 2.53–4 above. This includes aftercare provided under s 117 of the Mental Health Act 1983.[40] In so far as informal admission was resisted by P, required force or the threat of force to effect, or restricted P's liberty of movement, it would constitute restraint and would therefore be subject to the specific provisions discussed in paras 2.51–2 above. Indeed, if the admission constituted a violation of P's right to liberty under article 5 of the ECHR (see para 1.22 above), it could only be effected under the MCA by court order: see para 2.51 above. In practice, where the sole problematic issue is hospital admission, it will normally be more expeditious and less expensive to invoke the civil confinement sections of the Mental Health Act rather than to resort to the courts under the MCA.

3.42   Once admitted to hospital, informal patients are subject to the common law as regards treatment for their mental and other disorders. Informal patients lacking capacity are therefore to be treated under the MCA in much the same way as if they were outside the psychiatric facility. Donees of LPOAs and court-appointed deputies whose authority includes making treatment decisions have authority to make decisions related to treatment either for mental disorder or other disorder. Advance decisions to refuse medical treatment also apply, as long as the patient has informal status. Otherwise, treatment for mental or other disorder can be provided under the general defence unless it is governed by Part IV, as discussed above. In the event that a decision-maker is apparently not exercising his or her authority in the best interests of P, the usual remedies of contacting the Public Guardian or, if the decision-maker is acting in a professional capacity, raising the matter with his or her employer or professional organization remain available here.

3.43   If P remains on informal status, the procedural protections related to electro-convulsive therapy and treatment beyond three months will not apply, as the relevant section of that Act refers only to confined patients. These treatments will therefore not to be regulated by Part IV of the Mental Health Act 1983, and in law, it would appear that electro-convulsive therapy can therefore be given to an informal patient lacking capacity in his or her best interests, provided that the procedures in the MCA are followed. Some people will view this with concern,

---

[40] Explanatory notes to the Mental Capacity Bill (2004 HL Bill 13-EN) para 113.

particularly if the decision is made by a doctor relying on the general defence, rather than a donee of an LPOA or deputy specifically appointed to make medical decisions on behalf of P based on his or her knowledge of P. If a doctor has reservations about proceeding in these circumstances, it may well be appropriate to seek the advice of an independent colleague, or to call in the services of a Court of Protection Special Visitor or an independent advocate. Indeed, this sort of treatment may well be included in the regulation defining 'serious' treatment in s 37 when those regulations are drafted. This would trigger the involvement of an advocate as a matter of routine, where there is no LPOA, EPOA or court-appointed deputy. Unless that occurs, while the doctor has the option of seeking the advice of others, it will not be possible for others concerned about P to require it. They could instead notify the Public Guardian of concerns that P's best interests were not being met or apply to the Court of Protection. Either of these would however require factual circumstances calling into question whether P's best interests were being served; the mere provision of an unpopular treatment would not suffice.

There is nothing in the MCA to preclude the application of the confinement **3.44** provisions contained in Part II of the Mental Health Act 1983. The Mental Health Act is subject to substantive thresholds and procedural requirements of its own,[41] suggesting different advantages and disadvantages for people lacking capacity, their doctors, and their other carers relying upon the Act's provisions.

The substantive legal criteria are contained in s 2 (admission for assessment, **3.45** allowing confinement for twenty-eight days non-renewable) and s 3 (admission for treatment, allowing admission for six months, renewable) of the Mental Health Act 1983. This is not the place to examine them in detail. In essence, each requires the individual to be suffering from mental disorder of a 'nature or degree' that makes it appropriate for him or her to be admitted for assessment or treatment, as the case may be. Such admission must also be necessary for the health or safety of the person, or the protection of others. For s 3 admissions, if the individual is suffering from 'psychopathy' or 'mental impairment', both defined terms, a treatment must exist to alleviate or prevent a deterioration of the individual's condition. These 'nature or degree' criteria are not particularly strong—admission in the interests of the patient's health is sufficient. Meeting this threshold does not require a doctor to civilly confine the individual, however, and most doctors, aware perhaps both of the significance of the decision to confine an individual and the shortage of resources in this area of medical practice, avoid sectioning if reasonably possible.

Where the Mental Health Act 1983 does create a significant substantive **3.46** barrier is in its definitions of 'mental impairment' and 'severe mental impairment'. Section 3, unlike s 2, requires that the mental disorder of the individual

---

[41] The substantive and procedural rules regarding civil confinement are complex. For an explanation and discussion of their operation, see P. Bartlett and R. Sandland, *Mental Health Law: Policy and Practice*, 2nd edn (2003), chs 4 and 5; and R. Jones, *Mental Health Act Manual*, 8th edn (2003).

be specified as mental illness, mental impairment, severe mental impairment, or psychopathy. As discussed in paras 1.06–7 above, the definition of the mental impairments requires not merely impairment of intelligence and social functioning, but 'abnormally aggressive or seriously irresponsible conduct' on the part of the person as a result.[42] The courts have taken this restriction seriously. As a result, individuals with mental impairments may fall outside the scope of the longer-term confinement available in s 3. For these people, the MCA procedures may be the only long-term option.

3.47 The Mental Health Act provisions are procedurally stronger than the restraint provisions of the MCA, requiring certification by two doctors and a social worker. This may be important for P. The people who make decisions for P under the MCA will not necessarily be professionals, and may lack the knowledge of practical alternatives to hospital admission possessed by a competent social worker. If professional knowledge is at the core of the decision, whether it is the knowledge of social workers or medical professionals, the combination of individuals in the confinement process suggests stronger decision-making than that of a single doctor with or without a lay decision-maker under the MCA. In the Mental Health Act process, of course, the views of the individual while competent and the nuanced views of best interests contained in the MCA do not form a formal part of the consideration. That may work to the advantage or disadvantage of the patient according to the individual case. The substantive threshold criteria under the Mental Health Act are also relatively weak, as discussed above. The individual is therefore subject to some choice of criteria by the professional decision-makers. The principle of least restrictive alternative, for example, will be adopted by most of these professionals, but there is no formal requirement to that effect in the Mental Health Act.

3.48 The nearest relative of the patient normally has the right to block any compulsory admission under the Mental Health Act, unless the patient would be dangerous if not subject to confinement. If the nearest relative as defined by the Mental Health Act is the same person as a MCA deputy or donee of an LPOA with authority over the admission, the confinement process may offer a broader range of information and advice relevant to the merits of the decision, while still leaving the decision with the individual chosen by P or the court. Processes do however exist for substitution of the nearest relative when the individual prescribed by statute 'unreasonably objects' to the civil committal. The courts have in the past been primarily interested in the patient's best medical interests in assessing such unreasonable objection. If this trend continues, a deputy or donee of an LPOA who refused the admission based on MCA best interests criteria might find himself or herself being removed as nearest relative.

3.49 As part of the Mental Health Act's procedural strength, persons admitted under either s 2 or 3 or their nearest relatives have the right to a review tribunal

---

[42] Mental Health Act 1983, s 1(2).

hearing to challenge the confinement, complete with legal representation for which legal aid is available. There is no corresponding right under the MCA short of an application to the Court of Protection. Probably, success before the review tribunal does not preclude continuing the admission of the individual under the MCA processes. In practice, P might well be perturbed by this approach, and his or her continued admission might therefore be sufficiently intrusive to violate the right to liberty under article 5 of the ECHR. In that event, his or her continued detention would have to be by court order. In the event that the Court of Protection viewed the admission as in the best interests of P, there is nothing obvious in the MCA that would preclude the court ordering P's continued accommodation as an 'informal' patient in hospital, subject to the reservations raised in para 2.46 above as to whether the MCA best interests criteria are sufficiently clear to meet the standard of ECHR compliance. The informal admission of persons lacking capacity has been the subject of a government consultation.[43] The results of that consultation may alter the law in this area.

The Mental Health Act 1983 provides the right to a hearing, but it does not **3.50** provide an automatic hearing under s 2. The right to a hearing may therefore be largely illusory, if P lacks the ability to form the intent to apply for the hearing. In *R (on the application of MH) v Secretary of State for Health*,[44] this situation was taken to be a violation of article 5 of the ECHR, as P would not have the benefit of the process designed to test the legality of his or her confinement.[45] In this regard, the Mental Health Act provision was held to be incompatible with the Human Rights Act. In the view of Buxton LJ, it would be remedied only by routine hearings by the Mental Health Review Tribunal into the admissions of all persons in this position.[46] Where an individual is admitted under s 3, the Mental Health Act does provide an automatic hearing at the end of six months, and every three years thereafter for persons over the age of sixteen.[47] While not formally at issue in the case, a broad hint was given in *MH* that this too would violate the ECHR for similar reasons,[48] and presumably a similar programme of routine hearings would be required as a result.

Confinement is not always an end in itself, but is sometimes resorted to as a **3.51** way of circumventing a refusal by individuals to consent to treatment for their

---

[43] Department of Health, *'Bournewood' Consultation: The approach to be taken in response to the judgment of the European Court of Human Rights in the 'Bournewood' case*, DOH #267902 (2005), available at <http//:www.dh.gov.uk/Consultations/ClosedConsultations/fs/en>, accessed 20 June 2005.

[44] [2004] EWCA Civ 1609, [2005] 1 WLR 1209. At the time of writing, this case is under appeal to the House of Lords.

[45] [2004] EWCA Civ 1609, [2005] 1 WLR 1209 at [18].

[46] [2004] EWCA Civ 1609, [2005] 1 WLR 1209 at [25]–[26].

[47] Mental Health Act 1983, s 68.

[48] *R (on the application of MH) v Secretary of State for Health* [2004] EWCA Civ 1609, [2005] 1 WLR 1209 at [9].

mental disorder. This will no doubt be the case with the MCA. Indeed, civil confinement followed by treatment without consent is the only way to treat notwithstanding a valid and applicable advance decision to refuse treatment. That approach will be effective only for treatments for mental disorder, as these are the only treatments for which the requirement of consent is waived under the Mental Health Act. While the definition of medical treatment is broad in this context, including 'nursing, . . . care, habilitation, and rehabilitation under medical supervision',[49] it is not universal. Advance decisions regarding treatments for non-mental disorders cannot be overruled.

3.52 How far the confinement and resulting treatment powers can overrule the views of the patient when competent is something of an open question in any event. It does seem now that the refusal of proposed treatment by a competent patient must be taken into consideration as one of the factors in deciding whether compulsory treatment will be given under the Mental Health Act 1983, but it is only one factor. It does not determine whether treatment will be enforced.[50] An advance decision to refuse medical treatment, if valid and applicable, has the same status as if the decision had been made by P when competent at the time consent was called for (s 26(1)). It should therefore have the same impact on the decision to treat involuntarily as the refusal of a competent patient. Broader views would similarly appear to feed into the mix, although none would be able definitively to determine the outcome of the decision to treat involuntarily.

3.53 Particularly for people lacking capacity to make personal decisions who are expected to be resident outside hospitals, the guardianship provisions of the Mental Health Act warrant at least passing consideration. The criteria require the individual to be suffering from mental illness, mental impairment, severe mental impairment, or psychopathy. The limitations on the definitions of the mental impairments discussed in paras 1.06–7 above apply here, and may have the effect of rendering Mental Health Act guardianship unavailable to many individuals who lack capacity to make personal decisions. The norm in recent years has been that the guardian appointed is the social services authority, although that is not a requirement.

3.54 The powers that the Mental Health Act provisions convey to the guardian are limited. The guardian can require the patient to reside at a specific place (but does not have power to detain him or her there); the power to require the patient to attend for medical treatment, occupation, education, or training (but no power to consent to treatment); and the power to require access to the patient to be given to specified professionals such as doctors. These are not as powerful as those conveyed under an LPOA allowing the donee to make personal welfare decisions, nor as strong as those available to the court to award to deputies.

---

[49] Mental Health Act 1983, s 145.
[50] *R (on the application of PS) v G (RMO) and W (SOAD)* [2003] EWHC 2335 at [119].

Guardianship is therefore unlikely to be much use in these circumstances. For that reason, guardians ought not to be appointed in these situations. An individual is to be received into guardianship only if it is 'necessary' in the interests of his or her welfare or the protection of others, and it is difficult to see the necessity when an LPOA or deputy already exists. The reverse is not necessarily true. As the role of a deputy can be considerably broader than that of a Mental Health Act guardian, it may still be appropriate for the court to appoint a deputy even if a guardian under the Mental Health Act exists. Either way, the existence of the other decision-maker should be disclosed in the application for guardianship or for the appointment of a deputy, as the case may be. In the event that both a guardian and a donee of an LPOA or deputy exist, it is not clear whose views should prevail on matters within both authorities. The procedural rules do not assist here, guardianship may be challenged first at the review board and then at the High Court, but not in the Court of Protection, which has jurisdiction relating to LPOAs and deputies. The litigants might be in the Court of Appeal before both issues could be determined at the same time.

It is less obvious that the appointment of a Mental Health Act guardian will 3.55 be inappropriate when decisions are otherwise being made under the general defence. If the person lacking capacity meets the criteria, and where the issues of concern are within the guardian's powers listed above, a guardianship application may provide an expeditious way to introduce a specific decision-maker. Certainly, the process would be less cumbersome than an application to the Court of Protection for the appointment of a deputy. The MCA does not address whether the person relying on the general defence may make decisions in contravention of those of a Mental Health Act guardian. The MCA does not revoke Mental Health Act guardianship, however, and therefore must be taken to coexist with it. In that context, the general defence must be subject to the decisions of a guardian, acting within his or her scope of authority.

The above discussion has been intended to provide some guidance on the legal 3.56 tensions between the Mental Health Act 1983 and the MCA provisions. Where the jurisdiction of the statutes overlaps, there is still considerable scope for professional discretion. In particular, in some parts of psychiatric practice, traditions have grown up since the introduction of review tribunals almost half a century ago that patients aggrieved by their civil confinement ought to be able to challenge that confinement. While formal studies have not been done, anecdotal evidence would suggest that a significant proportion of those who are now challenging their Mental Health Act confinements lack capacity to decide where they should live. Theoretically, unless the force required to accommodate these people lacking capacity interfered with their rights to liberty under article 5 of the ECHR, they might now be dealt with under the MCA with fewer administrative requirements. This would have the effect of removing procedural rights from people who now enjoy them. It may well be that the traditions of psychiatric practice instead will continue to be followed, and the civil confinement provisions will be resorted to when patients firmly object to their admissions even when the MCA processes would also be available. While practitioners should exercise reasonable care not to subject people unduly to the stigma of confinement, the continuation of this tradition of rights would seem still to be highly appropriate. It would be ironic indeed if the MCA served to remove rights currently enjoyed by people lacking capacity.

3.57 As discussed in para 3.49 above, the practicalities of the situation of certain persons lacking capacity may mean that they will be unable to exercise their rights to a hearing under the Mental Health Act. Recourse to the Mental Health Act should not be used with the object of circumventing the substantive and procedural safeguards of the MCA in this situation, when P would in practice be unlikely to be able to apply for a hearing under the Mental Health Act. The Mental Health Act civil confinement powers must be justified by the objective condition of P, not by any potential administrative convenience of avoiding the MCA.

F. CONTINUATION OF THE COMMON LAW?

3.58 The first chapter of this book described the recent developments of the common law in the field of incapacity. There is therefore a pleasing symmetry in concluding the book by returning to those developments. The question to address here is how much of the common law is superseded by the MCA, and how much of it will be taken to coexist with the new legislation.

3.59 In its original conception by the Law Commission, the legislative developments would have supplanted little of the common law. Various tests of capacity that had been long established in laws of contract, crime, wills, equity, and other contexts would continue to exist.[51] The new legislation would instead provide new mechanisms creating new authorities to make decisions on behalf of those lacking capacity. The MCA as eventually passed has not departed from that original format. Nothing in the MCA expressly supersedes anything in common law; instead the Act is phrased as a collection of newly created legal responses.

3.60 The common law context of the Law Commission approach did not remain static, however. Indeed, since 1989, there has been a veritable explosion in judicial decision-making related to the law of incapacity. The two cases that serve as the cornerstones of recent thinking, *Re F (Mental Patient: Sterilization)*[52] regarding the doctrine of necessity and *Re C (Adult: Refusal of Medical Treatment)*[53] regarding the legal definition of incapacity, occurred during the Law Commission's deliberations, the latter very late in those deliberations. The other significant common law developments have occurred since the Law

---

[51] Law Com Report No 231, *Mental Incapacity* (February 1995), para 3.23, available at <http://www.lawcom.gov.uk>, accessed 20 June 2005.

[52] [1990] 2 AC 1.

[53] [1994] 1 All ER 819.

Commission report, and could not reasonably have been anticipated by it. These developments do overlap significantly with the MCA as enacted. As discussed in Chapter 1, they have refined the common law best interests test, given the court a new and broader jurisdiction in matters relating to incapacity, and introduced the appointment of substitute decision-makers. As already noted, these developments are problematic in practice and on shaky doctrinal foundations, but they cannot be ignored. They are not expressly overruled by the MCA; the question is how far they are overruled by implication, and how far they continue to stand.

Even in its original conception, prior to the recent developments in the com- **3.61** mon law, there was potential for discord. The law of testamentary capacity serves as an example. The test of such capacity at common law is contained in *Banks v Goodfellow*:

It is essential to the exercise of such a power that a testator shall understand the nature of the act and its effects; shall understand the extent of the property of which he is disposing; shall be able to comprehend and appreciate the claims to which he ought to give effect.[54]

This is quite a different wording to the definition of inability to make a decision in the MCA. Judicial interpretations of the *Banks* test show a further divergence from the approach of the MCA. In *Evans v Knight and Moore*, for example, it was held:

[W]here a mental aberration is proved to have shown itself in the alleged testator, the degree of evidence necessary to substantiate any testamentary act depends greatly on the character of the act itself. If it purports to give effect only to probable intentions, its validity may be established by comparatively slight evidence. But evidence, very different in kind and much weightier in degree, is required to the support of an act which purports to contain dispositions contrary to the testator's probable intentions, or savouring, in any degree, of folly or frenzy.[55]

This suggests that the wisdom or appropriateness of the decision is a factor in whether the testator will be deemed to have capacity. In that case, the fact that the will was 'precisely such a disposition as natural affection would dictate'[56] was apparently a significant factor in upholding the will. Such an approach is not consistent with the principle in the MCA that a person will not be treated as lacking capacity merely because he makes an unwise decision (s 1(4)).

Such incomplete alignments, at least in theory, have the potential to be **3.62** problematic. The test of incapacity that would allow a court to write a will on behalf of P is the statutory test under the MCA, not the common law test. Incomplete alignments between the tests in statute and common law mean that,

---

[54] (1870) 5 QB 549, 565.
[55] (1822) 1 Add 229, 237–8.
[56] (1822) 1 Add 229, 238.

potentially, either both the court and P might have the authority to write a will, or neither might. The former situation might result in a posthumous battle between two apparently valid wills; the latter would result in no one being able to draft a will, defeating the object of the statutory provision. While the courts may endeavour to interpret cases in ways that would minimize these anomalous results, and while the difficulties may be inevitable, the result is not ideal.

3.63   The issues surrounding the new powers of the court raise different issues. Where it is clear that the common law definitions of capacity will coexist with the MCA provisions, it is not clear how far the common law powers related to the doctrine of necessity will remain. They certainly will to some degree. The doctrine of necessity existed long before *Re F*. It is this doctrine that allows firefighters to enter burning buildings to fight fires, without liability for trespass. The passage of the MCA clearly does not remove this doctrine in that context. There can similarly be no doubt that the court retains a jurisdiction to make declarations on the law. As noted in Chapter 1, that power extends well beyond mental capacity; it is not revoked by the Act. The question is instead whether in areas closely related to the Act, the other jurisdictions should be taken to have been amended into closer conformity with the Act.

3.64   The advance decision to refuse treatment is a case where some elements of the common law are clearly superseded. The common law provided no formalities requirements for any advance decisions to refuse medical treatment. The MCA instead requires advance decisions of life-sustaining treatment to state expressly that they apply even though life may be put at risk, and requires them to be in writing, signed, and witnessed (s 25(5)–(6)).

3.65   The continuing extent of broader powers of the court regarding necessity and declarations is less clear. On the one hand, the continuation of these legal mechanisms may provide a safety valve allowing relief to be given in hard cases without unduly stretching the language of the MCA. On the other hand, overuse of the common law powers in these situations may excise from the MCA the very benefits it was designed to promote. Some examples may clarify this tension.

3.66   Consider a man suffering from a severe physical injury following an auto-mobile accident. When the ambulance arrives, he may be distracted by pain, and therefore unable to give meaningful consent. It would seem an unduly harsh result to fail to provide pain relief in that situation; yet can it really be said that he is suffering from an 'impairment of, or a disturbance in the functioning of, the mind or brain' (s 2(1))? The Law Commission viewed the provision of this diagnostic threshold as a safeguard.[57] Expanding the meaning to suit the facts would risk destroying its value as a safeguard. It might in this example be better to keep a firm grip on the scope of the diagnostic threshold, and refuse to apply

---

[57] Law Com Report No 231 (n 51 above) para 3.8.

the MCA. That would still leave necessity as an available defence,[58] and one that might better fit the facts of the situation. This would be an example of the continued use of necessity used to strengthen the safeguards in the Act.

At the same time, overuse of the alternative processes risks undermining the   **3.67**
Act. Decisions that are covered by the statutory general defence in s 5 will often be the same as the decisions previously made under the common law defence of necessity. The definition of best interests will vary however depending on which legal mechanism is applied. The MCA has a carefully considered and nuanced definition, much more precise than the simple balance-sheet approach of the common law. Allowing reliance on the common law in this context would circumvent the Act, and effectively undermine one of its key provisions.

This is not a merely abstract possibility. To be realistic, many (if not most)   **3.68**
people who are in caring relationships of people lacking capacity will be unaware of the MCA or the common law provisions. Indeed, the clarification of the rules surrounding such informal care was one of the objectives of the Law Commission proposals in this area.[59] They will not be the donees of LPOAs or in receipt of deputy powers from the court. They will, without their express knowledge, be relying on the general defence in s 5 or the doctrine of necessity. They will have no knowledge of the best interests test in s 4, so it will be unsurprising if they do not follow its specific provisions. Such carers may have been acting in good faith and with considerable personal sacrifice. How is the court to react in this situation? It would seem insulting to find that such carers acted illegally, let alone to hold them liable in damages or subject to a criminal punishment, particularly if their actions met the common law test of best interests.

One possibility for the court in this situation is to soft-pedal the legislative   **3.69**
requirements. It might do this, for example, by suggesting that the statutory best interest test is 'directive' rather than 'mandatory'. It might alternatively give particular weight to s 4(2), which allows 'all relevant circumstances' to be taken into account, at the expense of sidelining the specific determinations under the rest of the section. Best interests is a key concept, however, and such an approach would effectively gut the MCA. This approach cannot be the intent of the Act as drafted. Certainly, s 4(9) provides that a reasonable belief that a decision is taken in the best interests of P will suffice, but only if the processes are in compliance with s 4(2)–(7). These provisions are not meant to be sidelined.

Another possibility is for the court to hold that the statutory scheme is not   **3.70**
satisfied, but that the common law defence of necessity remains open. As

---

[58] This approach suits the understanding of necessity prior to *Re F* case in 1989: see R. Dias, *Clerk and Lindsell on Torts*, 15th edn (1982) para 1–154; J. Fleming, *Law of Torts*, 5th edn (1977) 92–4 and 9th edn (1998) 106.
[59] Law Com Report No 231 (n 51 above) para 4.2.

discussed above, this would be likely to have the same effect of rendering key provisions of the statute meaningless.

3.71   The third possibility is to hold that the MCA supersedes the law in this area, and that the carer has acted illegally. That seems to be the best result if the objective is to protect the integrity of the statutory regime, with the protections it provides to people lacking capacity in general. If the carer is an unattractive witness or of dubious character, this may be the result the court prefers. If, however, the carer has acted in good faith and with considerable personal sacrifice, there may well be considerable pressures to take one of the other approaches: hard cases make bad law. That said, it is difficult to see the justice in the result, when the carer did not even know of the law he or she should have followed. While ignorance may be no excuse in law, it does tug at the heartstrings.

3.72   The new-found common law jurisdiction of the court to appoint substitute decision-makers is easier to deal with. It is discretionary. The arguments in favour of the jurisdiction are eradicated by the new jurisdiction of the Court of Protection to appoint deputies. It may be a nice legal question as to whether the common law jurisdiction continues to exist—it was always on rather shaky legal foundations—but it is difficult to see a circumstance where it would be appropriate for the court to exercise it.

APPENDIX

Mental Capacity Act 2005

2005 CHAPTER 9

CONTENTS

PART 1
PERSONS WHO LACK CAPACITY

97

PART 2
THE COURT OF PROTECTION AND THE PUBLIC GUARDIAN

PART 3
MISCELLANEOUS AND GENERAL

An Act to make new provision relating to persons who lack capacity; to establish a superior court of record called the Court of Protection in place of the office of the Supreme Court called by that name; to make provision in connection with the Convention on the International Protection of Adults signed at the Hague on 13th January 2000; and for connected purposes.

[7th April 2005]

BEE IT ENACTED by the Queen's most Excellent Majesty, by and with the advice and consent of the Lords Spiritual and Temporal, and Commons, in this present Parliament assembled, and by the authority of the same, as follows:—

PART 1
PERSONS WHO LACK CAPACITY

The principles

1 The principles

(1) The following principles apply for the purposes of this Act.

(2) A person must be assumed to have capacity unless it is established that he lacks capacity.

(3) A person is not to be treated as unable to make a decision unless all practicable steps to help him to do so have been taken without success.

(4) A person is not to be treated as unable to make a decision merely because he makes an unwise decision.

(5) An act done, or decision made, under this Act for or on behalf of a person who lacks capacity must be done, or made, in his best interests.

(6) Before the act is done, or the decision is made, regard must be had to whether the purpose for which it is needed can be as effectively achieved in a way that is less restrictive of the person's rights and freedom of action.

Preliminary

2 People who lack capacity

(1) For the purposes of this Act, a person lacks capacity in relation to a matter if at the material time he is unable to make a decision for himself in relation to the matter because of an impairment of, or a disturbance in the functioning of, the mind or brain.

(2) It does not matter whether the impairment or disturbance is permanent or temporary.

(3) A lack of capacity cannot be established merely by reference to—
    (a) a person's age or appearance, or
    (b) a condition of his, or an aspect of his behaviour, which might lead others to make unjustified assumptions about his capacity.

(4) In proceedings under this Act or any other enactment, any question whether a person lacks capacity within the meaning of this Act must be decided on the balance of probabilities.

(5) No power which a person ('D') may exercise under this Act—
    (a) in relation to a person who lacks capacity, or
    (b) where D reasonably thinks that a person lacks capacity,
    is exercisable in relation to a person under 16.

(6) Subsection (5) is subject to section 18(3).

3 Inability to make decisions

(1) For the purposes of section 2, a person is unable to make a decision for himself if he is unable—
    (a) to understand the information relevant to the decision,
    (b) to retain that information,
    (c) to use or weigh that information as part of the process of making the decision, or

    (d) to communicate his decision (whether by talking, using sign language or any other means).

(2) A person is not to be regarded as unable to understand the information relevant to a decision if he is able to understand an explanation of it given to him in a way that is appropriate to his circumstances (using simple language, visual aids or any other means).

(3) The fact that a person is able to retain the information relevant to a decision for a short period only does not prevent him from being regarded as able to make the decision.

(4) The information relevant to a decision includes information about the reasonably foreseeable consequences of—

    (a) deciding one way or another, or

    (b) failing to make the decision.

4 Best interests

(1) In determining for the purposes of this Act what is in a person's best interests, the person making the determination must not make it merely on the basis of—

    (a) the person's age or appearance, or

    (b) a condition of his, or an aspect of his behaviour, which might lead others to make unjustified assumptions about what might be in his best interests.

(2) The person making the determination must consider all the relevant circumstances and, in particular, take the following steps.

(3) He must consider—

    (a) whether it is likely that the person will at some time have capacity in relation to the matter in question, and

    (b) if it appears likely that he will, when that is likely to be.

(4) He must, so far as reasonably practicable, permit and encourage the person to participate, or to improve his ability to participate, as fully as possible in any act done for him and any decision affecting him.

(5) Where the determination relates to life-sustaining treatment he must not, in considering whether the treatment is in the best interests of the person concerned, be motivated by a desire to bring about his death.

(6) He must consider, so far as is reasonably ascertainable—

    (a) the person's past and present wishes and feelings (and, in particular, any relevant written statement made by him when he had capacity),

    (b) the beliefs and values that would be likely to influence his decision if he had capacity, and

    (c) the other factors that he would be likely to consider if he were able to do so.

(7) He must take into account, if it is practicable and appropriate to consult them, the views of—

    (a) anyone named by the person as someone to be consulted on the matter in question or on matters of that kind,

    (b) anyone engaged in caring for the person or interested in his welfare,

    (c) any donee of a lasting power of attorney granted by the person, and

    (d) any deputy appointed for the person by the court,

as to what would be in the person's best interests and, in particular, as to the matters mentioned in subsection (6).

(8) The duties imposed by subsections (1) to (7) also apply in relation to the exercise of any powers which—
    (a) are exercisable under a lasting power of attorney, or
    (b) are exercisable by a person under this Act where he reasonably believes that another person lacks capacity.

(9) In the case of an act done, or a decision made, by a person other than the court, there is sufficient compliance with this section if (having complied with the requirements of subsections (1) to (7)) he reasonably believes that what he does or decides is in the best interests of the person concerned.

(10) 'Life-sustaining treatment' means treatment which in the view of a person providing health care for the person concerned is necessary to sustain life.

(11) 'Relevant circumstances' are those—
    (a) of which the person making the determination is aware, and
    (b) which it would be reasonable to regard as relevant.

5 Acts in connection with care or treatment

(1) If a person ('D') does an act in connection with the care or treatment of another person ('P'), the act is one to which this section applies if—
    (a) before doing the act, D takes reasonable steps to establish whether P lacks capacity in relation to the matter in question, and
    (b) when doing the act, D reasonably believes—
        (i) that P lacks capacity in relation to the matter, and
        (ii) that it will be in P's best interests for the act to be done.

(2) D does not incur any liability in relation to the act that he would not have incurred if P—
    (a) had had capacity to consent in relation to the matter, and
    (b) had consented to D's doing the act.

(3) Nothing in this section excludes a person's civil liability for loss or damage, or his criminal liability, resulting from his negligence in doing the act.

(4) Nothing in this section affects the operation of sections 24 to 26 (advance decisions to refuse treatment).

6 Section 5 acts: limitations

(1) If D does an act that is intended to restrain P, it is not an act to which section 5 applies unless two further conditions are satisfied.

(2) The first condition is that D reasonably believes that it is necessary to do the act in order to prevent harm to P.

(3) The second is that the act is a proportionate response to—
    (a) the likelihood of P's suffering harm, and
    (b) the seriousness of that harm.

(4) For the purposes of this section D restrains P if he—
    (a) uses, or threatens to use, force to secure the doing of an act which P resists, or
    (b) restricts P's liberty of movement, whether or not P resists.

(5) But D does more than merely restrain P if he deprives P of his liberty within the meaning of Article 5(1) of the Human Rights Convention (whether or not D is a public authority).

(6) Section 5 does not authorise a person to do an act which conflicts with a decision made, within the scope of his authority and in accordance with this Part, by—

(a) a donee of a lasting power of attorney granted by P, or

(b) a deputy appointed for P by the court.

(7) But nothing in subsection (6) stops a person—

    (a) providing life-sustaining treatment, or

    (b) doing any act which he reasonably believes to be necessary to prevent a serious deterioration in P's condition,

while a decision as respects any relevant issue is sought from the court.

7 Payment for necessary goods and services

(1) If necessary goods or services are supplied to a person who lacks capacity to contract for the supply, he must pay a reasonable price for them.

(2) 'Necessary' means suitable to a person's condition in life and to his actual requirements at the time when the goods or services are supplied.

8 Expenditure

(1) If an act to which section 5 applies involves expenditure, it is lawful for D—

    (a) to pledge P's credit for the purpose of the expenditure, and

    (b) to apply money in P's possession for meeting the expenditure.

(2) If the expenditure is borne for P by D, it is lawful for D—

    (a) to reimburse himself out of money in P's possession, or

    (b) to be otherwise indemnified by P.

(3) Subsections (1) and (2) do not affect any power under which (apart from those subsections) a person—

    (a) has lawful control of P's money or other property, and

    (b) has power to spend money for P's benefit.

Lasting powers of attorney

9 Lasting powers of attorney

(1) A lasting power of attorney is a power of attorney under which the donor ('P') confers on the donee (or donees) authority to make decisions about all or any of the following—

    (a) P's personal welfare or specified matters concerning P's personal welfare, and

    (b) P's property and affairs or specified matters concerning P's property and affairs,

and which includes authority to make such decisions in circumstances where P no longer has capacity.

(2) A lasting power of attorney is not created unless—

    (a) section 10 is complied with,

    (b) an instrument conferring authority of the kind mentioned in subsection (1) is made and registered in accordance with Schedule 1, and

    (c) at the time when P executes the instrument, P has reached 18 and has capacity to execute it.

(3) An instrument which—

    (a) purports to create a lasting power of attorney, but

    (b) does not comply with this section, section 10 or Schedule 1,

confers no authority.

(4) The authority conferred by a lasting power of attorney is subject to—

(a) the provisions of this Act and, in particular, sections 1 (the principles) and 4 (best interests), and

(b) any conditions or restrictions specified in the instrument.

10   Appointment of donees

(1) A donee of a lasting power of attorney must be—
   (a) an individual who has reached 18, or
   (b) if the power relates only to P's property and affairs, either such an individual or a trust corporation.

(2) An individual who is bankrupt may not be appointed as donee of a lasting power of attorney in relation to P's property and affairs.

(3) Subsections (4) to (7) apply in relation to an instrument under which two or more persons are to act as donees of a lasting power of attorney.

(4) The instrument may appoint them to act—
   (a) jointly,
   (b) jointly and severally, or
   (c) jointly in respect of some matters and jointly and severally in respect of others.

(5) To the extent to which it does not specify whether they are to act jointly or jointly and severally, the instrument is to be assumed to appoint them to act jointly.

(6) If they are to act jointly, a failure, as respects one of them, to comply with the requirements of subsection (1) or (2) or Part 1 or 2 of Schedule 1 prevents a lasting power of attorney from being created.

(7) If they are to act jointly and severally, a failure, as respects one of them, to comply with the requirements of subsection (1) or (2) or Part 1 or 2 of Schedule 1—
   (a) prevents the appointment taking effect in his case, but
   (b) does not prevent a lasting power of attorney from being created in the case of the other or others.

(8) An instrument used to create a lasting power of attorney—
   (a) cannot give the donee (or, if more than one, any of them) power to appoint a substitute or successor, but
   (b) may itself appoint a person to replace the donee (or, if more than one, any of them) on the occurrence of an event mentioned in section 13(6)(a) to (d) which has the effect of terminating the donee's appointment.

11   Lasting powers of attorney: restrictions

(1) A lasting power of attorney does not authorise the donee (or, if more than one, any of them) to do an act that is intended to restrain P, unless three conditions are satisfied.

(2) The first condition is that P lacks, or the donee reasonably believes that P lacks, capacity in relation to the matter in question.

(3) The second is that the donee reasonably believes that it is necessary to do the act in order to prevent harm to P.

(4) The third is that the act is a proportionate response to—
   (a) the likelihood of P's suffering harm, and
   (b) the seriousness of that harm.

(5) For the purposes of this section, the donee restrains P if he—
   (a) uses, or threatens to use, force to secure the doing of an act which P resists, or

(b) restricts P's liberty of movement, whether or not P resists,

or if he authorises another person to do any of those things.

(6) But the donee does more than merely restrain P if he deprives P of his liberty within the meaning of Article 5(1) of the Human Rights Convention.

(7) Where a lasting power of attorney authorises the donee (or, if more than one, any of them) to make decisions about P's personal welfare, the authority—

(a) does not extend to making such decisions in circumstances other than those where P lacks, or the donee reasonably believes that P lacks, capacity,

(b) is subject to sections 24 to 26 (advance decisions to refuse treatment), and

(c) extends to giving or refusing consent to the carrying out or continuation of a treatment by a person providing health care for P.

(8) But subsection (7)(c)—

(a) does not authorise the giving or refusing of consent to the carrying out or continuation of life-sustaining treatment, unless the instrument contains express provision to that effect, and

(b) is subject to any conditions or restrictions in the instrument.

12 Scope of lasting powers of attorney: gifts

(1) Where a lasting power of attorney confers authority to make decisions about P's property and affairs, it does not authorise a donee (or, if more than one, any of them) to dispose of the donor's property by making gifts except to the extent permitted by subsection (2).

(2) The donee may make gifts—

(a) on customary occasions to persons (including himself) who are related to or connected with the donor, or

(b) to any charity to whom the donor made or might have been expected to make gifts,

if the value of each such gift is not unreasonable having regard to all the circumstances and, in particular, the size of the donor's estate.

(3) 'Customary occasion' means—

(a) the occasion or anniversary of a birth, a marriage or the formation of a civil partnership, or

(b) any other occasion on which presents are customarily given within families or among friends or associates.

(4) Subsection (2) is subject to any conditions or restrictions in the instrument.

13 Revocation of lasting powers of attorney etc.

(1) This section applies if—

(a) P has executed an instrument with a view to creating a lasting power of attorney, or

(b) a lasting power of attorney is registered as having been conferred by P,

and in this section references to revoking the power include revoking the instrument.

(2) P may, at any time when he has capacity to do so, revoke the power.

(3) P's bankruptcy revokes the power so far as it relates to P's property and affairs.

(4) But where P is bankrupt merely because an interim bankruptcy restrictions order has effect in respect of him, the power is suspended, so far as it relates to P's property and affairs, for so long as the order has effect.

(5) The occurrence in relation to a donee of an event mentioned in subsection (6)—
  (a) terminates his appointment, and
  (b) except in the cases given in subsection (7), revokes the power.

(6) The events are—
  (a) the disclaimer of the appointment by the donee in accordance with such requirements as may be prescribed for the purposes of this section in regulations made by the Lord Chancellor,
  (b) subject to subsections (8) and (9), the death or bankruptcy of the donee or, if the donee is a trust corporation, its winding-up or dissolution,
  (c) subject to subsection (11), the dissolution or annulment of a marriage or civil partnership between the donor and the donee,
  (d) the lack of capacity of the donee.

(7) The cases are—
  (a) the donee is replaced under the terms of the instrument,
  (b) he is one of two or more persons appointed to act as donees jointly and severally in respect of any matter and, after the event, there is at least one remaining donee.

(8) The bankruptcy of a donee does not terminate his appointment, or revoke the power, in so far as his authority relates to P's personal welfare.

(9) Where the donee is bankrupt merely because an interim bankruptcy restrictions order has effect in respect of him, his appointment and the power are suspended, so far as they relate to P's property and affairs, for so long as the order has effect.

(10) Where the donee is one of two or more appointed to act jointly and severally under the power in respect of any matter, the reference in subsection (9) to the suspension of the power is to its suspension in so far as it relates to that donee.

(11) The dissolution or annulment of a marriage or civil partnership does not terminate the appointment of a donee, or revoke the power, if the instrument provided that it was not to do so.

14   Protection of donee and others if no power created or power revoked

(1) Subsections (2) and (3) apply if—
  (a) an instrument has been registered under Schedule 1 as a lasting power of attorney, but
  (b) a lasting power of attorney was not created,
  whether or not the registration has been cancelled at the time of the act or transaction in question.

(2) A donee who acts in purported exercise of the power does not incur any liability (to P or any other person) because of the non-existence of the power unless at the time of acting he—
  (a) knows that a lasting power of attorney was not created, or
  (b) is aware of circumstances which, if a lasting power of attorney had been created, would have terminated his authority to act as a donee.

(3) Any transaction between the donee and another person is, in favour of that person, as valid as if the power had been in existence, unless at the time of the transaction that person has knowledge of a matter referred to in subsection (2).

(4) If the interest of a purchaser depends on whether a transaction between the donee and the other person was valid by virtue of subsection (3), it is conclusively presumed in favour of the purchaser that the transaction was valid if—

    (a) the transaction was completed within 12 months of the date on which the instrument was registered, or

    (b) the other person makes a statutory declaration, before or within 3 months after the completion of the purchase, that he had no reason at the time of the transaction to doubt that the donee had authority to dispose of the property which was the subject of the transaction.

(5) In its application to a lasting power of attorney which relates to matters in addition to P's property and affairs, section 5 of the Powers of Attorney Act 1971 (c. 27) (protection where power is revoked) has effect as if references to revocation included the cessation of the power in relation to P's property and affairs.

(6) Where two or more donees are appointed under a lasting power of attorney, this section applies as if references to the donee were to all or any of them.

General powers of the court and appointment of deputies

15 Power to make declarations

(1) The court may make declarations as to—

    (a) whether a person has or lacks capacity to make a decision specified in the declaration;

    (b) whether a person has or lacks capacity to make decisions on such matters as are described in the declaration;

    (c) the lawfulness or otherwise of any act done, or yet to be done, in relation to that person.

(2) 'Act' includes an omission and a course of conduct.

16 Powers to make decisions and appoint deputies: general

(1) This section applies if a person ('P') lacks capacity in relation to a matter or matters concerning—

    (a) P's personal welfare, or

    (b) P's property and affairs.

(2) The court may—

    (a) by making an order, make the decision or decisions on P's behalf in relation to the matter or matters, or

    (b) appoint a person (a 'deputy') to make decisions on P's behalf in relation to the matter or matters.

(3) The powers of the court under this section are subject to the provisions of this Act and, in particular, to sections 1 (the principles) and 4 (best interests).

(4) When deciding whether it is in P's best interests to appoint a deputy, the court must have regard (in addition to the matters mentioned in section 4) to the principles that—

    (a) a decision by the court is to be preferred to the appointment of a deputy to make a decision, and

    (b) the powers conferred on a deputy should be as limited in scope and duration as is reasonably practicable in the circumstances.

(5) The court may make such further orders or give such directions, and confer on a deputy such powers or impose on him such duties, as it thinks necessary or expedient for giving effect to, or otherwise in connection with, an order or appointment made by it under subsection (2).

(6) Without prejudice to section 4, the court may make the order, give the directions or make the appointment on such terms as it considers are in P's best interests, even though no application is before the court for an order, directions or an appointment on those terms.

(7) An order of the court may be varied or discharged by a subsequent order.

(8) The court may, in particular, revoke the appointment of a deputy or vary the powers conferred on him if it is satisfied that the deputy—

   (a) has behaved, or is behaving, in a way that contravenes the authority conferred on him by the court or is not in P's best interests, or

   (b) proposes to behave in a way that would contravene that authority or would not be in P's best interests.

17 Section 16 powers: personal welfare

(1) The powers under section 16 as respects P's personal welfare extend in particular to—

   (a) deciding where P is to live;

   (b) deciding what contact, if any, P is to have with any specified persons;

   (c) making an order prohibiting a named person from having contact with P;

   (d) giving or refusing consent to the carrying out or continuation of a treatment by a person providing health care for P;

   (e) giving a direction that a person responsible for P's health care allow a different person to take over that responsibility.

(2) Subsection (1) is subject to section 20 (restrictions on deputies).

18 Section 16 powers: property and affairs

(1) The powers under section 16 as respects P's property and affairs extend in particular to—

   (a) the control and management of P's property;

   (b) the sale, exchange, charging, gift or other disposition of P's property;

   (c) the acquisition of property in P's name or on P's behalf;

   (d) the carrying on, on P's behalf, of any profession, trade or business;

   (e) the taking of a decision which will have the effect of dissolving a partnership of which P is a member;

   (f) the carrying out of any contract entered into by P;

   (g) the discharge of P's debts and of any of P's obligations, whether legally enforceable or not;

   (h) the settlement of any of P's property, whether for P's benefit or for the benefit of others;

   (i) the execution for P of a will;

   (j) the exercise of any power (including a power to consent) vested in P whether beneficially or as trustee or otherwise;

   (k) the conduct of legal proceedings in P's name or on P's behalf.

(2) No will may be made under subsection (1)(i) at a time when P has not reached 18.

(3) The powers under section 16 as respects any other matter relating to P's property and affairs may be exercised even though P has not reached 16, if the court considers it likely that P will still lack capacity to make decisions in respect of that matter when he reaches 18.

(4) Schedule 2 supplements the provisions of this section.

(5) Section 16(7) (variation and discharge of court orders) is subject to paragraph 6 of Schedule 2.

(6) Subsection (1) is subject to section 20 (restrictions on deputies).

19 Appointment of deputies

(1) A deputy appointed by the court must be—

    (a) an individual who has reached 18, or

    (b) as respects powers in relation to property and affairs, an individual who has reached 18 or a trust corporation.

(2) The court may appoint an individual by appointing the holder for the time being of a specified office or position.

(3) A person may not be appointed as a deputy without his consent.

(4) The court may appoint two or more deputies to act—

    (a) jointly,

    (b) jointly and severally, or

    (c) jointly in respect of some matters and jointly and severally in respect of others.

(5) When appointing a deputy or deputies, the court may at the same time appoint one or more other persons to succeed the existing deputy or those deputies—

    (a) in such circumstances, or on the happening of such events, as may be specified by the court;

    (b) for such period as may be so specified.

(6) A deputy is to be treated as P's agent in relation to anything done or decided by him within the scope of his appointment and in accordance with this Part.

(7) The deputy is entitled—

    (a) to be reimbursed out of P's property for his reasonable expenses in discharging his functions, and

    (b) if the court so directs when appointing him, to remuneration out of P's property for discharging them.

(8) The court may confer on a deputy powers to—

    (a) take possession or control of all or any specified part of P's property;

    (b) exercise all or any specified powers in respect of it, including such powers of investment as the court may determine.

(9) The court may require a deputy—

    (a) to give to the Public Guardian such security as the court thinks fit for the due discharge of his functions, and

    (b) to submit to the Public Guardian such reports at such times or at such intervals as the court may direct.

20 Restrictions on deputies

(1) A deputy does not have power to make a decision on behalf of P in relation to a matter if he knows or has reasonable grounds for believing that P has capacity in relation to the matter.

(2) Nothing in section 16(5) or 17 permits a deputy to be given power—

    (a) to prohibit a named person from having contact with P;

    (b) to direct a person responsible for P's health care to allow a different person to take over that responsibility.

(3) A deputy may not be given powers with respect to—
   (a) the settlement of any of P's property, whether for P's benefit or for the benefit of others,
   (b) the execution for P of a will, or
   (c) the exercise of any power (including a power to consent) vested in P whether beneficially or as trustee or otherwise.

(4) A deputy may not be given power to make a decision on behalf of P which is inconsistent with a decision made, within the scope of his authority and in accordance with this Act, by the donee of a lasting power of attorney granted by P (or, if there is more than one donee, by any of them).

(5) A deputy may not refuse consent to the carrying out or continuation of life-sustaining treatment in relation to P.

(6) The authority conferred on a deputy is subject to the provisions of this Act and, in particular, sections 1 (the principles) and 4 (best interests).

(7) A deputy may not do an act that is intended to restrain P unless four conditions are satisfied.

(8) The first condition is that, in doing the act, the deputy is acting within the scope of an authority expressly conferred on him by the court.

(9) The second is that P lacks, or the deputy reasonably believes that P lacks, capacity in relation to the matter in question.

(10) The third is that the deputy reasonably believes that it is necessary to do the act in order to prevent harm to P.

(11) The fourth is that the act is a proportionate response to—
   (a) the likelihood of P's suffering harm, or
   (b) the seriousness of that harm.

(12) For the purposes of this section, a deputy restrains P if he—
   (a) uses, or threatens to use, force to secure the doing of an act which P resists, or
   (b) restricts P's liberty of movement, whether or not P resists,
   or if he authorises another person to do any of those things.

(13) But a deputy does more than merely restrain P if he deprives P of his liberty within the meaning of Article 5(1) of the Human Rights Convention (whether or not the deputy is a public authority).

21 Transfer of proceedings relating to people under 18

The Lord Chancellor may by order make provision as to the transfer of proceedings relating to a person under 18, in such circumstances as are specified in the order—
(a) from the Court of Protection to a court having jurisdiction under the Children Act 1989 (c. 41), or
(b) from a court having jurisdiction under that Act to the Court of Protection.

Powers of the court in relation to lasting powers of attorney

22 Powers of court in relation to validity of lasting powers of attorney

(1) This section and section 23 apply if—
   (a) a person ('P') has executed or purported to execute an instrument with a view to creating a lasting power of attorney, or
   (b) an instrument has been registered as a lasting power of attorney conferred by P.

(2) The court may determine any question relating to—

    (a) whether one or more of the requirements for the creation of a lasting power of attorney have been met;

    (b) whether the power has been revoked or has otherwise come to an end.

(3) Subsection (4) applies if the court is satisfied—

    (a) that fraud or undue pressure was used to induce P—

        (i) to execute an instrument for the purpose of creating a lasting power of attorney, or

        (ii) to create a lasting power of attorney, or

    (b) that the donee (or, if more than one, any of them) of a lasting power of attorney—

        (i) has behaved, or is behaving, in a way that contravenes his authority or is not in P's best interests, or

        (ii) proposes to behave in a way that would contravene his authority or would not be in P's best interests.

(4) The court may—

    (a) direct that an instrument purporting to create the lasting power of attorney is not to be registered, or

    (b) if P lacks capacity to do so, revoke the instrument or the lasting power of attorney.

(5) If there is more than one donee, the court may under subsection (4)(b) revoke the instrument or the lasting power of attorney so far as it relates to any of them.

(6) 'Donee' includes an intended donee.

23   Powers of court in relation to operation of lasting powers of attorney

(1) The court may determine any question as to the meaning or effect of a lasting power of attorney or an instrument purporting to create one.

(2) The court may—

    (a) give directions with respect to decisions—

        (i) which the donee of a lasting power of attorney has authority to make, and

        (ii) which P lacks capacity to make;

    (b) give any consent or authorisation to act which the donee would have to obtain from P if P had capacity to give it.

(3) The court may, if P lacks capacity to do so—

    (a) give directions to the donee with respect to the rendering by him of reports or accounts and the production of records kept by him for that purpose;

    (b) require the donee to supply information or produce documents or things in his possession as donee;

    (c) give directions with respect to the remuneration or expenses of the donee;

    (d) relieve the donee wholly or partly from any liability which he has or may have incurred on account of a breach of his duties as donee.

(4) The court may authorise the making of gifts which are not within section 12(2) (permitted gifts).

(5) Where two or more donees are appointed under a lasting power of attorney, this section applies as if references to the donee were to all or any of them.

Advance decisions to refuse treatment

24 Advance decisions to refuse treatment: general

(1) 'Advance decision' means a decision made by a person ('P'), after he has reached 18 and when he has capacity to do so, that if—

    (a) at a later time and in such circumstances as he may specify, a specified treatment is proposed to be carried out or continued by a person providing health care for him, and

    (b) at that time he lacks capacity to consent to the carrying out or continuation of the treatment,

the specified treatment is not to be carried out or continued.

(2) For the purposes of subsection (1)(a), a decision may be regarded as specifying a treatment or circumstances even though expressed in layman's terms.

(3) P may withdraw or alter an advance decision at any time when he has capacity to do so.

(4) A withdrawal (including a partial withdrawal) need not be in writing.

(5) An alteration of an advance decision need not be in writing (unless section 25(5) applies in relation to the decision resulting from the alteration).

25 Validity and applicability of advance decisions

(1) An advance decision does not affect the liability which a person may incur for carrying out or continuing a treatment in relation to P unless the decision is at the material time—

    (a) valid, and

    (b) applicable to the treatment.

(2) An advance decision is not valid if P—

    (a) has withdrawn the decision at a time when he had capacity to do so,

    (b) has, under a lasting power of attorney created after the advance decision was made, conferred authority on the donee (or, if more than one, any of them) to give or refuse consent to the treatment to which the advance decision relates, or

    (c) has done anything else clearly inconsistent with the advance decision remaining his fixed decision.

(3) An advance decision is not applicable to the treatment in question if at the material time P has capacity to give or refuse consent to it.

(4) An advance decision is not applicable to the treatment in question if—

    (a) that treatment is not the treatment specified in the advance decision,

    (b) any circumstances specified in the advance decision are absent, or

    (c) there are reasonable grounds for believing that circumstances exist which P did not anticipate at the time of the advance decision and which would have affected his decision had he anticipated them.

(5) An advance decision is not applicable to life-sustaining treatment unless—

    (a) the decision is verified by a statement by P to the effect that it is to apply to that treatment even if life is at risk, and

    (b) the decision and statement comply with subsection (6).

(6) A decision or statement complies with this subsection only if—

    (a) it is in writing,

    (b) it is signed by P or by another person in P's presence and by P's direction,

(c) the signature is made or acknowledged by P in the presence of a witness, and

(d) the witness signs it, or acknowledges his signature, in P's presence.

(7) The existence of any lasting power of attorney other than one of a description mentioned in subsection (2)(b) does not prevent the advance decision from being regarded as valid and applicable.

26   Effect of advance decisions

(1) If P has made an advance decision which is—

   (a) valid, and

   (b) applicable to a treatment,

   the decision has effect as if he had made it, and had had capacity to make it, at the time when the question arises whether the treatment should be carried out or continued.

(2) A person does not incur liability for carrying out or continuing the treatment unless, at the time, he is satisfied that an advance decision exists which is valid and applicable to the treatment.

(3) A person does not incur liability for the consequences of withholding or withdrawing a treatment from P if, at the time, he reasonably believes that an advance decision exists which is valid and applicable to the treatment.

(4) The court may make a declaration as to whether an advance decision—

   (a) exists;

   (b) is valid;

   (c) is applicable to a treatment.

(5) Nothing in an apparent advance decision stops a person—

   (a) providing life-sustaining treatment, or

   (b) doing any act he reasonably believes to be necessary to prevent a serious deterioration in P's condition,

   while a decision as respects any relevant issue is sought from the court.

Excluded decisions

27   Family relationships etc.

(1) Nothing in this Act permits a decision on any of the following matters to be made on behalf of a person—

   (a) consenting to marriage or a civil partnership,

   (b) consenting to have sexual relations,

   (c) consenting to a decree of divorce being granted on the basis of two years' separation,

   (d) consenting to a dissolution order being made in relation to a civil partnership on the basis of two years' separation,

   (e) consenting to a child's being placed for adoption by an adoption agency,

   (f) consenting to the making of an adoption order,

   (g) discharging parental responsibilities in matters not relating to a child's property,

   (h) giving a consent under the Human Fertilisation and Embryology Act 1990 (c. 37).

(2) 'Adoption order' means—

   (a) an adoption order within the meaning of the Adoption and Children Act 2002 (c. 38) (including a future adoption order), and

(b) an order under section 84 of that Act (parental responsibility prior to adoption abroad).

28 Mental Health Act matters

(1) Nothing in this Act authorises anyone—
   (a) to give a patient medical treatment for mental disorder, or
   (b) to consent to a patient's being given medical treatment for mental disorder,
   if, at the time when it is proposed to treat the patient, his treatment is regulated by Part 4 of the Mental Health Act.
(2) 'Medical treatment', 'mental disorder' and 'patient' have the same meaning as in that Act.

29 Voting rights

(1) Nothing in this Act permits a decision on voting at an election for any public office, or at a referendum, to be made on behalf of a person.
(2) 'Referendum' has the same meaning as in section 101 of the Political Parties, Elections and Referendums Act 2000 (c. 41).

Research

30 Research

(1) Intrusive research carried out on, or in relation to, a person who lacks capacity to consent to it is unlawful unless it is carried out—
   (a) as part of a research project which is for the time being approved by the appropriate body for the purposes of this Act in accordance with section 31, and
   (b) in accordance with sections 32 and 33.
(2) Research is intrusive if it is of a kind that would be unlawful if it was carried out—
   (a) on or in relation to a person who had capacity to consent to it, but
   (b) without his consent.
(3) A clinical trial which is subject to the provisions of clinical trials regulations is not to be treated as research for the purposes of this section.
(4) 'Appropriate body', in relation to a research project, means the person, committee or other body specified in regulations made by the appropriate authority as the appropriate body in relation to a project of the kind in question.
(5) 'Clinical trials regulations' means—
   (a) the Medicines for Human Use (Clinical Trials) Regulations 2004 (S.I. 2004/1031) and any other regulations replacing those regulations or amending them, and
   (b) any other regulations relating to clinical trials and designated by the Secretary of State as clinical trials regulations for the purposes of this section.
(6) In this section, section 32 and section 34, 'appropriate authority' means—
   (a) in relation to the carrying out of research in England, the Secretary of State, and
   (b) in relation to the carrying out of research in Wales, the National Assembly for Wales.

31 Requirements for approval

(1) The appropriate body may not approve a research project for the purposes of this Act unless satisfied that the following requirements will be met in relation to research

carried out as part of the project on, or in relation to, a person who lacks capacity to consent to taking part in the project ('P').

(2) The research must be connected with—
   (a) an impairing condition affecting P, or
   (b) its treatment.

(3) 'Impairing condition' means a condition which is (or may be) attributable to, or which causes or contributes to (or may cause or contribute to), the impairment of, or disturbance in the functioning of, the mind or brain.

(4) There must be reasonable grounds for believing that research of comparable effectiveness cannot be carried out if the project has to be confined to, or relate only to, persons who have capacity to consent to taking part in it.

(5) The research must—
   (a) have the potential to benefit P without imposing on P a burden that is disproportionate to the potential benefit to P, or
   (b) be intended to provide knowledge of the causes or treatment of, or of the care of persons affected by, the same or a similar condition.

(6) If the research falls within paragraph (b) of subsection (5) but not within paragraph (a), there must be reasonable grounds for believing—
   (a) that the risk to P from taking part in the project is likely to be negligible, and
   (b) that anything done to, or in relation to, P will not—
      (i) interfere with P's freedom of action or privacy in a significant way, or
      (ii) be unduly invasive or restrictive.

(7) There must be reasonable arrangements in place for ensuring that the requirements of sections 32 and 33 will be met.

32 Consulting carers etc.

(1) This section applies if a person ('R')—
   (a) is conducting an approved research project, and
   (b) wishes to carry out research, as part of the project, on or in relation to a person ('P') who lacks capacity to consent to taking part in the project.

(2) R must take reasonable steps to identify a person who—
   (a) otherwise than in a professional capacity or for remuneration, is engaged in caring for P or is interested in P's welfare, and
   (b) is prepared to be consulted by R under this section.

(3) If R is unable to identify such a person he must, in accordance with guidance issued by the appropriate authority, nominate a person who—
   (a) is prepared to be consulted by R under this section, but
   (b) has no connection with the project.

(4) R must provide the person identified under subsection (2), or nominated under subsection (3), with information about the project and ask him—
   (a) for advice as to whether P should take part in the project, and
   (b) what, in his opinion, P's wishes and feelings about taking part in the project would be likely to be if P had capacity in relation to the matter.

(5) If, at any time, the person consulted advises R that in his opinion P's wishes and feelings would be likely to lead him to decline to take part in the project (or to wish to withdraw from it) if he had capacity in relation to the matter, R must ensure—

    (a) if P is not already taking part in the project, that he does not take part in it;

    (b) if P is taking part in the project, that he is withdrawn from it.

(6) But subsection (5)(b) does not require treatment that P has been receiving as part of the project to be discontinued if R has reasonable grounds for believing that there would be a significant risk to P's health if it were discontinued.

(7) The fact that a person is the donee of a lasting power of attorney given by P, or is P's deputy, does not prevent him from being the person consulted under this section.

(8) Subsection (9) applies if treatment is being, or is about to be, provided for P as a matter of urgency and R considers that, having regard to the nature of the research and of the particular circumstances of the case—

    (a) it is also necessary to take action for the purposes of the research as a matter of urgency, but

    (b) it is not reasonably practicable to consult under the previous provisions of this section.

(9) R may take the action if—

    (a) he has the agreement of a registered medical practitioner who is not involved in the organisation or conduct of the research project, or

    (b) where it is not reasonably practicable in the time available to obtain that agreement, he acts in accordance with a procedure approved by the appropriate body at the time when the research project was approved under section 31.

(10) But R may not continue to act in reliance on subsection (9) if he has reasonable grounds for believing that it is no longer necessary to take the action as a matter of urgency.

33   Additional safeguards

(1) This section applies in relation to a person who is taking part in an approved research project even though he lacks capacity to consent to taking part.

(2) Nothing may be done to, or in relation to, him in the course of the research—

    (a) to which he appears to object (whether by showing signs of resistance or otherwise) except where what is being done is intended to protect him from harm or to reduce or prevent pain or discomfort, or

    (b) which would be contrary to—

        (i) an advance decision of his which has effect, or

        (ii) any other form of statement made by him and not subsequently withdrawn, of which R is aware.

(3) The interests of the person must be assumed to outweigh those of science and society.

(4) If he indicates (in any way) that he wishes to be withdrawn from the project he must be withdrawn without delay.

(5) P must be withdrawn from the project, without delay, if at any time the person conducting the research has reasonable grounds for believing that one or more of the requirements set out in section 31(2) to (7) is no longer met in relation to research being carried out on, or in relation to, P.

(6) But neither subsection (4) nor subsection (5) requires treatment that P has been receiving as part of the project to be discontinued if R has reasonable grounds for believing that there would be a significant risk to P's health if it were discontinued.

34 Loss of capacity during research project

(1) This section applies where a person ('P')—
   (a) has consented to take part in a research project begun before the commencement of section 30, but
   (b) before the conclusion of the project, loses capacity to consent to continue to take part in it.

(2) The appropriate authority may by regulations provide that, despite P's loss of capacity, research of a prescribed kind may be carried out on, or in relation to, P if—
   (a) the project satisfies prescribed requirements,
   (b) any information or material relating to P which is used in the research is of a prescribed description and was obtained before P's loss of capacity, and
   (c) the person conducting the project takes in relation to P such steps as may be prescribed for the purpose of protecting him.

(3) The regulations may, in particular,—
   (a) make provision about when, for the purposes of the regulations, a project is to be treated as having begun;
   (b) include provision similar to any made by section 31, 32 or 33.

Independent mental capacity advocate service

35 Appointment of independent mental capacity advocates

(1) The appropriate authority must make such arrangements as it considers reasonable to enable persons ('independent mental capacity advocates') to be available to represent and support persons to whom acts or decisions proposed under sections 37, 38 and 39 relate.

(2) The appropriate authority may make regulations as to the appointment of independent mental capacity advocates.

(3) The regulations may, in particular, provide—
   (a) that a person may act as an independent mental capacity advocate only in such circumstances, or only subject to such conditions, as may be prescribed;
   (b) for the appointment of a person as an independent mental capacity advocate to be subject to approval in accordance with the regulations.

(4) In making arrangements under subsection (1), the appropriate authority must have regard to the principle that a person to whom a proposed act or decision relates should, so far as practicable, be represented and supported by a person who is independent of any person who will be responsible for the act or decision.

(5) The arrangements may include provision for payments to be made to, or in relation to, persons carrying out functions in accordance with the arrangements.

(6) For the purpose of enabling him to carry out his functions, an independent mental capacity advocate—
   (a) may interview in private the person whom he has been instructed to represent, and
   (b) may, at all reasonable times, examine and take copies of—
      (i) any health record,
      (ii) any record of, or held by, a local authority and compiled in connection with a social services function, and
      (iii) any record held by a person registered under Part 2 of the Care Standards Act 2000 (c. 14),

which the person holding the record considers may be relevant to the independent mental capacity advocate's investigation.

(7) In this section, section 36 and section 37, 'the appropriate authority' means—

    (a) in relation to the provision of the services of independent mental capacity advocates in England, the Secretary of State, and

    (b) in relation to the provision of the services of independent mental capacity advocates in Wales, the National Assembly for Wales.

36 Functions of independent mental capacity advocates

(1) The appropriate authority may make regulations as to the functions of independent mental capacity advocates.

(2) The regulations may, in particular, make provision requiring an advocate to take such steps as may be prescribed for the purpose of—

    (a) providing support to the person whom he has been instructed to represent ('P') so that P may participate as fully as possible in any relevant decision;

    (b) obtaining and evaluating relevant information;

    (c) ascertaining what P's wishes and feelings would be likely to be, and the beliefs and values that would be likely to influence P, if he had capacity;

    (d) ascertaining what alternative courses of action are available in relation to P;

    (e) obtaining a further medical opinion where treatment is proposed and the advocate thinks that one should be obtained.

(3) The regulations may also make provision as to circumstances in which the advocate may challenge, or provide assistance for the purpose of challenging, any relevant decision.

37 Provision of serious medical treatment by NHS body

(1) This section applies if an NHS body—

    (a) is proposing to provide, or secure the provision of, serious medical treatment for a person ('P') who lacks capacity to consent to the treatment, and

    (b) is satisfied that there is no person, other than one engaged in providing care or treatment for P in a professional capacity or for remuneration, whom it would be appropriate to consult in determining what would be in P's best interests.

(2) But this section does not apply if P's treatment is regulated by Part 4 of the Mental Health Act.

(3) Before the treatment is provided, the NHS body must instruct an independent mental capacity advocate to represent P.

(4) If the treatment needs to be provided as a matter of urgency, it may be provided even though the NHS body has not been able to comply with subsection (3).

(5) The NHS body must, in providing or securing the provision of treatment for P, take into account any information given, or submissions made, by the independent mental capacity advocate.

(6) 'Serious medical treatment' means treatment which involves providing, withholding or withdrawing treatment of a kind prescribed by regulations made by the appropriate authority.

(7) 'NHS body' has such meaning as may be prescribed by regulations made for the purposes of this section by—

(a) the Secretary of State, in relation to bodies in England, or

(b) the National Assembly for Wales, in relation to bodies in Wales.

38 Provision of accommodation by NHS body

(1) This section applies if an NHS body proposes to make arrangements—

    (a) for the provision of accommodation in a hospital or care home for a person ('P') who lacks capacity to agree to the arrangements, or

    (b) for a change in P's accommodation to another hospital or care home,

and is satisfied that there is no person, other than one engaged in providing care or treatment for P in a professional capacity or for remuneration, whom it would be appropriate for it to consult in determining what would be in P's best interests.

(2) But this section does not apply if P is accommodated as a result of an obligation imposed on him under the Mental Health Act.

(3) Before making the arrangements, the NHS body must instruct an independent mental capacity advocate to represent P unless it is satisfied that—

    (a) the accommodation is likely to be provided for a continuous period which is less than the applicable period, or

    (b) the arrangements need to be made as a matter of urgency.

(4) If the NHS body—

    (a) did not instruct an independent mental capacity advocate to represent P before making the arrangements because it was satisfied that subsection (3)(a) or (b) applied, but

    (b) subsequently has reason to believe that the accommodation is likely to be provided for a continuous period—

        (i) beginning with the day on which accommodation was first provided in accordance with the arrangements, and

        (ii) ending on or after the expiry of the applicable period,

it must instruct an independent mental capacity advocate to represent P.

(5) The NHS body must, in deciding what arrangements to make for P, take into account any information given, or submissions made, by the independent mental capacity advocate.

(6) 'Care home' has the meaning given in section 3 of the Care Standards Act 2000 (c. 14).

(7) 'Hospital' means—

    (a) a health service hospital as defined by section 128 of the National Health Service Act 1977 (c. 49), or

    (b) an independent hospital as defined by section 2 of the Care Standards Act 2000.

(8) 'NHS body' has such meaning as may be prescribed by regulations made for the purposes of this section by—

    (a) the Secretary of State, in relation to bodies in England, or

    (b) the National Assembly for Wales, in relation to bodies in Wales.

(9) 'Applicable period' means—

    (a) in relation to accommodation in a hospital, 28 days, and

    (b) in relation to accommodation in a care home, 8 weeks.

39 Provision of accommodation by local authority

(1) This section applies if a local authority propose to make arrangements—

(a) for the provision of residential accommodation for a person ('P') who lacks capacity to agree to the arrangements, or

(b) for a change in P's residential accommodation,

and are satisfied that there is no person, other than one engaged in providing care or treatment for P in a professional capacity or for remuneration, whom it would be appropriate for them to consult in determining what would be in P's best interests.

(2) But this section applies only if the accommodation is to be provided in accordance with—

(a) section 21 or 29 of the National Assistance Act 1948 (c. 29), or

(b) section 117 of the Mental Health Act,

as the result of a decision taken by the local authority under section 47 of the National Health Service and Community Care Act 1990 (c. 19).

(3) This section does not apply if P is accommodated as a result of an obligation imposed on him under the Mental Health Act.

(4) Before making the arrangements, the local authority must instruct an independent mental capacity advocate to represent P unless they are satisfied that—

(a) the accommodation is likely to be provided for a continuous period of less than 8 weeks, or

(b) the arrangements need to be made as a matter of urgency.

(5) If the local authority—

(a) did not instruct an independent mental capacity advocate to represent P before making the arrangements because they were satisfied that subsection (4)(a) or (b) applied, but

(b) subsequently have reason to believe that the accommodation is likely to be provided for a continuous period that will end 8 weeks or more after the day on which accommodation was first provided in accordance with the arrangements,

they must instruct an independent mental capacity advocate to represent P.

(6) The local authority must, in deciding what arrangements to make for P, take into account any information given, or submissions made, by the independent mental capacity advocate.

40   Exceptions

Sections 37(3), 38(3) and (4) and 39(4) and (5) do not apply if there is—

(a) a person nominated by P (in whatever manner) as a person to be consulted in matters affecting his interests,

(b) a donee of a lasting power of attorney created by P,

(c) a deputy appointed by the court for P, or

(d) a donee of an enduring power of attorney (within the meaning of Schedule 4) created by P.

41   Power to adjust role of independent mental capacity advocate

(1) The appropriate authority may make regulations—

(a) expanding the role of independent mental capacity advocates in relation to persons who lack capacity, and

(b) adjusting the obligation to make arrangements imposed by section 35.

(2) The regulations may, in particular—

(a) prescribe circumstances (different to those set out in sections 37, 38 and 39) in which an independent mental capacity advocate must, or circumstances in which one may, be instructed by a person of a prescribed description to represent a person who lacks capacity, and

(b) include provision similar to any made by section 37, 38, 39 or 40.

(3) 'Appropriate authority' has the same meaning as in section 35.

Miscellaneous and supplementary

42 Codes of practice

(1) The Lord Chancellor must prepare and issue one or more codes of practice—

    (a) for the guidance of persons assessing whether a person has capacity in relation to any matter,

    (b) for the guidance of persons acting in connection with the care or treatment of another person (see section 5),

    (c) for the guidance of donees of lasting powers of attorney,

    (d) for the guidance of deputies appointed by the court,

    (e) for the guidance of persons carrying out research in reliance on any provision made by or under this Act (and otherwise with respect to sections 30 to 34),

    (f) for the guidance of independent mental capacity advocates,

    (g) with respect to the provisions of sections 24 to 26 (advance decisions and apparent advance decisions), and

    (h) with respect to such other matters concerned with this Act as he thinks fit.

(2) The Lord Chancellor may from time to time revise a code.

(3) The Lord Chancellor may delegate the preparation or revision of the whole or any part of a code so far as he considers expedient.

(4) It is the duty of a person to have regard to any relevant code if he is acting in relation to a person who lacks capacity and is doing so in one or more of the following ways—

    (a) as the donee of a lasting power of attorney,

    (b) as a deputy appointed by the court,

    (c) as a person carrying out research in reliance on any provision made by or under this Act (see sections 30 to 34),

    (d) as an independent mental capacity advocate,

    (e) in a professional capacity,

    (f) for remuneration.

(5) If it appears to a court or tribunal conducting any criminal or civil proceedings that—

    (a) a provision of a code, or

    (b) a failure to comply with a code,

is relevant to a question arising in the proceedings, the provision or failure must be taken into account in deciding the question.

(6) A code under subsection (1)(d) may contain separate guidance for deputies appointed by virtue of paragraph 1(2) of Schedule 5 (functions of deputy conferred on receiver appointed under the Mental Health Act).

(7) In this section and in section 43, 'code' means a code prepared or revised under this section.

43 Codes of practice: procedure

(1) Before preparing or revising a code, the Lord Chancellor must consult—
   (a) the National Assembly for Wales, and
   (b) such other persons as he considers appropriate.
(2) The Lord Chancellor may not issue a code unless—
   (a) a draft of the code has been laid by him before both Houses of Parliament, and
   (b) the 40 day period has elapsed without either House resolving not to approve the draft.
(3) The Lord Chancellor must arrange for any code that he has issued to be published in such a way as he considers appropriate for bringing it to the attention of persons likely to be concerned with its provisions.
(4) '40 day period', in relation to the draft of a proposed code, means—
   (a) if the draft is laid before one House on a day later than the day on which it is laid before the other House, the period of 40 days beginning with the later of the two days;
   (b) in any other case, the period of 40 days beginning with the day on which it is laid before each House.
(5) In calculating the period of 40 days, no account is to be taken of any period during which Parliament is dissolved or prorogued or during which both Houses are adjourned for more than 4 days.

44 Ill-treatment or neglect

(1) Subsection (2) applies if a person ('D')—
   (a) has the care of a person ('P') who lacks, or whom D reasonably believes to lack, capacity,
   (b) is the donee of a lasting power of attorney, or an enduring power of attorney (within the meaning of Schedule 4), created by P, or
   (c) is a deputy appointed by the court for P.
(2) D is guilty of an offence if he ill-treats or wilfully neglects P.
(3) A person guilty of an offence under this section is liable—
   (a) on summary conviction, to imprisonment for a term not exceeding 12 months or a fine not exceeding the statutory maximum or both;
   (b) on conviction on indictment, to imprisonment for a term not exceeding 5 years or a fine or both.

PART 2
THE COURT OF PROTECTION AND THE PUBLIC GUARDIAN

The Court of Protection

45 The Court of Protection

(1) There is to be a superior court of record known as the Court of Protection.
(2) The court is to have an official seal.
(3) The court may sit at any place in England and Wales, on any day and at any time.
(4) The court is to have a central office and registry at a place appointed by the Lord Chancellor.

(5) The Lord Chancellor may designate as additional registries of the court any district registry of the High Court and any county court office.

(6) The office of the Supreme Court called the Court of Protection ceases to exist.

46   The judges of the Court of Protection

(1) Subject to Court of Protection Rules under section 51(2)(d), the jurisdiction of the court is exercisable by a judge nominated for that purpose by—
   (a) the Lord Chancellor, or
   (b) a person acting on the Lord Chancellor's behalf.

(2) To be nominated, a judge must be—
   (a) the President of the Family Division,
   (b) the Vice-Chancellor,
   (c) a puisne judge of the High Court,
   (d) a circuit judge, or
   (e) a district judge.

(3) The Lord Chancellor must—
   (a) appoint one of the judges nominated by virtue of subsection (2)(a) to (c) to be President of the Court of Protection, and
   (b) appoint another of those judges to be Vice-President of the Court of Protection.

(4) The Lord Chancellor must appoint one of the judges nominated by virtue of subsection (2)(d) or (e) to be Senior Judge of the Court of Protection, having such administrative functions in relation to the court as the Lord Chancellor may direct.

Supplementary powers

47   General powers and effect of orders etc.

(1) The court has in connection with its jurisdiction the same powers, rights, privileges and authority as the High Court.

(2) Section 204 of the Law of Property Act 1925 (c. 20) (orders of High Court conclusive in favour of purchasers) applies in relation to orders and directions of the court as it applies to orders of the High Court.

(3) Office copies of orders made, directions given or other instruments issued by the court and sealed with its official seal are admissible in all legal proceedings as evidence of the originals without any further proof.

48   Interim orders and directions

The court may, pending the determination of an application to it in relation to a person ('P'), make an order or give directions in respect of any matter if—
(a) there is reason to believe that P lacks capacity in relation to the matter,
(b) the matter is one to which its powers under this Act extend, and
(c) it is in P's best interests to make the order, or give the directions, without delay.

49   Power to call for reports

(1) This section applies where, in proceedings brought in respect of a person ('P') under Part 1, the court is considering a question relating to P.

(2) The court may require a report to be made to it by the Public Guardian or by a Court of Protection Visitor.

(3) The court may require a local authority, or an NHS body, to arrange for a report to be made—
   (a) by one of its officers or employees, or
   (b) by such other person (other than the Public Guardian or a Court of Protection Visitor) as the authority, or the NHS body, considers appropriate.

(4) The report must deal with such matters relating to P as the court may direct.

(5) Court of Protection Rules may specify matters which, unless the court directs otherwise, must also be dealt with in the report.

(6) The report may be made in writing or orally, as the court may direct.

(7) In complying with a requirement, the Public Guardian or a Court of Protection Visitor may, at all reasonable times, examine and take copies of—
   (a) any health record,
   (b) any record of, or held by, a local authority and compiled in connection with a social services function, and
   (c) any record held by a person registered under Part 2 of the Care Standards Act 2000 (c. 14),
   so far as the record relates to P.

(8) If the Public Guardian or a Court of Protection Visitor is making a visit in the course of complying with a requirement, he may interview P in private.

(9) If a Court of Protection Visitor who is a Special Visitor is making a visit in the course of complying with a requirement, he may if the court so directs carry out in private a medical, psychiatric or psychological examination of P's capacity and condition.

(10) 'NHS body' has the meaning given in section 148 of the Health and Social Care (Community Health and Standards) Act 2003 (c. 43).

(11) 'Requirement' means a requirement imposed under subsection (2) or (3).

Practice and procedure

50 Applications to the Court of Protection

(1) No permission is required for an application to the court for the exercise of any of its powers under this Act—
   (a) by a person who lacks, or is alleged to lack, capacity,
   (b) if such a person has not reached 18, by anyone with parental responsibility for him,
   (c) by the donor or a donee of a lasting power of attorney to which the application relates,
   (d) by a deputy appointed by the court for a person to whom the application relates, or
   (e) by a person named in an existing order of the court, if the application relates to the order.

(2) But, subject to Court of Protection Rules and to paragraph 20(2) of Schedule 3 (declarations relating to private international law), permission is required for any other application to the court.

(3) In deciding whether to grant permission the court must, in particular, have regard to—
   (a) the applicant's connection with the person to whom the application relates,
   (b) the reasons for the application,

(c) the benefit to the person to whom the application relates of a proposed order or directions, and

(d) whether the benefit can be achieved in any other way.

(4) 'Parental responsibility' has the same meaning as in the Children Act 1989 (c. 41).

51 Court of Protection Rules

(1) The Lord Chancellor may make rules of court (to be called 'Court of Protection Rules') with respect to the practice and procedure of the court.

(2) Court of Protection Rules may, in particular, make provision—

(a) as to the manner and form in which proceedings are to be commenced;

(b) as to the persons entitled to be notified of, and be made parties to, the proceedings;

(c) for the allocation, in such circumstances as may be specified, of any specified description of proceedings to a specified judge or to specified descriptions of judges;

(d) for the exercise of the jurisdiction of the court, in such circumstances as may be specified, by its officers or other staff;

(e) for enabling the court to appoint a suitable person (who may, with his consent, be the Official Solicitor) to act in the name of, or on behalf of, or to represent the person to whom the proceedings relate;

(f) for enabling an application to the court to be disposed of without a hearing;

(g) for enabling the court to proceed with, or with any part of, a hearing in the absence of the person to whom the proceedings relate;

(h) for enabling or requiring the proceedings or any part of them to be conducted in private and for enabling the court to determine who is to be admitted when the court sits in private and to exclude specified persons when it sits in public;

(i) as to what may be received as evidence (whether or not admissible apart from the rules) and the manner in which it is to be presented;

(j) for the enforcement of orders made and directions given in the proceedings.

(3) Court of Protection Rules may, instead of providing for any matter, refer to provision made or to be made about that matter by directions.

(4) Court of Protection Rules may make different provision for different areas.

52 Practice directions

(1) The President of the Court of Protection may, with the concurrence of the Lord Chancellor, give directions as to the practice and procedure of the court.

(2) Directions as to the practice and procedure of the court may not be given by anyone other than the President of the Court of Protection without the approval of the President of the Court of Protection and the Lord Chancellor.

(3) Nothing in this section prevents the President of the Court of Protection, without the concurrence of the Lord Chancellor, giving directions which contain guidance as to law or making judicial decisions.

53 Rights of appeal

(1) Subject to the provisions of this section, an appeal lies to the Court of Appeal from any decision of the court.

(2) Court of Protection Rules may provide that where a decision of the court is made by—

    (a) a person exercising the jurisdiction of the court by virtue of rules made under section 51(2)(d),

    (b) a district judge, or

    (c) a circuit judge,

an appeal from that decision lies to a prescribed higher judge of the court and not to the Court of Appeal.

(3) For the purposes of this section the higher judges of the court are—

    (a) in relation to a person mentioned in subsection (2)(a), a circuit judge or a district judge;

    (b) in relation to a person mentioned in subsection (2)(b), a circuit judge;

    (c) in relation to any person mentioned in subsection (2), one of the judges nominated by virtue of section 46(2)(a) to (c).

(4) Court of Protection Rules may make provision—

    (a) that, in such cases as may be specified, an appeal from a decision of the court may not be made without permission;

    (b) as to the person or persons entitled to grant permission to appeal;

    (c) as to any requirements to be satisfied before permission is granted;

    (d) that where a higher judge of the court makes a decision on an appeal, no appeal may be made to the Court of Appeal from that decision unless the Court of Appeal considers that—

        (i) the appeal would raise an important point of principle or practice, or

        (ii) there is some other compelling reason for the Court of Appeal to hear it;

    (e) as to any considerations to be taken into account in relation to granting or refusing permission to appeal.

Fees and costs

54 Fees

(1) The Lord Chancellor may with the consent of the Treasury by order prescribe fees payable in respect of anything dealt with by the court.

(2) An order under this section may in particular contain provision as to—

    (a) scales or rates of fees;

    (b) exemptions from and reductions in fees;

    (c) remission of fees in whole or in part.

(3) Before making an order under this section, the Lord Chancellor must consult—

    (a) the President of the Court of Protection,

    (b) the Vice-President of the Court of Protection, and

    (c) the Senior Judge of the Court of Protection.

(4) The Lord Chancellor must take such steps as are reasonably practicable to bring information about fees to the attention of persons likely to have to pay them.

(5) Fees payable under this section are recoverable summarily as a civil debt.

55 Costs

(1) Subject to Court of Protection Rules, the costs of and incidental to all proceedings in the court are in its discretion.

(2) The rules may in particular make provision for regulating matters relating to the costs of those proceedings, including prescribing scales of costs to be paid to legal or other representatives.

(3) The court has full power to determine by whom and to what extent the costs are to be paid.

(4) The court may, in any proceedings—
   (a) disallow, or
   (b) order the legal or other representatives concerned to meet,
   the whole of any wasted costs or such part of them as may be determined in accordance with the rules.

(5) 'Legal or other representative', in relation to a party to proceedings, means any person exercising a right of audience or right to conduct litigation on his behalf.

(6) 'Wasted costs' means any costs incurred by a party—
   (a) as a result of any improper, unreasonable or negligent act or omission on the part of any legal or other representative or any employee of such a representative, or
   (b) which, in the light of any such act or omission occurring after they were incurred, the court considers it is unreasonable to expect that party to pay.

56 Fees and costs: supplementary

(1) Court of Protection Rules may make provision—
   (a) as to the way in which, and funds from which, fees and costs are to be paid;
   (b) for charging fees and costs upon the estate of the person to whom the proceedings relate;
   (c) for the payment of fees and costs within a specified time of the death of the person to whom the proceedings relate or the conclusion of the proceedings.

(2) A charge on the estate of a person created by virtue of subsection (1)(b) does not cause any interest of the person in any property to fail or determine or to be prevented from recommencing.

The Public Guardian

57 The Public Guardian

(1) For the purposes of this Act, there is to be an officer, to be known as the Public Guardian.

(2) The Public Guardian is to be appointed by the Lord Chancellor.

(3) There is to be paid to the Public Guardian out of money provided by Parliament such salary as the Lord Chancellor may determine.

(4) The Lord Chancellor may, after consulting the Public Guardian—
   (a) provide him with such officers and staff, or
   (b) enter into such contracts with other persons for the provision (by them or their sub-contractors) of officers, staff or services,
   as the Lord Chancellor thinks necessary for the proper discharge of the Public Guardian's functions.

(5) Any functions of the Public Guardian may, to the extent authorised by him, be performed by any of his officers.

58 Functions of the Public Guardian

(1) The Public Guardian has the following functions—

    (a) establishing and maintaining a register of lasting powers of attorney,

    (b) establishing and maintaining a register of orders appointing deputies,

    (c) supervising deputies appointed by the court,

    (d) directing a Court of Protection Visitor to visit—

        (i) a donee of a lasting power of attorney,

        (ii) a deputy appointed by the court, or

        (iii) the person granting the power of attorney or for whom the deputy is appointed ('P'),

    and to make a report to the Public Guardian on such matters as he may direct,

    (e) receiving security which the court requires a person to give for the discharge of his functions,

    (f) receiving reports from donees of lasting powers of attorney and deputies appointed by the court,

    (g) reporting to the court on such matters relating to proceedings under this Act as the court requires,

    (h) dealing with representations (including complaints) about the way in which a donee of a lasting power of attorney or a deputy appointed by the court is exercising his powers,

    (i) publishing, in any manner the Public Guardian thinks appropriate, any information he thinks appropriate about the discharge of his functions.

(2) The functions conferred by subsection (1)(c) and (h) may be discharged in co-operation with any other person who has functions in relation to the care or treatment of P.

(3) The Lord Chancellor may by regulations make provision—

    (a) conferring on the Public Guardian other functions in connection with this Act;

    (b) in connection with the discharge by the Public Guardian of his functions.

(4) Regulations made under subsection (3)(b) may in particular make provision as to—

    (a) the giving of security by deputies appointed by the court and the enforcement and discharge of security so given;

    (b) the fees which may be charged by the Public Guardian;

    (c) the way in which, and funds from which, such fees are to be paid;

    (d) exemptions from and reductions in such fees;

    (e) remission of such fees in whole or in part;

    (f) the making of reports to the Public Guardian by deputies appointed by the court and others who are directed by the court to carry out any transaction for a person who lacks capacity.

(5) For the purpose of enabling him to carry out his functions, the Public Guardian may, at all reasonable times, examine and take copies of—

    (a) any health record,

    (b) any record of, or held by, a local authority and compiled in connection with a social services function, and

    (c) any record held by a person registered under Part 2 of the Care Standards Act 2000 (c. 14),

    so far as the record relates to P.

(6) The Public Guardian may also for that purpose interview P in private.

59 Public Guardian Board

(1) There is to be a body, to be known as the Public Guardian Board.

(2) The Board's duty is to scrutinise and review the way in which the Public Guardian discharges his functions and to make such recommendations to the Lord Chancellor about that matter as it thinks appropriate.

(3) The Lord Chancellor must, in discharging his functions under sections 57 and 58, give due consideration to recommendations made by the Board.

(4) The members of the Board are to be appointed by the Lord Chancellor.

(5) The Board must have—

    (a) at least one member who is a judge of the court, and

    (b) at least four members who are persons appearing to the Lord Chancellor to have appropriate knowledge or experience of the work of the Public Guardian.

(6) The Lord Chancellor may by regulations make provision as to—

    (a) the appointment of members of the Board (and, in particular, the procedures to be followed in connection with appointments);

    (b) the selection of one of the members to be the chairman;

    (c) the term of office of the chairman and members;

    (d) their resignation, suspension or removal;

    (e) the procedure of the Board (including quorum);

    (f) the validation of proceedings in the event of a vacancy among the members or a defect in the appointment of a member.

(7) Subject to any provision made in reliance on subsection (6)(c) or (d), a person is to hold and vacate office as a member of the Board in accordance with the terms of the instrument appointing him.

(8) The Lord Chancellor may make such payments to or in respect of members of the Board by way of reimbursement of expenses, allowances and remuneration as he may determine.

(9) The Board must make an annual report to the Lord Chancellor about the discharge of its functions.

60 Annual report

(1) The Public Guardian must make an annual report to the Lord Chancellor about the discharge of his functions.

(2) The Lord Chancellor must, within one month of receiving the report, lay a copy of it before Parliament.

Court of Protection Visitors

61 Court of Protection Visitors

(1) A Court of Protection Visitor is a person who is appointed by the Lord Chancellor to—

    (a) a panel of Special Visitors, or

    (b) a panel of General Visitors.

(2) A person is not qualified to be a Special Visitor unless he—

    (a) is a registered medical practitioner or appears to the Lord Chancellor to have other suitable qualifications or training, and

    (b) appears to the Lord Chancellor to have special knowledge of and experience in cases of impairment of or disturbance in the functioning of the mind or brain.

(3) A General Visitor need not have a medical qualification.

(4) A Court of Protection Visitor—

(a) may be appointed for such term and subject to such conditions, and

(b) may be paid such remuneration and allowances,

as the Lord Chancellor may determine.

(5) For the purpose of carrying out his functions under this Act in relation to a person who lacks capacity ('P'), a Court of Protection Visitor may, at all reasonable times, examine and take copies of—

(a) any health record,

(b) any record of, or held by, a local authority and compiled in connection with a social services function, and

(c) any record held by a person registered under Part 2 of the Care Standards Act 2000 (c. 14),

so far as the record relates to P.

(6) A Court of Protection Visitor may also for that purpose interview P in private.

PART 3
MISCELLANEOUS AND GENERAL

Declaratory provision

62 Scope of the act

For the avoidance of doubt, it is hereby declared that nothing in this Act is to be taken to affect the law relating to murder or manslaughter or the operation of section 2 of the Suicide Act 1961 (c. 60) (assisting suicide).

Private international law

63 International protection of adults

Schedule 3—

(a) gives effect in England and Wales to the Convention on the International Protection of Adults signed at the Hague on 13th January 2000 (Cm. 5881) (in so far as this Act does not otherwise do so), and

(b) makes related provision as to the private international law of England and Wales.

General

64 Interpretation

(1) In this Act—

'the 1985 Act' means the Enduring Powers of Attorney Act 1985 (c. 29),

'advance decision' has the meaning given in section 24(1),

'the court' means the Court of Protection established by section 45,

'Court of Protection Rules' has the meaning given in section 51(1),

'Court of Protection Visitor' has the meaning given in section 61,

'deputy' has the meaning given in section 16(2)(b),

'enactment' includes a provision of subordinate legislation (within the meaning of the Interpretation Act 1978 (c. 30)), 'health record' has the meaning given in section 68 of the Data Protection Act 1998 (c. 29) (as read with section 69 of that Act),

'the Human Rights Convention' has the same meaning as 'the Convention' in the Human Rights Act 1998 (c. 42),

'independent mental capacity advocate' has the meaning given in section 35(1),

'lasting power of attorney' has the meaning given in section 9,

'life-sustaining treatment' has the meaning given in section 4(10),

'local authority' means—

(a) the council of a county in England in which there are no district councils,

(b) the council of a district in England,

(c) the council of a county or county borough in Wales,

(d) the council of a London borough,

(e) the Common Council of the City of London, or

(f) the Council of the Isles of Scilly,

'Mental Health Act' means the Mental Health Act 1983 (c. 20),

'prescribed', in relation to regulations made under this Act, means prescribed by those regulations,

'property' includes any thing in action and any interest in real or personal property,

'public authority' has the same meaning as in the Human Rights Act 1998,

'Public Guardian' has the meaning given in section 57,

'purchaser' and 'purchase' have the meaning given in section 205(1) of the Law of Property Act 1925 (c. 20),

'social services function' has the meaning given in section 1A of the Local Authority Social Services Act 1970 (c. 42),

'treatment' includes a diagnostic or other procedure,

'trust corporation' has the meaning given in section 68(1) of the Trustee Act 1925 (c. 19), and

'will' includes codicil.

(2) In this Act, references to making decisions, in relation to a donee of a lasting power of attorney or a deputy appointed by the court, include, where appropriate, acting on decisions made.

(3) In this Act, references to the bankruptcy of an individual include a case where a bankruptcy restrictions order under the Insolvency Act 1986 (c. 45) has effect in respect of him.

(4) 'Bankruptcy restrictions order' includes an interim bankruptcy restrictions order.

65   Rules, regulations and orders

(1) Any power to make rules, regulations or orders under this Act—

(a) is exercisable by statutory instrument;

(b) includes power to make supplementary, incidental, consequential, transitional or saving provision;

(c) includes power to make different provision for different cases.

(2) Any statutory instrument containing rules, regulations or orders made by the Lord Chancellor or the Secretary of State under this Act, other than—

(a) regulations under section 34 (loss of capacity during research project),
(b) regulations under section 41 (adjusting role of independent mental capacity advocacy service),
(c) regulations under paragraph 32(1)(b) of Schedule 3 (private international law relating to the protection of adults),
(d) an order of the kind mentioned in section 67(6) (consequential amendments of primary legislation), or
(e) an order under section 68 (commencement),
is subject to annulment in pursuance of a resolution of either House of Parliament.

(3) A statutory instrument containing an Order in Council under paragraph 31 of Schedule 3 (provision to give further effect to Hague Convention) is subject to annulment in pursuance of a resolution of either House of Parliament.

(4) A statutory instrument containing regulations made by the Secretary of State under section 34 or 41 or by the Lord Chancellor under paragraph 32(1)(b) of Schedule 3 may not be made unless a draft has been laid before and approved by resolution of each House of Parliament.

66 Existing receivers and enduring powers of attorney etc.

(1) The following provisions cease to have effect—
(a) Part 7 of the Mental Health Act,
(b) the Enduring Powers of Attorney Act 1985 (c. 29).

(2) No enduring power of attorney within the meaning of the 1985 Act is to be created after the commencement of subsection (1)(b).

(3) Schedule 4 has effect in place of the 1985 Act in relation to any enduring power of attorney created before the commencement of subsection (1)(b).

(4) Schedule 5 contains transitional provisions and savings in relation to Part 7 of the Mental Health Act and the 1985 Act.

67 Minor and consequential amendments and repeals

(1) Schedule 6 contains minor and consequential amendments.

(2) Schedule 7 contains repeals.

(3) The Lord Chancellor may by order make supplementary, incidental, consequential, transitional or saving provision for the purposes of, in consequence of, or for giving full effect to a provision of this Act.

(4) An order under subsection (3) may, in particular—
(a) provide for a provision of this Act which comes into force before another provision of this Act has come into force to have effect, until the other provision has come into force, with specified modifications;
(b) amend, repeal or revoke an enactment, other than one contained in an Act or Measure passed in a Session after the one in which this Act is passed.

(5) The amendments that may be made under subsection (4)(b) are in addition to those made by or under any other provision of this Act.

(6) An order under subsection (3) which amends or repeals a provision of an Act or Measure may not be made unless a draft has been laid before and approved by resolution of each House of Parliament.

68 Commencement and extent

(1) This Act, other than sections 30 to 41, comes into force in accordance with provision made by order by the Lord Chancellor.

(2) Sections 30 to 41 come into force in accordance with provision made by order by—
   (a) the Secretary of State, in relation to England, and
   (b) the National Assembly for Wales, in relation to Wales.

(3) An order under this section may appoint different days for different provisions and different purposes.

(4) Subject to subsections (5) and (6), this Act extends to England and Wales only.

(5) The following provisions extend to the United Kingdom—
   (a) paragraph 16(1) of Schedule 1 (evidence of instruments and of registration of lasting powers of attorney),
   (b) paragraph 15(3) of Schedule 4 (evidence of instruments and of registration of enduring powers of attorney).

(6) Subject to any provision made in Schedule 6, the amendments and repeals made by Schedules 6 and 7 have the same extent as the enactments to which they relate.

69 Short title

This Act may be cited as the Mental Capacity Act 2005.

SCHEDULES

Section 9 SCHEDULE 1

LASTING POWERS OF ATTORNEY: FORMALITIES

PART 1
MAKING INSTRUMENTS

General requirements as to making instruments

1 (1) An instrument is not made in accordance with this Schedule unless—
   (a) it is in the prescribed form,
   (b) it complies with paragraph 2, and
   (c) any prescribed requirements in connection with its execution are satisfied.

(2) Regulations may make different provision according to whether—
   (a) the instrument relates to personal welfare or to property and affairs (or to both);
   (b) only one or more than one donee is to be appointed (and if more than one, whether jointly or jointly and severally).

(3) In this Schedule—
   (a) 'prescribed' means prescribed by regulations, and
   (b) 'regulations' means regulations made for the purposes of this Schedule by the Lord Chancellor.

Requirements as to content of instruments

2 (1) The instrument must include—

(a) the prescribed information about the purpose of the instrument and the effect of a lasting power of attorney,

(b) a statement by the donor to the effect that he—

  (i) has read the prescribed information or a prescribed part of it (or has had it read to him), and

  (ii) intends the authority conferred under the instrument to include authority to make decisions on his behalf in circumstances where he no longer has capacity,

(c) a statement by the donor—

  (i) naming a person or persons whom the donor wishes to be notified of any application for the registration of the instrument, or

  (ii) stating that there are no persons whom he wishes to be notified of any such application,

(d) a statement by the donee (or, if more than one, each of them) to the effect that he—

  (i) has read the prescribed information or a prescribed part of it (or has had it read to him), and

  (ii) understands the duties imposed on a donee of a lasting power of attorney under sections 1 (the principles) and 4 (best interests), and

(e) a certificate by a person of a prescribed description that, in his opinion, at the time when the donor executes the instrument—

  (i) the donor understands the purpose of the instrument and the scope of the authority conferred under it,

  (ii) no fraud or undue pressure is being used to induce the donor to create a lasting power of attorney, and

  (iii) there is nothing else which would prevent a lasting power of attorney from being created by the instrument.

(2) Regulations may—

  (a) prescribe a maximum number of named persons;

  (b) provide that, where the instrument includes a statement under sub-paragraph (1)(c)(ii), two persons of a prescribed description must each give a certificate under sub-paragraph (1)(e).

(3) The persons who may be named persons do not include a person who is appointed as donee under the instrument.

(4) In this Schedule, 'named person' means a person named under sub-paragraph (1)(c).

(5) A certificate under sub-paragraph (1)(e)—

  (a) must be made in the prescribed form, and

  (b) must include any prescribed information.

(6) The certificate may not be given by a person appointed as donee under the instrument.

Failure to comply with prescribed form

3 (1) If an instrument differs in an immaterial respect in form or mode of expression from the prescribed form, it is to be treated by the Public Guardian as sufficient in point of form and expression.

(2) The court may declare that an instrument which is not in the prescribed form is to be treated as if it were, if it is satisfied that the persons executing the instrument intended it to create a lasting power of attorney.

PART 2
REGISTRATION

Applications and procedure for registration

4 (1) An application to the Public Guardian for the registration of an instrument intended to create a lasting power of attorney—
   (a) must be made in the prescribed form, and
   (b) must include any prescribed information.
(2) The application may be made—
   (a) by the donor,
   (b) by the donee or donees, or
   (c) if the instrument appoints two or more donees to act jointly and severally in respect of any matter, by any of the donees.
(3) The application must be accompanied by—
   (a) the instrument, and
   (b) any fee provided for under section 58(4)(b).
(4) A person who, in an application for registration, makes a statement which he knows to be false in a material particular is guilty of an offence and is liable—
   (a) on summary conviction, to imprisonment for a term not exceeding 12 months or a fine not exceeding the statutory maximum or both;
   (b) on conviction on indictment, to imprisonment for a term not exceeding 2 years or a fine or both.
5 Subject to paragraphs 11 to 14, the Public Guardian must register the instrument as a lasting power of attorney at the end of the prescribed period.

Notification requirements

6 (1) A donor about to make an application under paragraph 4(2)(a) must notify any named persons that he is about to do so.
(2) The donee (or donees) about to make an application under paragraph 4(2)(b) or (c) must notify any named persons that he is (or they are) about to do so.
7 As soon as is practicable after receiving an application by the donor under paragraph 4(2)(a), the Public Guardian must notify the donee (or donees) that the application has been received.
8 (1) As soon as is practicable after receiving an application by a donee (or donees) under paragraph 4(2)(b), the Public Guardian must notify the donor that the application has been received.
(2) As soon as is practicable after receiving an application by a donee under paragraph 4(2)(c), the Public Guardian must notify—
   (a) the donor, and
   (b) the donee or donees who did not join in making the application,
   that the application has been received.

9   (1) A notice under paragraph 6 must be made in the prescribed form.
    (2) A notice under paragraph 6, 7 or 8 must include such information, if any, as may
         be prescribed.

Power to dispense with notification requirements

10 The court may—
         (a) on the application of the donor, dispense with the requirement to notify
             under paragraph 6(1), or
         (b) on the application of the donee or donees concerned, dispense with the
             requirement to notify under paragraph 6(2),
    if satisfied that no useful purpose would be served by giving the notice.

Instrument not made properly or containing ineffective provision

11 (1) If it appears to the Public Guardian that an instrument accompanying an appli-
         cation under paragraph 4 is not made in accordance with this Schedule, he must
         not register the instrument unless the court directs him to do so.
    (2) Sub-paragraph (3) applies if it appears to the Public Guardian that the instru-
         ment contains a provision which—
         (a) would be ineffective as part of a lasting power of attorney, or
         (b) would prevent the instrument from operating as a valid lasting power of
             attorney.
    (3) The Public Guardian—
         (a) must apply to the court for it to determine the matter under section 23(1),
             and
         (b) pending the determination by the court, must not register the
             instrument.
    (4) Sub-paragraph (5) applies if the court determines under section 23(1) (whether
         or not on an application by the Public Guardian) that the instrument contains a
         provision which—
         (a) would be ineffective as part of a lasting power of attorney, or
         (b) would prevent the instrument from operating as a valid lasting power of
             attorney.
    (5) The court must—
         (a) notify the Public Guardian that it has severed the provision, or
         (b) direct him not to register the instrument.
    (6) Where the court notifies the Public Guardian that it has severed a provision, he
         must register the instrument with a note to that effect attached to it.

Deputy already appointed

12 (1) Sub-paragraph (2) applies if it appears to the Public Guardian that
         (a) there is a deputy appointed by the court for the donor, and
         (b) the powers conferred on the deputy would, if the instrument were registered,
             to any extent conflict with the powers conferred on the attorney.
    (2) The Public Guardian must not register the instrument unless the court directs
         him to do so.

Objection by donee or named person

13 (1) Sub-paragraph (2) applies if a donee or a named person—

    (a) receives a notice under paragraph 6, 7 or 8 of an application for the registration of an instrument, and

    (b) before the end of the prescribed period, gives notice to the Public Guardian of an objection to the registration on the ground that an event mentioned in section 13(3) or (6)(a) to (d) has occurred which has revoked the instrument.

  (2) If the Public Guardian is satisfied that the ground for making the objection is established, he must not register the instrument unless the court, on the application of the person applying for the registration—

    (a) is satisfied that the ground is not established, and

    (b) directs the Public Guardian to register the instrument.

  (3) Sub-paragraph (4) applies if a donee or a named person—

    (a) receives a notice under paragraph 6, 7 or 8 of an application for the registration of an instrument, and

    (b) before the end of the prescribed period—

      (i) makes an application to the court objecting to the registration on a prescribed ground, and

      (ii) notifies the Public Guardian of the application.

  (4) The Public Guardian must not register the instrument unless the court directs him to do so.

Objection by donor

14 (1) This paragraph applies if the donor—

    (a) receives a notice under paragraph 8 of an application for the registration of an instrument, and

    (b) before the end of the prescribed period, gives notice to the Public Guardian of an objection to the registration.

  (2) The Public Guardian must not register the instrument unless the court, on the application of the donee or, if more than one, any of them—

    (a) is satisfied that the donor lacks capacity to object to the registration, and

    (b) directs the Public Guardian to register the instrument.

Notification of registration

15 Where an instrument is registered under this Schedule, the Public Guardian must give notice of the fact in the prescribed form to—

    (a) the donor, and

    (b) the donee or, if more than one, each of them.

Evidence of registration

16 (1) A document purporting to be an office copy of an instrument registered under this Schedule is, in any part of the United Kingdom, evidence of—

    (a) the contents of the instrument, and

    (b) the fact that it has been registered.

  (2) Sub-paragraph (1) is without prejudice to—

    (a) section 3 of the Powers of Attorney Act 1971 (c. 27) (proof by certified copy), and

    (b) any other method of proof authorised by law.

PART 3
CANCELLATION OF REGISTRATION AND NOTIFICATION OF SEVERANCE

17 (1) The Public Guardian must cancel the registration of an instrument as a lasting power of attorney on being satisfied that the power has been revoked—

    (a) as a result of the donor's bankruptcy, or

    (b) on the occurrence of an event mentioned in section 13(6)(a) to (d).

  (2) If the Public Guardian cancels the registration of an instrument he must notify—

    (a) the donor, and

    (b) the donee or, if more than one, each of them.

18 The court must direct the Public Guardian to cancel the registration of an instrument as a lasting power of attorney if it—

    (a) determines under section 22(2)(a) that a requirement for creating the power was not met,

    (b) determines under section 22(2)(b) that the power has been revoked or has otherwise come to an end, or

    (c) revokes the power under section 22(4)(b) (fraud etc.).

19 (1) Sub-paragraph (2) applies if the court determines under section 23(1) that a lasting power of attorney contains a provision which—

    (a) is ineffective as part of a lasting power of attorney, or

    (b) prevents the instrument from operating as a valid lasting power of attorney.

  (2) The court must—

    (a) notify the Public Guardian that it has severed the provision, or

    (b) direct him to cancel the registration of the instrument as a lasting power of attorney.

20 On the cancellation of the registration of an instrument, the instrument and any office copies of it must be delivered up to the Public Guardian to be cancelled.

PART 4
RECORDS OF ALTERATIONS IN REGISTERED POWERS

Partial revocation or suspension of power as a result of bankruptcy

21 If in the case of a registered instrument it appears to the Public Guardian that under section 13 a lasting power of attorney is revoked, or suspended, in relation to the donor's property and affairs (but not in relation to other matters), the Public Guardian must attach to the instrument a note to that effect.

Termination of appointment of donee which does not revoke power

22 If in the case of a registered instrument it appears to the Public Guardian that an event has occurred—

(a) which has terminated the appointment of the donee, but

(b) which has not revoked the instrument,

the Public Guardian must attach to the instrument a note to that effect.

Replacement of donee

23 If in the case of a registered instrument it appears to the Public Guardian that the donee has been replaced under the terms of the instrument the Public Guardian must attach to the instrument a note to that effect.

Severance of ineffective provisions

24 If in the case of a registered instrument the court notifies the Public Guardian under paragraph 19(2)(a) that it has severed a provision of the instrument, the Public Guardian must attach to it a note to that effect.

Notification of alterations

25 If the Public Guardian attaches a note to an instrument under paragraph 21, 22, 23 or 24 he must give notice of the note to the donee or donees of the power (or, as the case may be, to the other donee or donees of the power).

Section 18(4)   SCHEDULE 2

PROPERTY AND AFFAIRS: SUPPLEMENTARY PROVISIONS

Wills: general

1 Paragraphs 2 to 4 apply in relation to the execution of a will, by virtue of section 18, on behalf of P.

Provision that may be made in will

2 The will may make any provision (whether by disposing of property or exercising a power or otherwise) which could be made by a will executed by P if he had capacity to make it.

Wills: requirements relating to execution

3 (1) Sub-paragraph (2) applies if under section 16 the court makes an order or gives directions requiring or authorising a person ('the authorised person') to execute a will on behalf of P.

   (2) Any will executed in pursuance of the order or direction—

      (a) must state that it is signed by P acting by the authorised person,

      (b) must be signed by the authorised person with the name of P and his own name, in the presence of two or more witnesses present at the same time,

      (c) must be attested and subscribed by those witnesses in the presence of the authorised person, and

      (d) must be sealed with the official seal of the court.

Wills: effect of execution

4   (1) This paragraph applies where a will is executed in accordance with paragraph 3.
    (2) The Wills Act 1837 (c. 26) has effect in relation to the will as if it were signed by P by his own hand, except that—
         (a) section 9 of the 1837 Act (requirements as to signing and attestation) does not apply, and
         (b) in the subsequent provisions of the 1837 Act any reference to execution in the manner required by the previous provisions is to be read as a reference to execution in accordance with paragraph 3.
    (3) The will has the same effect for all purposes as if—
         (a) P had had the capacity to make a valid will, and
         (b) the will had been executed by him in the manner required by the 1837 Act.
    (4) But sub-paragraph (3) does not have effect in relation to the will—
         (a) in so far as it disposes of immovable property outside England and Wales, or
         (b) in so far as it relates to any other property or matter if, when the will is executed—
              (i)   P is domiciled outside England and Wales, and
              (ii) the condition in sub-paragraph (5) is met.
    (5) The condition is that, under the law of P's domicile, any question of his testamentary capacity would fall to be determined in accordance with the law of a place outside England and Wales.

Vesting orders ancillary to settlement etc.

5   (1) If provision is made by virtue of section 18 for—
         (a) the settlement of any property of P, or
         (b) the exercise of a power vested in him of appointing trustees or retiring from a trust,
         the court may also make as respects the property settled or the trust property such consequential vesting or other orders as the case may require.
    (2) The power under sub-paragraph (1) includes, in the case of the exercise of such a power, any order which could have been made in such a case under Part 4 of the Trustee Act 1925 (c. 19).

Variation of settlements

6   (1) If a settlement has been made by virtue of section 18, the court may by order vary or revoke the settlement if—
         (a) the settlement makes provision for its variation or revocation,
         (b) the court is satisfied that a material fact was not disclosed when the settlement was made, or
         (c) the court is satisfied that there has been a substantial change of circumstances.
    (2) Any such order may give such consequential directions as the court thinks fit.

Vesting of stock in curator appointed outside England and Wales

7 (1) Sub-paragraph (2) applies if the court is satisfied—

(a) that under the law prevailing in a place outside England and Wales a person ('M') has been appointed to exercise powers in respect of the property or affairs of P on the ground (however formulated) that P lacks capacity to make decisions with respect to the management and administration of his property and affairs, and

(b) that, having regard to the nature of the appointment and to the circumstances of the case, it is expedient that the court should exercise its powers under this paragraph.

(2) The court may direct—

(a) any stocks standing in the name of P, or

(b) the right to receive dividends from the stocks,

to be transferred into M's name or otherwise dealt with as required by M, and may give such directions as the court thinks fit for dealing with accrued dividends from the stocks.

(3) 'Stocks' includes—

(a) shares, and

(b) any funds, annuity or security transferable in the books kept by any body corporate or unincorporated company or society or by an instrument of transfer either alone or accompanied by other formalities,

and 'dividends' is to be construed accordingly.

Preservation of interests in property disposed of on behalf of person lacking capacity

8 (1) Sub-paragraphs (2) and (3) apply if—

(a) P's property has been disposed of by virtue of section 18,

(b) under P's will or intestacy, or by a gift perfected or nomination taking effect on his death, any other person would have taken an interest in the property but for the disposal, and

(c) on P's death, any property belonging to P's estate represents the property disposed of.

(2) The person takes the same interest, if and so far as circumstances allow, in the property representing the property disposed of.

(3) If the property disposed of was real property, any property representing it is to be treated, so long as it remains part of P's estate, as if it were real property.

(4) The court may direct that, on a disposal of P's property—

(a) which is made by virtue of section 18, and

(b) which would apart from this paragraph result in the conversion of personal property into real property,

property representing the property disposed of is to be treated, so long as it remains P's property or forms part of P's estate, as if it were personal property.

(5) References in sub-paragraphs (1) to (4) to the disposal of property are to—

(a) the sale, exchange, charging of or other dealing (otherwise than by will) with property other than money;

(b) the removal of property from one place to another;

    (c) the application of money in acquiring property;

    (d) the transfer of money from one account to another;

and references to property representing property disposed of are to be construed accordingly and as including the result of successive disposals.

(6) The court may give such directions as appear to it necessary or expedient for the purpose of facilitating the operation of sub-paragraphs (1) to (3), including the carrying of money to a separate account and the transfer of property other than money.

9   (1) Sub-paragraph (2) applies if the court has ordered or directed the expenditure of money—

    (a) for carrying out permanent improvements on any of P's property, or

    (b) otherwise for the permanent benefit of any of P's property.

   (2) The court may order that—

    (a) the whole of the money expended or to be expended, or

    (b) any part of it,

is to be a charge on the property either without interest or with interest at a specified rate.

   (3) An order under sub-paragraph (2) may provide for excluding or restricting the operation of paragraph 8(1) to (3).

   (4) A charge under sub-paragraph (2) may be made in favour of such person as may be just and, in particular, where the money charged is paid out of P's general estate, may be made in favour of a person as trustee for P.

   (5) No charge under sub-paragraph (2) may confer any right of sale or foreclosure during P's lifetime.

Powers as patron of benefice

10 (1) Any functions which P has as patron of a benefice may be discharged only by a person ('R') appointed by the court.

   (2) R must be an individual capable of appointment under section 8(1)(b) of the 1986 Measure (which provides for an individual able to make a declaration of communicant status, a clerk in Holy Orders, etc. to be appointed to discharge a registered patron's functions).

   (3) The 1986 Measure applies to R as it applies to an individual appointed by the registered patron of the benefice under section 8(1)(b) or (3) of that Measure to discharge his functions as patron.

   (4) 'The 1986 Measure' means the Patronage (Benefices) Measure 1986 (No. 3).

Section 63   **SCHEDULE 3**

INTERNATIONAL PROTECTION OF ADULTS

PART 1
PRELIMINARY

Introduction

1   This Part applies for the purposes of this Schedule.

The Convention

2 (1) 'Convention' means the Convention referred to in section 63.

(2) 'Convention country' means a country in which the Convention is in force.

(3) A reference to an Article or Chapter is to an Article or Chapter of the Convention.

(4) An expression which appears in this Schedule and in the Convention is to be construed in accordance with the Convention.

Countries, territories and nationals

3 (1) 'Country' includes a territory which has its own system of law.

(2) Where a country has more than one territory with its own system of law, a reference to the country, in relation to one of its nationals, is to the territory with which the national has the closer, or the closest, connection.

Adults with incapacity

4 'Adult' means a person who—

(a) as a result of an impairment or insufficiency of his personal faculties, cannot protect his interests, and

(b) has reached 16.

Protective measures

5 (1) 'Protective measure' means a measure directed to the protection of the person or property of an adult; and it may deal in particular with any of the following—

(a) the determination of incapacity and the institution of a protective regime,

(b) placing the adult under the protection of an appropriate authority,

(c) guardianship, curatorship or any corresponding system,

(d) the designation and functions of a person having charge of the adult's person or property, or representing or otherwise helping him,

(e) placing the adult in a place where protection can be provided,

(f) administering, conserving or disposing of the adult's property,

(g) authorising a specific intervention for the protection of the person or property of the adult.

(2) Where a measure of like effect to a protective measure has been taken in relation to a person before he reaches 16, this Schedule applies to the measure in so far as it has effect in relation to him once he has reached 16.

Central Authority

6 (1) Any function under the Convention of a Central Authority is exercisable in England and Wales by the Lord Chancellor.

(2) A communication may be sent to the Central Authority in relation to England and Wales by sending it to the Lord Chancellor.

PART 2
JURISDICTION OF COMPETENT AUTHORITY

Scope of jurisdiction

7   (1) The court may exercise its functions under this Act (in so far as it cannot otherwise do so) in relation to—

    (a) an adult habitually resident in England and Wales,

    (b) an adult's property in England and Wales,

    (c) an adult present in England and Wales or who has property there, if the matter is urgent, or

    (d) an adult present in England and Wales, if a protective measure which is temporary and limited in its effect to England and Wales is proposed in relation to him.

  (2) An adult present in England and Wales is to be treated for the purposes of this paragraph as habitually resident there if—

    (a) his habitual residence cannot be ascertained,

    (b) he is a refugee, or

    (c) he has been displaced as a result of disturbance in the country of his habitual residence.

8   (1) The court may also exercise its functions under this Act (in so far as it cannot otherwise do so) in relation to an adult if sub-paragraph (2) or (3) applies in relation to him.

  (2) This sub-paragraph applies in relation to an adult if—

    (a) he is a British citizen,

    (b) he has a closer connection with England and Wales than with Scotland or Northern Ireland, and

    (c) Article 7 has, in relation to the matter concerned, been complied with.

  (3) This sub-paragraph applies in relation to an adult if the Lord Chancellor, having consulted such persons as he considers appropriate, agrees to a request under Article 8 in relation to the adult.

Exercise of jurisdiction

9   (1) This paragraph applies where jurisdiction is exercisable under this Schedule in connection with a matter which involves a Convention country other than England and Wales.

  (2) Any Article on which the jurisdiction is based applies in relation to the matter in so far as it involves the other country (and the court must, accordingly, comply with any duty conferred on it as a result).

  (3) Article 12 also applies, so far as its provisions allow, in relation to the matter in so far as it involves the other country.

10 A reference in this Schedule to the exercise of jurisdiction under this Schedule is to the exercise of functions under this Act as a result of this Part of this Schedule.

PART 3
APPLICABLE LAW

Applicable law

11 In exercising jurisdiction under this Schedule, the court may, if it thinks that the matter has a substantial connection with a country other than England and Wales, apply the law of that other country.

12 Where a protective measure is taken in one country but implemented in another, the conditions of implementation are governed by the law of the other country.

Lasting powers of attorney, etc.

13 (1) If the donor of a lasting power is habitually resident in England and Wales at the time of granting the power, the law applicable to the existence, extent, modification or extinction of the power is—
    (a) the law of England and Wales, or
    (b) if he specifies in writing the law of a connected country for the purpose, that law.

    (2) If he is habitually resident in another country at that time, but England and Wales is a connected country, the law applicable in that respect is—
    (a) the law of the other country, or
    (b) if he specifies in writing the law of England and Wales for the purpose, that law.

    (3) A country is connected, in relation to the donor, if it is a country—
    (a) of which he is a national,
    (b) in which he was habitually resident, or
    (c) in which he has property.

    (4) Where this paragraph applies as a result of sub-paragraph (3)(c), it applies only in relation to the property which the donor has in the connected country.

    (5) The law applicable to the manner of the exercise of a lasting power is the law of the country where it is exercised.

    (6) In this Part of this Schedule, 'lasting power' means—
    (a) a lasting power of attorney (see section 9),
    (b) an enduring power of attorney within the meaning of Schedule 4, or
    (c) any other power of like effect.

14 (1) Where a lasting power is not exercised in a manner sufficient to guarantee the protection of the person or property of the donor, the court, in exercising jurisdiction under this Schedule, may disapply or modify the power.

    (2) Where, in accordance with this Part of this Schedule, the law applicable to the power is, in one or more respects, that of a country other than England and Wales, the court must, so far as possible, have regard to the law of the other country in that respect (or those respects).

15 Regulations may provide for Schedule 1 (lasting powers of attorney: formalities) to apply with modifications in relation to a lasting power which comes within paragraph 13(6)(c) above.

Protection of third parties

16 (1) This paragraph applies where a person (a 'representative') in purported exercise of an authority to act on behalf of an adult enters into a transaction with a third party.

(2) The validity of the transaction may not be questioned in proceedings, nor may the third party be held liable, merely because—

(a) where the representative and third party are in England and Wales when entering into the transaction, sub-paragraph (3) applies;

(b) where they are in another country at that time, sub-paragraph (4) applies.

(3) This sub-paragraph applies if—

(a) the law applicable to the authority in one or more respects is, as a result of this Schedule, the law of a country other than England and Wales, and

(b) the representative is not entitled to exercise the authority in that respect (or those respects) under the law of that other country.

(4) This sub-paragraph applies if—

(a) the law applicable to the authority in one or more respects is, as a result of this Part of this Schedule, the law of England and Wales, and

(b) the representative is not entitled to exercise the authority in that respect (or those respects) under that law.

(5) This paragraph does not apply if the third party knew or ought to have known that the applicable law was—

(a) in a case within sub-paragraph (3), the law of the other country;

(b) in a case within sub-paragraph (4), the law of England and Wales.

Mandatory rules

17 Where the court is entitled to exercise jurisdiction under this Schedule, the mandatory provisions of the law of England and Wales apply, regardless of any system of law which would otherwise apply in relation to the matter.

Public policy

18 Nothing in this Part of this Schedule requires or enables the application in England and Wales of a provision of the law of another country if its application would be manifestly contrary to public policy.

PART 4
RECOGNITION AND ENFORCEMENT

Recognition

19 (1) A protective measure taken in relation to an adult under the law of a country other than England and Wales is to be recognised in England and Wales if it was taken on the ground that the adult is habitually resident in the other country.

(2) A protective measure taken in relation to an adult under the law of a Convention country other than England and Wales is to be recognised in England and Wales if it was taken on a ground mentioned in Chapter 2 (jurisdiction).

(3) But the court may disapply this paragraph in relation to a measure if it thinks that—

(a) the case in which the measure was taken was not urgent,

(b) the adult was not given an opportunity to be heard, and

(c) that omission amounted to a breach of natural justice.

(4) It may also disapply this paragraph in relation to a measure if it thinks that—

(a) recognition of the measure would be manifestly contrary to public policy,

(b) the measure would be inconsistent with a mandatory provision of the law of England and Wales, or

(c) the measure is inconsistent with one subsequently taken, or recognised, in England and Wales in relation to the adult.

(5) And the court may disapply this paragraph in relation to a measure taken under the law of a Convention country in a matter to which Article 33 applies, if the court thinks that that Article has not been complied with in connection with that matter.

20 (1) An interested person may apply to the court for a declaration as to whether a protective measure taken under the law of a country other than England and Wales is to be recognised in England and Wales.

(2) No permission is required for an application to the court under this paragraph.

21 For the purposes of paragraphs 19 and 20, any finding of fact relied on when the measure was taken is conclusive.

Enforcement

22 (1) An interested person may apply to the court for a declaration as to whether a protective measure taken under the law of, and enforceable in, a country other than England and Wales is enforceable, or to be registered, in England and Wales in accordance with Court of Protection Rules.

(2) The court must make the declaration if—

(a) the measure comes within sub-paragraph (1) or (2) of paragraph 19, and

(b) the paragraph is not disapplied in relation to it as a result of sub-paragraph (3), (4) or (5).

(3) A measure to which a declaration under this paragraph relates is enforceable in England and Wales as if it were a measure of like effect taken by the court.

Measures taken in relation to those aged under 16

23 (1) This paragraph applies where—

(a) provision giving effect to, or otherwise deriving from, the Convention in a country other than England and Wales applies in relation to a person who has not reached 16, and

(b) a measure is taken in relation to that person in reliance on that provision.

(2) This Part of this Schedule applies in relation to that measure as it applies in relation to a protective measure taken in relation to an adult under the law of a Convention country other than England and Wales.

Supplementary

24 The court may not review the merits of a measure taken outside England and Wales except to establish whether the measure complies with this Schedule in so far as it is, as a result of this Schedule, required to do so.

25 Court of Protection Rules may make provision about an application under paragraph 20 or 22.

PART 5
CO-OPERATION

Proposal for cross-border placement

26 (1) This paragraph applies where a public authority proposes to place an adult in an establishment in a Convention country other than England and Wales.
  (2) The public authority must consult an appropriate authority in that other country about the proposed placement and, for that purpose, must send it—
   (a) a report on the adult, and
   (b) a statement of its reasons for the proposed placement.
  (3) If the appropriate authority in the other country opposes the proposed placement within a reasonable time, the public authority may not proceed with it.

27 A proposal received by a public authority under Article 33 in relation to an adult is to proceed unless the authority opposes it within a reasonable time.

Adult in danger etc.

28 (1) This paragraph applies if a public authority is told that an adult—
   (a) who is in serious danger, and
   (b) in relation to whom the public authority has taken, or is considering taking, protective measures,
  is, or has become resident, in a Convention country other than England and Wales.
  (2) The public authority must tell an appropriate authority in that other country about—
   (a) the danger, and
   (b) the measures taken or under consideration.

29 A public authority may not request from, or send to, an appropriate authority in a Convention country information in accordance with Chapter 5 (co-operation) in relation to an adult if it thinks that doing so—
   (a) would be likely to endanger the adult or his property, or
   (b) would amount to a serious threat to the liberty or life of a member of the adult's family.

PART 6
GENERAL

Certificates

30 A certificate given under Article 38 by an authority in a Convention country other than England and Wales is, unless the contrary is shown, proof of the matters contained in it.

Powers to make further provision as to private international law

31 Her Majesty may by Order in Council confer on the Lord Chancellor, the court or another public authority functions for enabling the Convention to be given effect in England and Wales.

32 (1) Regulations may make provision—
   (a) giving further effect to the Convention, or
   (b) otherwise about the private international law of England and Wales in relation to the protection of adults.

(2) The regulations may—
   (a) confer functions on the court or another public authority;
   (b) amend this Schedule;
   (c) provide for this Schedule to apply with specified modifications;
   (d) make provision about countries other than Convention countries.

Exceptions

33 Nothing in this Schedule applies, and no provision made under paragraph 32 is to apply, to any matter to which the Convention, as a result of Article 4, does not apply.

Regulations and orders

34 A reference in this Schedule to regulations or an order (other than an Order in Council) is to regulations or an order made for the purposes of this Schedule by the Lord Chancellor.

Commencement

35 The following provisions of this Schedule have effect only if the Convention is in force in accordance with Article 57—
   (a) paragraph 8,
   (b) paragraph 9,
   (c) paragraph 19(2) and (5),
   (d) Part 5,
   (e) paragraph 30.

Section 66(3)
SCHEDULE 4

PROVISIONS APPLYING TO EXISTING ENDURING POWERS OF ATTORNEY

PART 1
ENDURING POWERS OF ATTORNEY

Enduring power of attorney to survive mental incapacity of donor

1 (1) Where an individual has created a power of attorney which is an enduring power within the meaning of this Schedule—

(a) the power is not revoked by any subsequent mental incapacity of his,

(b) upon such incapacity supervening, the donee of the power may not do anything under the authority of the power except as provided by sub-paragraph (2) unless or until the instrument creating the power is registered under paragraph 13, and

(c) if and so long as paragraph (b) operates to suspend the donee's authority to act under the power, section 5 of the Powers of Attorney Act 1971 (c. 27) (protection of donee and third persons), so far as applicable, applies as if the power had been revoked by the donor's mental incapacity,

and, accordingly, section 1 of this Act does not apply.

(2) Despite sub-paragraph (1)(b), where the attorney has made an application for registration of the instrument then, until it is registered, the attorney may take action under the power—

(a) to maintain the donor or prevent loss to his estate, or

(b) to maintain himself or other persons in so far as paragraph 3(2) permits him to do so.

(3) Where the attorney purports to act as provided by sub-paragraph (2) then, in favour of a person who deals with him without knowledge that the attorney is acting otherwise than in accordance with sub-paragraph (2)(a) or (b), the transaction between them is as valid as if the attorney were acting in accordance with sub-paragraph (2)(a) or (b).

Characteristics of an enduring power of attorney

2 (1) Subject to sub-paragraphs (5) and (6) and paragraph 20, a power of attorney is an enduring power within the meaning of this Schedule if the instrument which creates the power—

(a) is in the prescribed form,

(b) was executed in the prescribed manner by the donor and the attorney, and

(c) incorporated at the time of execution by the donor the prescribed explanatory information.

(2) In this paragraph, 'prescribed' means prescribed by such of the following regulations as applied when the instrument was executed—

(a) the Enduring Powers of Attorney (Prescribed Form) Regulations 1986 (S.I. 1986/126),

(b) the Enduring Powers of Attorney (Prescribed Form) Regulations 1987 (S.I. 1987/1612),

(c) the Enduring Powers of Attorney (Prescribed Form) Regulations 1990 (S.I. 1990/1376),

(d) the Enduring Powers of Attorney (Welsh Language Prescribed Form) Regulations 2000 (S.I. 2000/289).

(3) An instrument in the prescribed form purporting to have been executed in the prescribed manner is to be taken, in the absence of evidence to the contrary, to be a document which incorporated at the time of execution by the donor the prescribed explanatory information.

(4) If an instrument differs in an immaterial respect in form or mode of expression from the prescribed form it is to be treated as sufficient in point of form and expression.

(5) A power of attorney cannot be an enduring power unless, when he executes the instrument creating it, the attorney is—
   (a) an individual who has reached 18 and is not bankrupt, or
   (b) a trust corporation.

(6) A power of attorney which gives the attorney a right to appoint a substitute or successor cannot be an enduring power.

(7) An enduring power is revoked by the bankruptcy of the donor or attorney.

(8) But where the donor or attorney is bankrupt merely because an interim bankruptcy restrictions order has effect in respect of him, the power is suspended for so long as the order has effect.

(9) An enduring power is revoked if the court—
   (a) exercises a power under sections 16 to 20 in relation to the donor, and
   (b) directs that the enduring power is to be revoked.

(10) No disclaimer of an enduring power, whether by deed or otherwise, is valid unless and until the attorney gives notice of it to the donor or, where paragraph 4(6) or 15(1) applies, to the Public Guardian.

Scope of authority etc. of attorney under enduring power

3   (1) If the instrument which creates an enduring power of attorney is expressed to confer general authority on the attorney, the instrument operates to confer, subject to—
   (a) the restriction imposed by sub-paragraph (3), and
   (b) any conditions or restrictions contained in the instrument,
authority to do on behalf of the donor anything which the donor could lawfully do by an attorney at the time when the donor executed the instrument.

(2) Subject to any conditions or restrictions contained in the instrument, an attorney under an enduring power, whether general or limited, may (without obtaining any consent) act under the power so as to benefit himself or other persons than the donor to the following extent but no further—
   (a) he may so act in relation to himself or in relation to any other person if the donor might be expected to provide for his or that person's needs respectively, and
   (b) he may do whatever the donor might be expected to do to meet those needs.

(3) Without prejudice to sub-paragraph (2) but subject to any conditions or restrictions contained in the instrument, an attorney under an enduring power, whether general or limited, may (without obtaining any consent) dispose of the property of the donor by way of gift to the following extent but no further—
   (a) he may make gifts of a seasonal nature or at a time, or on an anniversary, of a birth, a marriage or the formation of a civil partnership, to persons (including himself) who are related to or connected with the donor, and
   (b) he may make gifts to any charity to whom the donor made or might be expected to make gifts,
provided that the value of each such gift is not unreasonable having regard to all the circumstances and in particular the size of the donor's estate.

PART 2
ACTION ON ACTUAL OR IMPENDING INCAPACITY OF DONOR

Duties of attorney in event of actual or impending incapacity of donor

4 (1) Sub-paragraphs (2) to (6) apply if the attorney under an enduring power has reason to believe that the donor is or is becoming mentally incapable.

(2) The attorney must, as soon as practicable, make an application to the Public Guardian for the registration of the instrument creating the power.

(3) Before making an application for registration the attorney must comply with the provisions as to notice set out in Part 3 of this Schedule.

(4) An application for registration—
   (a) must be made in the prescribed form, and
   (b) must contain such statements as may be prescribed.

(5) The attorney—
   (a) may, before making an application for the registration of the instrument, refer to the court for its determination any question as to the validity of the power, and
   (b) must comply with any direction given to him by the court on that determination.

(6) No disclaimer of the power is valid unless and until the attorney gives notice of it to the Public Guardian; and the Public Guardian must notify the donor if he receives a notice under this sub-paragraph.

(7) A person who, in an application for registration, makes a statement which he knows to be false in a material particular is guilty of an offence and is liable—
   (a) on summary conviction, to imprisonment for a term not exceeding 12 months or a fine not exceeding the statutory maximum or both;
   (b) on conviction on indictment, to imprisonment for a term not exceeding 2 years or a fine or both.

(8) In this paragraph, 'prescribed' means prescribed by regulations made for the purposes of this Schedule by the Lord Chancellor.

PART 3
NOTIFICATION PRIOR TO REGISTRATION

Duty to give notice to relatives

5 Subject to paragraph 7, before making an application for registration the attorney must give notice of his intention to do so to all those persons (if any) who are entitled to receive notice by virtue of paragraph 6.

6 (1) Subject to sub-paragraphs (2) to (4), persons of the following classes ('relatives') are entitled to receive notice under paragraph 5—
   (a) the donor's spouse or civil partner,
   (b) the donor's children,
   (c) the donor's parents,
   (d) the donor's brothers and sisters, whether of the whole or half blood,
   (e) the widow, widower or surviving civil partner of a child of the donor,

    (f) the donor's grandchildren,

    (g) the children of the donor's brothers and sisters of the whole blood,

    (h) the children of the donor's brothers and sisters of the half blood,

    (i) the donor's uncles and aunts of the whole blood,

    (j) the children of the donor's uncles and aunts of the whole blood.

(2) A person is not entitled to receive notice under paragraph 5 if—

    (a) his name or address is not known to the attorney and cannot be reasonably ascertained by him, or

    (b) the attorney has reason to believe that he has not reached 18 or is mentally incapable.

(3) Except where sub-paragraph (4) applies—

    (a) no more than 3 persons are entitled to receive notice under paragraph 5, and

    (b) in determining the persons who are so entitled, persons falling within the class in sub-paragraph (1)(a) are to be preferred to persons falling within the class in sub-paragraph (1)(b), those falling within the class in sub-paragraph (1)(b) are to be preferred to those falling within the class in sub-paragraph (1)(c), and so on.

(4) Despite the limit of 3 specified in sub-paragraph (3), where—

    (a) there is more than one person falling within any of classes (a) to (j) of sub-paragraph (1), and

    (b) at least one of those persons would be entitled to receive notice under paragraph 5,

then, subject to sub-paragraph (2), all the persons falling within that class are entitled to receive notice under paragraph 5.

7   (1) An attorney is not required to give notice under paragraph 5—

    (a) to himself, or

    (b) to any other attorney under the power who is joining in making the application,

even though he or, as the case may be, the other attorney is entitled to receive notice by virtue of paragraph 6.

(2) In the case of any person who is entitled to receive notice by virtue of paragraph 6, the attorney, before applying for registration, may make an application to the court to be dispensed from the requirement to give him notice; and the court must grant the application if it is satisfied—

    (a) that it would be undesirable or impracticable for the attorney to give him notice, or

    (b) that no useful purpose is likely to be served by giving him notice.

Duty to give notice to donor

8   (1) Subject to sub-paragraph (2), before making an application for registration the attorney must give notice of his intention to do so to the donor.

(2) Paragraph 7(2) applies in relation to the donor as it applies in relation to a person who is entitled to receive notice under paragraph 5.

Contents of notices

9   A notice to relatives under this Part of this Schedule must—

(a) be in the prescribed form,

(b) state that the attorney proposes to make an application to the Public Guardian for the registration of the instrument creating the enduring power in question,

(c) inform the person to whom it is given of his right to object to the registration under paragraph 13(4), and

(d) specify, as the grounds on which an objection to registration may be made, the grounds set out in paragraph 13(9).

10 A notice to the donor under this Part of this Schedule—

(a) must be in the prescribed form,

(b) must contain the statement mentioned in paragraph 9(b), and

(c) must inform the donor that, while the instrument remains registered, any revocation of the power by him will be ineffective unless and until the revocation is confirmed by the court.

Duty to give notice to other attorneys

11 (1) Subject to sub-paragraph (2), before making an application for registration an attorney under a joint and several power must give notice of his intention to do so to any other attorney under the power who is not joining in making the application; and paragraphs 7(2) and 9 apply in relation to attorneys entitled to receive notice by virtue of this paragraph as they apply in relation to persons entitled to receive notice by virtue of paragraph 6.

(2) An attorney is not entitled to receive notice by virtue of this paragraph if—

(a) his address is not known to the applying attorney and cannot reasonably be ascertained by him, or

(b) the applying attorney has reason to believe that he has not reached 18 or is mentally incapable.

Supplementary

12 Despite section 7 of the Interpretation Act 1978 (c. 30) (construction of references to service by post), for the purposes of this Part of this Schedule a notice given by post is to be regarded as given on the date on which it was posted.

PART 4
REGISTRATION

Registration of instrument creating power

13 (1) If an application is made in accordance with paragraph 4(3) and (4) the Public Guardian must, subject to the provisions of this paragraph, register the instrument to which the application relates.

(2) If it appears to the Public Guardian that—

(a) there is a deputy appointed for the donor of the power created by the instrument, and

(b) the powers conferred on the deputy would, if the instrument were registered, to any extent conflict with the powers conferred on the attorney,

the Public Guardian must not register the instrument except in accordance with the court's directions.

(3) The court may, on the application of the attorney, direct the Public Guardian to register an instrument even though notice has not been given as required by paragraph 4(3) and Part 3 of this Schedule to a person entitled to receive it, if the court is satisfied—

    (a) that it was undesirable or impracticable for the attorney to give notice to that person, or

    (b) that no useful purpose is likely to be served by giving him notice.

(4) Sub-paragraph (5) applies if, before the end of the period of 5 weeks beginning with the date (or the latest date) on which the attorney gave notice under paragraph 5 of an application for registration, the Public Guardian receives a valid notice of objection to the registration from a person entitled to notice of the application.

(5) The Public Guardian must not register the instrument except in accordance with the court's directions.

(6) Sub-paragraph (7) applies if, in the case of an application for registration—

    (a) it appears from the application that there is no one to whom notice has been given under paragraph 5, or

    (b) the Public Guardian has reason to believe that appropriate inquiries might bring to light evidence on which he could be satisfied that one of the grounds of objection set out in sub-paragraph (9) was established.

(7) The Public Guardian—

    (a) must not register the instrument, and

    (b) must undertake such inquiries as he thinks appropriate in all the circumstances.

(8) If, having complied with sub-paragraph (7)(b), the Public Guardian is satisfied that one of the grounds of objection set out in sub-paragraph (9) is established—

    (a) the attorney may apply to the court for directions, and

    (b) the Public Guardian must not register the instrument except in accordance with the court's directions.

(9) A notice of objection under this paragraph is valid if made on one or more of the following grounds—

    (a) that the power purported to have been created by the instrument was not valid as an enduring power of attorney,

    (b) that the power created by the instrument no longer subsists,

    (c) that the application is premature because the donor is not yet becoming mentally incapable,

    (d) that fraud or undue pressure was used to induce the donor to create the power,

    (e) that, having regard to all the circumstances and in particular the attorney's relationship to or connection with the donor, the attorney is unsuitable to be the donor's attorney.

(10) If any of those grounds is established to the satisfaction of the court it must direct the Public Guardian not to register the instrument, but if not so satisfied it must direct its registration.

(11) If the court directs the Public Guardian not to register an instrument because it is satisfied that the ground in sub-paragraph (9)(d) or (e) is established, it must by order revoke the power created by the instrument.

(12) If the court directs the Public Guardian not to register an instrument because it is satisfied that any ground in sub-paragraph (9) except that in paragraph (c) is established, the instrument must be delivered up to be cancelled unless the court otherwise directs.

Register of enduring powers

14 The Public Guardian has the function of establishing and maintaining a register of enduring powers for the purposes of this Schedule.

PART 5
LEGAL POSITION AFTER REGISTRATION

Effect and proof of registration

15 (1) The effect of the registration of an instrument under paragraph 13 is that—
       (a) no revocation of the power by the donor is valid unless and until the court confirms the revocation under paragraph 16(3);
       (b) no disclaimer of the power is valid unless and until the attorney gives notice of it to the Public Guardian;
       (c) the donor may not extend or restrict the scope of the authority conferred by the instrument and no instruction or consent given by him after registration, in the case of a consent, confers any right and, in the case of an instruction, imposes or confers any obligation or right on or creates any liability of the attorney or other persons having notice of the instruction or consent.
     (2) Sub-paragraph (1) applies for so long as the instrument is registered under paragraph 13 whether or not the donor is for the time being mentally incapable.
     (3) A document purporting to be an office copy of an instrument registered under this Schedule is, in any part of the United Kingdom, evidence of—
       (a) the contents of the instrument, and
       (b) the fact that it has been so registered.
     (4) Sub-paragraph (3) is without prejudice to section 3 of the Powers of Attorney Act 1971 (c. 27) (proof by certified copies) and to any other method of proof authorised by law.

Functions of court with regard to registered power

16 (1) Where an instrument has been registered under paragraph 13, the court has the following functions with respect to the power and the donor of and the attorney appointed to act under the power.
     (2) The court may—
       (a) determine any question as to the meaning or effect of the instrument;
       (b) give directions with respect to—
          (i) the management or disposal by the attorney of the property and affairs of the donor;
          (ii) the rendering of accounts by the attorney and the production of the records kept by him for the purpose;

      (iii) the remuneration or expenses of the attorney whether or not in default of or in accordance with any provision made by the instrument, including directions for the repayment of excessive or the payment of additional remuneration;

  (c) require the attorney to supply information or produce documents or things in his possession as attorney;

  (d) give any consent or authorisation to act which the attorney would have to obtain from a mentally capable donor;

  (e) authorise the attorney to act so as to benefit himself or other persons than the donor otherwise than in accordance with paragraph 3(2) and (3) (but subject to any conditions or restrictions contained in the instrument);

  (f) relieve the attorney wholly or partly from any liability which he has or may have incurred on account of a breach of his duties as attorney.

(3) On application made for the purpose by or on behalf of the donor, the court must confirm the revocation of the power if satisfied that the donor—

  (a) has done whatever is necessary in law to effect an express revocation of the power, and

  (b) was mentally capable of revoking a power of attorney when he did so (whether or not he is so when the court considers the application).

(4) The court must direct the Public Guardian to cancel the registration of an instrument registered under paragraph 13 in any of the following circumstances—

  (a) on confirming the revocation of the power under sub-paragraph (3),

  (b) on directing under paragraph 2(9)(b) that the power is to be revoked,

  (c) on being satisfied that the donor is and is likely to remain mentally capable,

  (d) on being satisfied that the power has expired or has been revoked by the mental incapacity of the attorney,

  (e) on being satisfied that the power was not a valid and subsisting enduring power when registration was effected,

  (f) on being satisfied that fraud or undue pressure was used to induce the donor to create the power,

  (g) on being satisfied that, having regard to all the circumstances and in particular the attorney's relationship to or connection with the donor, the attorney is unsuitable to be the donor's attorney.

(5) If the court directs the Public Guardian to cancel the registration of an instrument on being satisfied of the matters specified in sub-paragraph (4)(f) or (g) it must by order revoke the power created by the instrument.

(6) If the court directs the cancellation of the registration of an instrument under sub-paragraph (4) except paragraph (c) the instrument must be delivered up to the Public Guardian to be cancelled, unless the court otherwise directs.

Cancellation of registration by Public Guardian

17 The Public Guardian must cancel the registration of an instrument creating an enduring power of attorney—

  (a) on receipt of a disclaimer signed by the attorney;

(b) if satisfied that the power has been revoked by the death or bankruptcy of the donor or attorney or, if the attorney is a body corporate, by its winding up or dissolution;

(c) on receipt of notification from the court that the court has revoked the power;

(d) on confirmation from the court that the donor has revoked the power.

PART 6
PROTECTION OF ATTORNEY AND THIRD PARTIES

Protection of attorney and third persons where power is invalid or revoked

18 (1) Sub-paragraphs (2) and (3) apply where an instrument which did not create a valid power of attorney has been registered under paragraph 13 (whether or not the registration has been cancelled at the time of the act or transaction in question).

(2) An attorney who acts in pursuance of the power does not incur any liability (either to the donor or to any other person) because of the non-existence of the power unless at the time of acting he knows—

(a) that the instrument did not create a valid enduring power,

(b) that an event has occurred which, if the instrument had created a valid enduring power, would have had the effect of revoking the power, or

(c) that, if the instrument had created a valid enduring power, the power would have expired before that time.

(3) Any transaction between the attorney and another person is, in favour of that person, as valid as if the power had then been in existence, unless at the time of the transaction that person has knowledge of any of the matters mentioned in sub-paragraph (2).

(4) If the interest of a purchaser depends on whether a transaction between the attorney and another person was valid by virtue of sub-paragraph (3), it is conclusively presumed in favour of the purchaser that the transaction was valid if—

(a) the transaction between that person and the attorney was completed within 12 months of the date on which the instrument was registered, or

(b) that person makes a statutory declaration, before or within 3 months after the completion of the purchase, that he had no reason at the time of the transaction to doubt that the attorney had authority to dispose of the property which was the subject of the transaction.

(5) For the purposes of section 5 of the Powers of Attorney Act 1971 (c. 27) (protection where power is revoked) in its application to an enduring power the revocation of which by the donor is by virtue of paragraph 15 invalid unless and until confirmed by the court under paragraph 16—

(a) knowledge of the confirmation of the revocation is knowledge of the revocation of the power, but

(b) knowledge of the unconfirmed revocation is not.

Further protection of attorney and third persons

19 (1) If—

159

(a) an instrument framed in a form prescribed as mentioned in paragraph 2(2) creates a power which is not a valid enduring power, and

(b) the power is revoked by the mental incapacity of the donor,

sub-paragraphs (2) and (3) apply, whether or not the instrument has been registered.

(2) An attorney who acts in pursuance of the power does not, by reason of the revocation, incur any liability (either to the donor or to any other person) unless at the time of acting he knows—

(a) that the instrument did not create a valid enduring power, and

(b) that the donor has become mentally incapable.

(3) Any transaction between the attorney and another person is, in favour of that person, as valid as if the power had then been in existence, unless at the time of the transaction that person knows—

(a) that the instrument did not create a valid enduring power, and

(b) that the donor has become mentally incapable.

(4) Paragraph 18(4) applies for the purpose of determining whether a transaction was valid by virtue of sub-paragraph (3) as it applies for the purpose or deter-mining whether a transaction was valid by virtue of paragraph 18(3).

PART 7
JOINT AND JOINT AND SEVERAL ATTORNEYS

Application to joint and joint and several attorneys

20 (1) An instrument which appoints more than one person to be an attorney cannot create an enduring power unless the attorneys are appointed to act—

(a) jointly, or

(b) jointly and severally.

(2) This Schedule, in its application to joint attorneys, applies to them collectively as it applies to a single attorney but subject to the modifications specified in paragraph 21.

(3) This Schedule, in its application to joint and several attorneys, applies with the modifications specified in sub-paragraphs (4) to (7) and in paragraph 22.

(4) A failure, as respects any one attorney, to comply with the requirements for the creation of enduring powers—

(a) prevents the instrument from creating such a power in his case, but

(b) does not affect its efficacy for that purpose as respects the other or others or its efficacy in his case for the purpose of creating a power of attorney which is not an enduring power.

(5) If one or more but not both or all the attorneys makes or joins in making an application for registration of the instrument—

(a) an attorney who is not an applicant as well as one who is may act pending the registration of the instrument as provided in paragraph 1(2),

(b) notice of the application must also be given under Part 3 of this Schedule to the other attorney or attorneys, and

(c) objection may validly be taken to the registration on a ground relating to an attorney or to the power of an attorney who is not an applicant as well as to one or the power of one who is an applicant.

(6) The Public Guardian is not precluded by paragraph 13(5) or (8) from registering an instrument and the court must not direct him not to do so under paragraph 13(10) if an enduring power subsists as respects some attorney who is not affected by the ground or grounds of the objection in question; and where the Public Guardian registers an instrument in that case, he must make against the registration an entry in the prescribed form.

(7) Sub-paragraph (6) does not preclude the court from revoking a power in so far as it confers a power on any other attorney in respect of whom the ground in paragraph 13(9)(d) or (e) is established; and where any ground in paragraph 13(9) affecting any other attorney is established the court must direct the Public Guardian to make against the registration an entry in the prescribed form.

(8) In sub-paragraph (4), 'the requirements for the creation of enduring powers' means the provisions of—

    (a) paragraph 2 other than sub-paragraphs (8) and (9), and

    (b) the regulations mentioned in paragraph 2.

Joint attorneys

21 (1) In paragraph 2(5), the reference to the time when the attorney executes the instrument is to be read as a reference to the time when the second or last attorney executes the instrument.

    (2) In paragraph 2(6) to (8), the reference to the attorney is to be read as a reference to any attorney under the power.

    (3) Paragraph 13 has effect as if the ground of objection to the registration of the instrument specified in sub-paragraph (9)(e) applied to any attorney under the power.

    (4) In paragraph 16(2), references to the attorney are to be read as including references to any attorney under the power.

    (5) In paragraph 16(4), references to the attorney are to be read as including references to any attorney under the power.

    (6) In paragraph 17, references to the attorney are to be read as including references to any attorney under the power.

Joint and several attorneys

22 (1) In paragraph 2(7), the reference to the bankruptcy of the attorney is to be read as a reference to the bankruptcy of the last remaining attorney under the power; and the bankruptcy of any other attorney under the power causes that person to cease to be an attorney under the power.

    (2) In paragraph 2(8), the reference to the suspension of the power is to be read as a reference to its suspension in so far as it relates to the attorney in respect of whom the interim bankruptcy restrictions order has effect.

    (3) The restriction upon disclaimer imposed by paragraph 4(6) applies only to those attorneys who have reason to believe that the donor is or is becoming mentally incapable.

PART 8
INTERPRETATION

23 (1) In this Schedule—

'enduring power' is to be construed in accordance with paragraph 2,
'mentally incapable' or 'mental incapacity', except where it refers to revocation at common law, means in relation to any person, that he is incapable by reason of mental disorder (within the meaning of the Mental Health Act) of managing and administering his property and affairs and 'mentally capable' and 'mental capacity' are to be construed accordingly,
'notice' means notice in writing, and
'prescribed', except for the purposes of paragraph 2, means prescribed by regulations made for the purposes of this Schedule by the Lord Chancellor.

(2) Any question arising under or for the purposes of this Schedule as to what the donor of the power might at any time be expected to do is to be determined by assuming that he had full mental capacity at the time but otherwise by reference to the circumstances existing at that time.

Section 66(4)   SCHEDULE 5

TRANSITIONAL PROVISIONS AND SAVINGS

PART 1
REPEAL OF PART 7 OF THE MENTAL HEALTH ACT 1983

Existing receivers

1 (1) This paragraph applies where, immediately before the commencement day, there is a receiver ('R') for a person ('P') appointed under section 99 of the Mental Health Act.

(2) On and after that day—
    (a) this Act applies as if R were a deputy appointed for P by the court, but with the functions that R had as receiver immediately before that day, and
    (b) a reference in any other enactment to a deputy appointed by the court includes a person appointed as a deputy as a result of paragraph (a).

(3) On any application to it by R, the court may end R's appointment as P's deputy.

(4) Where, as a result of section 20(1), R may not make a decision on behalf of P in relation to a relevant matter, R must apply to the court.

(5) If, on the application, the court is satisfied that P is capable of managing his property and affairs in relation to the relevant matter—
    (a) it must make an order ending R's appointment as P's deputy in relation to that matter, but
    (b) it may, in relation to any other matter, exercise in relation to P any of the powers which it has under sections 15 to 19.

(6) If it is not satisfied, the court may exercise in relation to P any of the powers which it has under sections 15 to 19.

(7) R's appointment as P's deputy ceases to have effect if P dies.

(8) 'Relevant matter' means a matter in relation to which, immediately before the commencement day, R was authorised to act as P's receiver.

(9) In sub-paragraph (1), the reference to a receiver appointed under section 99 of the Mental Health Act includes a reference to a person who by virtue of Schedule 5 to that Act was deemed to be a receiver appointed under that section.

Orders, appointments etc.

2 (1) Any order or appointment made, direction or authority given or other thing done which has, or by virtue of Schedule 5 to the Mental Health Act was deemed to have, effect under Part 7 of the Act immediately before the commencement day is to continue to have effect despite the repeal of Part 7.

(2) In so far as any such order, appointment, direction, authority or thing could have been made, given or done under sections 15 to 20 if those sections had then been in force—
  (a) it is to be treated as made, given or done under those sections, and
  (b) the powers of variation and discharge conferred by section 16(7) apply accordingly.

(3) Sub-paragraph (1)—
  (a) does not apply to nominations under section 93(1) or (4) of the Mental Health Act, and
  (b) as respects receivers, has effect subject to paragraph 1.

(4) This Act does not affect the operation of section 109 of the Mental Health Act (effect and proof of orders etc.) in relation to orders made and directions given under Part 7 of that Act.

(5) This paragraph is without prejudice to section 16 of the Interpretation Act 1978 (c. 30) (general savings on repeal).

Pending proceedings

3 (1) Any application for the exercise of a power under Part 7 of the Mental Health Act which is pending immediately before the commencement day is to be treated, in so far as a corresponding power is exercisable under sections 16 to 20, as an application for the exercise of that power.

(2) For the purposes of sub-paragraph (1) an application for the appointment of a receiver is to be treated as an application for the appointment of a deputy.

Appeals

4 (1) Part 7 of the Mental Health Act and the rules made under it are to continue to apply to any appeal brought by virtue of section 105 of that Act which has not been determined before the commencement day.

(2) If in the case of an appeal brought by virtue of section 105(1) (appeal to nominated judge) the judge nominated under section 93 of the Mental Health Act has begun to hear the appeal, he is to continue to do so but otherwise it is to be heard by a puisne judge of the High Court nominated under section 46.

Fees

5 All fees and other payments which, having become due, have not been paid to the former Court of Protection before the commencement day, are to be paid to the new Court of Protection.

Court records

6 (1) The records of the former Court of Protection are to be treated, on and after the commencement day, as records of the new Court of Protection and are to be dealt with accordingly under the Public Records Act 1958 (c. 51).

(2) On and after the commencement day, the Public Guardian is, for the purpose of exercising any of his functions, to be given such access as he may require to such of the records mentioned in sub-paragraph (1) as relate to the appointment of receivers under section 99 of the Mental Health Act.

Existing charges

7 This Act does not affect the operation in relation to a charge created before the commencement day of—

(a) so much of section 101(6) of the Mental Health Act as precludes a charge created under section 101(5) from conferring a right of sale or foreclosure during the lifetime of the patient, or

(b) section 106(6) of the Mental Health Act (charge created by virtue of section 106(5) not to cause interest to fail etc.).

Preservation of interests on disposal of property

8 Paragraph 8(1) of Schedule 2 applies in relation to any disposal of property (within the meaning of that provision) by a person living on 1st November 1960, being a disposal effected under the Lunacy Act 1890 (c. 5) as it applies in relation to the disposal of property effected under sections 16 to 20.

Accounts

9 Court of Protection Rules may provide that, in a case where paragraph 1 applies, R is to have a duty to render accounts—

(a) while he is receiver;

(b) after he is discharged.

Interpretation

10 In this Part of this Schedule—

(a) 'the commencement day' means the day on which section 66(1)(a) (repeal of Part 7 of the Mental Health Act) comes into force,

(b) 'the former Court of Protection' means the office abolished by section 45, and

(c) 'the new Court of Protection' means the court established by that section.

PART 2
REPEAL OF THE ENDURING POWERS OF ATTORNEY ACT 1985

Orders, determinations, etc.

11 (1) Any order or determination made, or other thing done, under the 1985 Act which has effect immediately before the commencement day continues to have effect despite the repeal of that Act.

(2) In so far as any such order, determination or thing could have been made or done under Schedule 4 if it had then been in force—

(a) it is to be treated as made or done under that Schedule, and

(b) the powers of variation and discharge exercisable by the court apply accordingly.

(3) Any instrument registered under the 1985 Act is to be treated as having been registered by the Public Guardian under Schedule 4.

(4) This paragraph is without prejudice to section 16 of the Interpretation Act 1978 (c. 30) (general savings on repeal).

Pending proceedings

12 (1) An application for the exercise of a power under the 1985 Act which is pending immediately before the commencement day is to be treated, in so far as a corresponding power is exercisable under Schedule 4, as an application for the exercise of that power.

(2) For the purposes of sub-paragraph (1)—

(a) a pending application under section 4(2) of the 1985 Act for the registration of an instrument is to be treated as an application to the Public Guardian under paragraph 4 of Schedule 4 and any notice given in connection with that application under Schedule 1 to the 1985 Act is to be treated as given under Part 3 of Schedule 4,

(b) a notice of objection to the registration of an instrument is to be treated as a notice of objection under paragraph 13 of Schedule 4, and

(c) pending proceedings under section 5 of the 1985 Act are to be treated as proceedings on an application for the exercise by the court of a power which would become exercisable in relation to an instrument under paragraph 16(2) of Schedule 4 on its registration.

Appeals

13 (1) The 1985 Act and, so far as relevant, the provisions of Part 7 of the Mental Health Act and the rules made under it as applied by section 10 of the 1985 Act are to continue to have effect in relation to any appeal brought by virtue of section 10(1)(c) of the 1985 Act which has not been determined before the commencement day.

(2) If, in the case of an appeal brought by virtue of section 105(1) of the Mental Health Act as applied by section 10(1)(c) of the 1985 Act (appeal to nominated judge), the judge nominated under section 93 of the Mental Health Act has begun to hear the appeal, he is to continue to do so but otherwise the appeal is to be heard by a puisne judge of the High Court nominated under section 46.

Exercise of powers of donor as trustee

14 (1) Section 2(8) of the 1985 Act (which prevents a power of attorney under section 25 of the Trustee Act 1925 (c. 19) as enacted from being an enduring power) is to continue to apply to any enduring power—

(a) created before 1st March 2000, and

(b) having effect immediately before the commencement day.

(2) Section 3(3) of the 1985 Act (which entitles the donee of an enduring power to exercise the donor's powers as trustee) is to continue to apply to any enduring power to which, as a result of the provision mentioned in sub-paragraph (3), it applies immediately before the commencement day.

(3) The provision is section 4(3)(a) of the Trustee Delegation Act 1999 (c. 15) (which provides for section 3(3) of the 1985 Act to cease to apply to an enduring power when its registration is cancelled, if it was registered in response to an application made before 1st March 2001).

(4) Even though section 4 of the 1999 Act is repealed by this Act, that section is to continue to apply in relation to an enduring power—

(a) to which section 3(3) of the 1985 Act applies as a result of sub-paragraph (2), or

(b) to which, immediately before the repeal of section 4 of the 1999 Act, section 1 of that Act applies as a result of section 4 of it.

(5) The reference in section 1(9) of the 1999 Act to section 4(6) of that Act is to be read with sub-paragraphs (2) to (4).

Interpretation

15 In this Part of this Schedule, 'the commencement day' means the day on which section 66(1)(b) (repeal of the 1985 Act) comes into force.

Section 67(1)   SCHEDULE 6

MINOR AND CONSEQUENTIAL AMENDMENTS

Fines and Recoveries Act 1833 (c. 74)

1 (1) The Fines and Recoveries Act 1833 (c. 74) is amended as follows.

(2) In section 33 (case where protector of settlement lacks capacity to act), for the words from 'shall be incapable' to 'is incapable as aforesaid' substitute 'lacks capacity (within the meaning of the Mental Capacity Act 2005) to manage his property and affairs, the Court of Protection is to take his place as protector of the settlement while he lacks capacity'.

(3) In sections 48 and 49 (mental health jurisdiction), for each reference to the judge having jurisdiction under Part 7 of the Mental Health Act substitute a reference to the Court of Protection.

Improvement of Land Act 1864 (c. 114)

2 In section 68 of the Improvement of Land Act 1864 (c. 114) (apportionment of rentcharges)—

166

(a) for, 'curator, or receiver of' substitute 'or curator of, or a deputy with powers in relation to property and affairs appointed by the Court of Protection for,', and

(b) for 'or patient within the meaning of Part VII of the Mental Health Act 1983' substitute 'person who lacks capacity (within the meaning of the Mental Capacity Act 2005) to receive the notice'.

Trustee Act 1925 (c. 19)

3   (1) The Trustee Act 1925 (c. 19) is amended as follows.

(2) In section 36 (appointment of new trustee)—

(a) in subsection (6C), for the words from 'a power of attorney' to the end, substitute 'an enduring power of attorney or lasting power of attorney registered under the Mental Capacity Act 2005', and

(b) in subsection (9)—

(i) for the words from 'is incapable' to 'exercising' substitute 'lacks capacity to exercise', and

(ii) for the words from 'the authority' to the end substitute 'the Court of Protection'.

(3) In section 41(1) (power of court to appoint new trustee) for the words from 'is incapable' to 'exercising' substitute 'lacks capacity to exercise'.

(4) In section 54 (mental health jurisdiction)—

(a) for subsection (1) substitute—

'(1) Subject to subsection (2), the Court of Protection may not make an order, or give a direction or authority, in relation to a person who lacks capacity to exercise his functions as trustee, if the High Court may make an order to that effect under this Act.',

(b) in subsection (2)—

(i) for the words from the beginning to 'of a receiver' substitute 'Where a person lacks capacity to exercise his functions as a trustee and a deputy is appointed for him by the Court of Protection or an application for the appointment of a deputy',

(ii) for 'the said authority', in each place, substitute 'the Court of Protection', and

(iii) for 'the patient', in each place, substitute 'the person concerned', and

(c) omit subsection (3).

(5) In section 55 (order made on particular allegation to be conclusive evidence of it)—

(a) for the words from 'Part VII' to 'Northern Ireland' substitute 'sections 15 to 20 of the Mental Capacity Act 2005 or any corresponding provisions having effect in Northern Ireland', and

(b) for paragraph (a) substitute—

'(a) that a trustee or mortgagee lacks capacity in relation to the matter in question;'.

(6) In section 68 (definitions), at the end add—

'(3) Any reference in this Act to a person who lacks capacity in relation to a matter is to a person—

      (a) who lacks capacity within the meaning of the Mental Capacity Act 2005 in relation to that matter, or

      (b) in respect of whom the powers conferred by section 48 of that Act are exercisable and have been exercised in relation to that matter.'.

Law of Property Act 1925 (c. 20)

4   (1) The Law of Property Act 1925 (c. 20) is amended as follows.

    (2) In section 22 (conveyances on behalf of persons who lack capacity)—

      (a) in subsection (1)—

         (i) for the words from 'in a person suffering' to 'is acting' substitute, 'either solely or jointly with any other person or persons, in a person lacking capacity (within the meaning of the Mental Capacity Act 2005) to convey or create a legal estate, a deputy appointed for him by the Court of Protection or (if no deputy is appointed', and

         (ii) for 'the authority having jurisdiction under Part VII of the Mental Health Act 1983' substitute 'the Court of Protection',

      (b) in subsection (2), for 'is incapable, by reason of mental disorder, of exercising' substitute 'lacks capacity (within the meaning of that Act) to exercise', and

      (c) in subsection (3), for the words from 'an enduring power' to the end substitute 'an enduring power of attorney or lasting power of attorney (within the meaning of the 2005 Act) is entitled to act for the trustee who lacks capacity in relation to the dealing.'.

    (3) In section 205(1) (interpretation), omit paragraph (xiii).

Administration of Estates Act 1925 (c. 23)

5   (1) The Administration of Estates Act 1925 (c. 23) is amended as follows.

    (2) In section 41(1) (powers of personal representatives to appropriate), in the proviso—

      (a) in paragraph (ii)—

         (i) for the words from 'is incapable' to 'the consent' substitute 'lacks capacity (within the meaning of the Mental Capacity Act 2005) to give the consent, it', and

         (ii) for 'or receiver' substitute 'or a person appointed as deputy for him by the Court of Protection', and

      (b) in paragraph (iv), for 'no receiver is acting for a person suffering from mental disorder' substitute 'no deputy is appointed for a person who lacks capacity to consent'.

    (3) Omit section 55(1)(viii) (definitions of 'person of unsound mind' and 'defective').

National Assistance Act 1948 (c. 29)

6   In section 49 of the National Assistance Act 1948 (c. 29) (expenses of council officers acting for persons who lack capacity)—

    (a) for the words from 'applies' to 'affairs of a patient' substitute 'applies for appointment by the Court of Protection as a deputy', and

    (b) for 'such functions' substitute 'his functions as deputy'.

U.S.A. Veterans' Pensions (Administration) Act 1949 (c. 45)

7 In section 1 of the U.S.A. Veterans' Pensions (Administration) Act 1949 (c. 45) (administration of pensions)—
(a) in subsection (4), omit the words from 'or for whom' to '1983', and
(b) after subsection (4), insert—
'(4A) An agreement under subsection (1) is not to be made in relation to a person who lacks capacity (within the meaning of the Mental Capacity Act 2005) for the purposes of this Act if—
(a) there is a donee of an enduring power of attorney or lasting power of attorney (within the meaning of the 2005 Act), or a deputy appointed for the person by the Court of Protection, and
(b) the donee or deputy has power in relation to the person for the purposes of this Act.
(4B) The proviso at the end of subsection (4) also applies in relation to subsection (4A).'.

Intestates' Estates Act 1952 (c. 64)

8 In Schedule 2 to the Intestates' Estates Act 1952 (c. 64) (rights of surviving spouse or civil partner in relation to home), for paragraph 6(1) substitute—
'(1) Where the surviving spouse or civil partner lacks capacity (within the meaning of the Mental Capacity Act 2005) to make a requirement or give a consent under this Schedule, the requirement or consent may be made or given by a deputy appointed by the Court of Protection with power in that respect or, if no deputy has that power, by that court'.

Variation of Trusts Act 1958 (c. 53)

9 In section 1 of the Variation of Trusts Act 1958 (c. 53) (jurisdiction of courts to vary trusts)—
(a) in subsection (3), for the words from 'shall be determined' to the end substitute 'who lacks capacity (within the meaning of the Mental Capacity Act 2005) to give his assent is to be determined by the Court of Protection', and
(b) in subsection (6), for the words from 'the powers' to the end substitute 'the powers of the Court of Protection'.

Administration of Justice Act 1960 (c. 65)

10 In section 12(1)(b) of the Administration of Justice Act 1960 (c. 65) (contempt of court to publish information about proceedings in private relating to persons with incapacity) for the words from 'under Part VIII' to 'that Act' substitute 'under the Mental Capacity Act 2005, or under any provision of the Mental Health Act 1983'.

Industrial and Provident Societies Act 1965 (c. 12)

11 In section 26 of the Industrial and Provident Societies Act 1965 (c. 12) (payments for mentally incapable people), for subsection (2) substitute—

'(2) Subsection (1) does not apply where the member or person concerned lacks capacity (within the meaning of the Mental Capacity Act 2005) for the purposes of this Act and—

    (a) there is a donee of an enduring power of attorney or lasting power of attorney (within the meaning of the 2005 Act), or a deputy appointed for the member or person by the Court of Protection, and

    (b) the donee or deputy has power in relation to the member or person for the purposes of this Act.'.

Compulsory Purchase Act 1965 (c. 56)

12 In Schedule 1 to the Compulsory Purchase Act 1965 (c. 56) (persons without power to sell their interests), for paragraph 1(2)(b) substitute—

'(b) do not have effect in relation to a person who lacks capacity (within the meaning of the Mental Capacity Act 2005) for the purposes of this Act if—

    (i) there is a donee of an enduring power of attorney or lasting power of attorney (within the meaning of the 2005 Act), or a deputy appointed for the person by the Court of Protection, and

    (ii) the donee or deputy has power in relation to the person for the purposes of this Act.'.

Leasehold Reform Act 1967 (c. 88)

13 (1) For section 26(2) of the Leasehold Reform Act 1967 (c. 88) (landlord lacking capacity) substitute—

'(2) Where a landlord lacks capacity (within the meaning of the Mental Capacity Act 2005) to exercise his functions as a landlord, those functions are to be exercised—

    (a) by a donee of an enduring power of attorney or lasting power of attorney (within the meaning of the 2005 Act), or a deputy appointed for him by the Court of Protection, with power to exercise those functions, or

    (b) if no donee or deputy has that power, by a person authorised in that respect by that court.'.

  (2) That amendment does not affect any proceedings pending at the commencement of this paragraph in which a receiver or a person authorised under Part 7 of the Mental Health Act is acting on behalf of the landlord.

Medicines Act 1968 (c. 67)

14 In section 72 of the Medicines Act 1968 (c. 67) (pharmacist lacking capacity)—

    (a) in subsection (1)(c), for the words from 'a receiver' to '1959' substitute 'he becomes a person who lacks capacity (within the meaning of the Mental Capacity Act 2005) to carry on the business',

    (b) after subsection (1) insert—

'(1A) In subsection (1)(c), the reference to a person who lacks capacity to carry on the business is to a person—

    (a) in respect of whom there is a donee of an enduring power of attorney or lasting power of attorney (within the meaning of the Mental Capacity Act 2005), or

(b) for whom a deputy is appointed by the Court of Protection,
and in relation to whom the donee or deputy has power for the purposes of this Act.',
    (c) in subsection (3)(d)—
        (i) for 'receiver' substitute 'deputy', and
        (ii) after 'guardian' insert 'or from the date of registration of the instrument appointing the donee', and
    (d) in subsection (4)(c), for 'receiver' substitute 'donee, deputy'.

Family Law Reform Act 1969 (c. 46)

15 For section 21(4) of the Family Law Reform Act 1969 (c. 46) (consent required for taking of bodily sample from person lacking capacity), substitute—
'(4) A bodily sample may be taken from a person who lacks capacity (within the meaning of the Mental Capacity Act 2005) to give his consent, if consent is given by the court giving the direction under section 20 or by—
    (a) a donee of an enduring power of attorney or lasting power of attorney (within the meaning of that Act), or
    (b) a deputy appointed, or any other person authorised, by the Court of Protection,
with power in that respect.'.

Local Authority Social Services Act 1970 (c. 42)

16 (1) Schedule 1 to the Local Authority Social Services Act 1970 (c. 42) (enactments conferring functions assigned to social services committee) is amended as follows.
    (2) In the entry for section 49 of the National Assistance Act 1948 (expenses of local authority officer appointed for person who lacks capacity) for 'receiver' substitute 'deputy'.
    (3) At the end, insert—

'Mental Capacity Act 2005

Section 39	Instructing independent mental capacity advocate before providing accommodation for person lacking capacity.
Section 49	Reports in proceedings.'

Courts Act 1971 (c. 23)

17 In Part 1A of Schedule 2 to the Courts Act 1971 (c. 23) (office-holders eligible for appointment as circuit judges), omit the reference to a Master of the Court of Protection.

Local Government Act 1972 (c. 70)

18 (1) Omit section 118 of the Local Government Act 1972 (c. 70) (payment of pension etc. where recipient lacks capacity).

(2) Sub-paragraph (3) applies where, before the commencement of this paragraph, a local authority has, in respect of a person referred to in that section as 'the patient', made payments under that section—

(a) to an institution or person having the care of the patient, or

(b) in accordance with subsection (1)(a) or (b) of that section.

(3) The local authority may, in respect of the patient, continue to make payments under that section to that institution or person, or in accordance with subsection (1)(a) or (b) of that section, despite the repeal made by sub-paragraph (1).

Matrimonial Causes Act 1973 (c. 18)

19 In section 40 of the Matrimonial Causes Act 1973 (c. 18) (payments to person who lacks capacity) (which becomes subsection (1))—

(a) for the words from 'is incapable' to 'affairs' substitute '("P") lacks capacity (within the meaning of the Mental Capacity Act 2005) in relation to the provisions of the order',

(b) for 'that person under Part VIII of that Act' substitute 'P under that Act',

(c) for the words from 'such persons' to the end substitute 'such person ("D") as it may direct', and

(d) at the end insert—

'(2) In carrying out any functions of his in relation to an order made under subsection (1), D must act in P's best interests (within the meaning of that Act).'.

Juries Act 1974 (c. 23)

20 In Schedule 1 to the Juries Act 1974 (c. 23) (disqualification for jury service), for paragraph 3 substitute—

'3 A person who lacks capacity, within the meaning of the Mental Capacity Act 2005, to serve as a juror.'.

Consumer Credit Act 1974 (c. 39)

21 For section 37(1)(c) of the Consumer Credit Act 1974 (c. 39) (termination of consumer credit licence if holder lacks capacity) substitute—

'(c) becomes a person who lacks capacity (within the meaning of the Mental Capacity Act 2005) to carry on the activities covered by the licence.'.

Solicitors Act 1974 (c. 47)

22 (1) The Solicitors Act 1974 (c. 47) is amended as follows.

(2) For section 12(1)(j) (application for practising certificate by solicitor lacking capacity) substitute—

'(j) while he lacks capacity (within the meaning of the Mental Capacity Act 2005) to act as a solicitor and powers under sections 15 to 20 or section 48 of that Act are exercisable in relation to him;'.

(3) In section 62(4) (contentious business agreements made by clients) for paragraphs (c) and (d) substitute—

'(c) as a deputy for him appointed by the Court of Protection with powers in relation to his property and affairs, or

(d) as another person authorised under that Act to act on his behalf.'.

(4) In paragraph 1(1) of Schedule 1 (circumstances in which Law Society may intervene in solicitor's practice), for paragraph (f) substitute—

'(f) a solicitor lacks capacity (within the meaning of the Mental Capacity Act 2005) to act as a solicitor and powers under sections 15 to 20 or section 48 of that Act are exercisable in relation to him;'.

Local Government (Miscellaneous Provisions) Act 1976 (c. 57)

23 In section 31 of the Local Government (Miscellaneous Provisions) Act 1976 (c. 57) (the title to which becomes 'Indemnities for local authority officers appointed as deputies or administrators'), for the words from 'as a receiver' to '1959' substitute 'as a deputy for a person by the Court of Protection'.

Sale of Goods Act 1979 (c. 54)

24 In section 3(2) of the Sale of Goods Act 1979 (c. 54) (capacity to buy and sell) the words 'mental incapacity or' cease to have effect in England and Wales.

Limitation Act 1980 (c. 58)

25 In section 38 of the Limitation Act 1980 (c. 58) (interpretation) substitute—

(a) in subsection (2) for 'of unsound mind' substitute 'lacks capacity (within the meaning of the Mental Capacity Act 2005) to conduct legal proceedings', and

(b) omit subsections (3) and (4).

Public Passenger Vehicles Act 1981 (c. 14)

26 In section 57(2)(c) of the Public Passenger Vehicles Act 1981 (c. 14) (termination of public service vehicle licence if holder lacks capacity) for the words from 'becomes a patient' to 'or' substitute 'becomes a person who lacks capacity (within the meaning of the Mental Capacity Act 2005) to use a vehicle under the licence, or'.

Judicial Pensions Act 1981 (c. 20)

27 In Schedule 1 to the Judicial Pensions Act 1981 (c. 20) (pensions of Supreme Court officers, etc.), in paragraph 1, omit the reference to a Master of the Court of Protection except in the case of a person holding that office immediately before the commencement of this paragraph or who had previously retired from that office or died.

Supreme Court Act 1981 (c. 54)

28 In Schedule 2 to the Supreme Court Act 1981 (c. 54) (qualifications for appointment to office in Supreme Court), omit paragraph 11 (Master of the Court of Protection).

Mental Health Act 1983 (c. 20)

29 (1) The Mental Health Act is amended as follows.

(2) In section 134(3) (cases where correspondence of detained patients may not be withheld) for paragraph (b) substitute—

'(b) any judge or officer of the Court of Protection, any of the Court of Protection Visitors or any person asked by that Court for a report under section 49 of the Mental Capacity Act 2005 concerning the patient;'.

(3) In section 139 (protection for acts done in pursuance of 1983 Act), in subsection (1), omit from 'or in, or in pursuance' to 'Part VII of this Act,'.

(4) Section 142 (payment of pension etc. where recipient lacks capacity) ceases to have effect in England and Wales.

(5) Sub-paragraph (6) applies where, before the commencement of sub-paragraph (4), an authority has, in respect of a person referred to in that section as 'the patient', made payments under that section—

(a) to an institution or person having the care of the patient, or

(b) in accordance with subsection (2)(a) or (b) of that section.

(6) The authority may, in respect of the patient, continue to make payments under that section to that institution or person, or in accordance with subsection (2)(a) or (b) of that section, despite the amendment made by sub-paragraph (4).

(7) In section 145(1) (interpretation), in the definition of 'patient', omit '(except in Part VII of this Act)'.

(8) In section 146 (provisions having effect in Scotland), omit from '104(4)' to 'section),'.

(9) In section 147 (provisions having effect in Northern Ireland), omit from '104(4)' to 'section),'.

Administration of Justice Act 1985 (c. 61)

30   In section 18(3) of the Administration of Justice Act 1985 (c. 61) (licensed conveyancer who lacks capacity), for the words from 'that person' to the end substitute 'he becomes a person who lacks capacity (within the meaning of the Mental Capacity Act 2005) to practise as a licensed conveyancer.'.

Insolvency Act 1986 (c. 45)

31   (1) The Insolvency Act 1986 (c. 45) is amended as follows.

(2) In section 389A (people not authorised to act as nominee or supervisor in voluntary arrangement), in subsection (3)—

(a) omit the 'or' immediately after paragraph (b),

(b) in paragraph (c), omit 'Part VII of the Mental Health Act 1983 or', and

(c) after that paragraph, insert', or

(d) he lacks capacity (within the meaning of the Mental Capacity Act 2005) to act as nominee or supervisor'.

(3) In section 390 (people not qualified to be insolvency practitioners), in subsection (4)—

(a) omit the 'or' immediately after paragraph (b),

(b) in paragraph (c), omit 'Part VII of the Mental Health Act 1983 or', and

(c) after that paragraph, insert', or

(d) he lacks capacity (within the meaning of the Mental Capacity Act 2005) to act as an insolvency practitioner.'.

Building Societies Act 1986 (c. 53)

32 In section 102D(9) of the Building Societies Act 1986 (c. 53) (references to a person holding an account on trust for another)—
   (a) in paragraph (a), for 'Part VII of the Mental Health Act 1983' substitute 'the Mental Capacity Act 2005', and
   (b) for paragraph (b) substitute—
      '(b) to an attorney holding an account for another person under—
         (i) an enduring power of attorney or lasting power of attorney registered under the Mental Capacity Act 2005, or
         (ii) an enduring power registered under the Enduring Powers of Attorney (Northern Ireland) Order 1987;'.

Public Trustee and Administration of Funds Act 1986 (c. 57)

33 In section 3 of the Public Trustee and Administration of Funds Act 1986 (c. 57) (functions of the Public Trustee)—
   (a) for subsections (1) to (5) substitute—
      '(1) The Public Trustee may exercise the functions of a deputy appointed by the Court of Protection.',
   (b) in subsection (6), for 'the 1906 Act' substitute 'the Public Trustee Act 1906', and
   (c) omit subsection (7).

Patronage (Benefices) Measure 1986 (No.3)

34 (1) The Patronage (Benefices) Measure 1986 (No. 3) is amended as follows.
   (2) In section 5 (rights of patronage exercisable otherwise than by registered patron), after subsection (3) insert—
      '(3A) The reference in subsection (3) to a power of attorney does not include an enduring power of attorney or lasting power of attorney (within the meaning of the Mental Capacity Act 2005).'
   (3) In section 9 (information to be sent to designated officer when benefice becomes vacant), after subsection (5) insert—
      '(5A) Subsections (5B) and (5C) apply where the functions of a registered patron are, as a result of paragraph 10 of Schedule 2 to the Mental Capacity Act 2005 (patron's loss of capacity to discharge functions), to be discharged by an individual appointed by the Court of Protection.
      (5B) If the individual is a clerk in Holy Orders, subsection (5) applies to him as it applies to the registered patron.
      (5C) If the individual is not a clerk in Holy Orders, subsection (1) (other than paragraph (b)) applies to him as it applies to the registered patron.'

Courts and Legal Services Act 1990 (c. 41)

35 (1) The Courts and Legal Services Act 1990 (c. 41) is amended as follows.
   (2) In Schedule 11 (judges etc. barred from legal practice), for the reference to a Master of the Court of Protection substitute a reference to each of the following—

    (a) Senior Judge of the Court of Protection,
    (b) President of the Court of Protection,
    (c) Vice-President of the Court of Protection.
(3) In paragraph 5(3) of Schedule 14 (exercise of powers of intervention in registered foreign lawyer's practice), for paragraph (f) substitute—
    '(f) he lacks capacity (within the meaning of the Mental Capacity Act 2005) to act as a registered foreign lawyer and powers under sections 15 to 20 or section 48 are exercisable in relation to him;'.

Child Support Act 1991 (c. 48)

36 In section 50 of the Child Support Act 1991 (c. 48) (unauthorised disclosure of information)—
    (a) in subsection (8)—
        (i) immediately after paragraph (a), insert 'or',
        (ii) omit paragraphs (b) and (d) and the 'or' immediately after paragraph (c), and
        (iii) for ', receiver, custodian or appointee' substitute 'or custodian', and
    (b) after that subsection, insert—
    '(9) Where the person to whom the information relates lacks capacity (within the meaning of the Mental Capacity Act 2005) to consent to its disclosure, the appropriate person is—
        (a) a donee of an enduring power of attorney or lasting power of attorney (within the meaning of that Act), or
        (b) a deputy appointed for him, or any other person authorised, by the Court of Protection,
with power in that respect.'.

Social Security Administration Act 1992 (c. 5)

37 In section 123 of the Social Security Administration Act 1992 (c. 5) (unauthorised disclosure of information)—
    (a) in subsection (10), omit—
        (i) in paragraph (b), 'a receiver appointed under section 99 of the Mental Health Act 1983 or',
        (ii) in paragraph (d)(i), 'sub-paragraph (a) of rule 41(1) of the Court of Protection Rules 1984 or',
        (iii) in paragraph (d)(ii), 'a receiver ad interim appointed under sub-paragraph (b) of the said rule 41(1) or', and
        (iv) 'receiver,', and
    (b) after that subsection, insert—
    '(11) Where the person to whom the information relates lacks capacity (within the meaning of the Mental Capacity Act 2005) to consent to its disclosure, the appropriate person is—
        (a) a donee of an enduring power of attorney or lasting power of attorney (within the meaning of that Act), or
        (b) a deputy appointed for him, or any other person authorised, by the Court of Protection,
with power in that respect.'.

Judicial Pensions and Retirement Act 1993 (c. 8)

38 (1) The Judicial Pensions and Retirement Act 1993 (c. 8) is amended as follows.

(2) In Schedule 1 (qualifying judicial offices), in Part 2, under the cross-heading 'Court officers', omit the reference to a Master of the Court of Protection except in the case of a person holding that office immediately before the commencement of this sub-paragraph or who had previously retired from that office or died.

(3) In Schedule 5 (retirement: the relevant offices), omit the entries relating to the Master and Deputy or temporary Master of the Court of Protection, except in the case of a person holding any of those offices immediately before the commencement of this sub-paragraph.

(4) In Schedule 7 (retirement: transitional provisions), omit paragraph 5(5)(i)(g) except in the case of a person holding office as a deputy or temporary Master of the Court of Protection immediately before the commencement of this sub-paragraph.

Leasehold Reform, Housing and Urban Development Act 1993 (c. 28)

39 (1) For paragraph 4 of Schedule 2 to the Leasehold Reform, Housing and Urban Development Act 1993 (c. 28) (landlord under a disability), substitute—

'4 (1) This paragraph applies where a Chapter I or Chapter II landlord lacks capacity (within the meaning of the Mental Capacity Act 2005) to exercise his functions as a landlord.

(2) For the purposes of the Chapter concerned, the landlord's place is to be taken—

(a) by a donee of an enduring power of attorney or lasting power of attorney (within the meaning of the 2005 Act), or a deputy appointed for him by the Court of Protection, with power to exercise those functions, or

(b) if no deputy or donee has that power, by a person authorised in that respect by that court.'.

(2) That amendment does not affect any proceedings pending at the commencement of this paragraph in which a receiver or a person authorised under Part 7 of the Mental Health Act 1983 (c. 20) is acting on behalf of the landlord.

Goods Vehicles (Licensing of Operators) Act 1995 (c. 23)

40 (1) The Goods Vehicles (Licensing of Operators) Act 1995 (c. 23) is amended as follows.

(2) In section 16(5) (termination of licence), for 'he becomes a patient within the meaning of Part VII of the Mental Health Act 1983' substitute 'he becomes a person who lacks capacity (within the meaning of the Mental Capacity Act 2005) to use a vehicle under the licence'.

(3) In section 48 (licence not to be transferable, etc.)—

(a) in subsection (2)—

(i) for 'or become a patient within the meaning of Part VII of the Mental Health Act 1983' substitute, 'or become a person who lacks capacity (within the meaning of the Mental Capacity Act 2005) to use a vehicle under the licence,', and

(ii) in paragraph (a), for 'became a patient' substitute 'became a person who lacked capacity in that respect', and

(b) in subsection (5), for 'a patient within the meaning of Part VII of the Mental Health Act 1983' substitute 'a person lacking capacity'.

Disability Discrimination Act 1995 (c. 50)

41 In section 20(7) of the Disability Discrimination Act 1995 (c. 50) (regulations to disapply provisions about incapacity), in paragraph (b), for 'Part VII of the Mental Health Act 1983' substitute 'the Mental Capacity Act 2005'.

Trusts of Land and Appointment of Trustees Act 1996 (c. 47)

42 (1) The Trusts of Land and Appointment of Trustees Act 1996 (c. 47) is amended as follows.

(2) In section 9 (delegation by trustees), in subsection (6), for the words from 'an enduring power' to the end substitute 'an enduring power of attorney or lasting power of attorney within the meaning of the Mental Capacity Act 2005'.

(3) In section 20 (the title to which becomes 'Appointment of substitute for trustee who lacks capacity')—

(a) in subsection (1)(a), for 'is incapable by reason of mental disorder of exercising' substitute 'lacks capacity (within the meaning of the Mental Capacity Act 2005) to exercise', and

(b) in subsection (2)—

(i) for paragraph (a) substitute—

'(a) a deputy appointed for the trustee by the Court of Protection,',

(ii) in paragraph (b), for the words from 'a power of attorney' to the end substitute 'an enduring power of attorney or lasting power of attorney registered under the Mental Capacity Act 2005', and

(iii) in paragraph (c), for the words from 'the authority' to the end substitute 'the Court of Protection'.

Human Rights Act 1998 (c. 42)

43 In section 4(5) of the Human Rights Act 1998 (c. 42) (courts which may make declarations of incompatibility), after paragraph (e) insert—

'(f) the Court of Protection, in any matter being dealt with by the President of the Family Division, the Vice-Chancellor or a puisne judge of the High Court.'

Access to Justice Act 1999 (c. 22)

44 In paragraph 1 of Schedule 2 to the Access to Justice Act 1999 (c. 22) (services excluded from the Community Legal Service), after paragraph (e) insert—

'(ea) the creation of lasting powers of attorney under the Mental Capacity Act 2005, (eb) the making of advance decisions under that Act,'.

Adoption and Children Act 2002 (c. 38)

45   In section 52(1)(a) of the Adoption and Children Act 2002 (c. 38) (parental consent to adoption), for 'is incapable of giving consent' substitute 'lacks capacity (within the meaning of the Mental Capacity Act 2005) to give consent'.

Licensing Act 2003 (c. 17)

46   (1)   The Licensing Act 2003 (c.17) is amended as follows.
      (2)   In section 27(1) (lapse of premises licence), for paragraph (b) substitute—
            '(b) becomes a person who lacks capacity (within the meaning of the Mental Capacity Act 2005) to hold the licence,'.
      (3)   In section 47 (interim authority notice in relation to premises licence)—
            (a) in subsection (5), for paragraph (b) substitute—
                 '(b) the former holder lacks capacity (within the meaning of the Mental Capacity Act 2005) to hold the licence and that person acts for him under an enduring power of attorney or lasting power of attorney registered under that Act,', and
            (b) in subsection (10), omit the definition of 'mentally incapable'.

Courts Act 2003 (c. 39)

47   (1)   The Courts Act 2003 (c. 39) is amended as follows.
      (2)   In section 1(1) (the courts in relation to which the Lord Chancellor must discharge his general duty), after paragraph (a) insert—
            '(aa) the Court of Protection,'.
      (3)   In section 64(2) (judicial titles which the Lord Chancellor may by order alter)—
            (a) omit the reference to a Master of the Court of Protection, and
            (b) at the appropriate place insert a reference to each of the following—
                 (i)   Senior Judge of the Court of Protection,
                 (ii) President of the Court of Protection,
                 (iii) Vice-president of the Court of Protection.

Section 67(2)   SCHEDULE 7

                                          REPEALS

Short title and chapter	Extent of repeal
Trustee Act 1925 (c. 19)	Section 54(3).
Law of Property Act 1925 (c. 20)	Section 205(1)(xiii).
Administration of Estates Act 1925 (c. 23)	Section 55(1)(viii)
U.S.A. Veterans' Pensions (Administration) Act 1949 (c. 45)	In section 1(4), the words from 'or for whom' to '1983'.
Mental Health Act 1959 (c. 72)	In Schedule 7, in Part 1, the entries relating to— section 33 of the Fines and Recoveries Act 1833, section 68 of the Improvement of Land Act 1864,

179

Short title and chapter	Extent of repeal
	section 55 of the Trustee Act 1925, section 205(1) of the Law of Property Act 1925, section 49 of the National Assistance Act 1948, and section 1 of the Variation of Trusts Act 1958.
Courts Act 1971 (c. 23)	In Schedule 2, in Part 1A, the words 'Master of the Court of Protection'.
Local Government Act 1972 (c. 70)	Section 118.
Limitation Act 1980 (c. 58)	Section 38(3) and (4).
Supreme Court Act 1981 (c. 54)	In Schedule 2, in Part 2, paragraph 11.
Mental Health Act 1983 (c. 20)	Part 7. In section 139(1) the words from 'or in, or in pursuance' to 'Part VII of this Act,'. In section 145(1), in the definition of 'patient' the words '(except in Part VII of this Act)'. In sections 146 and 147 the words from '104(4)' to 'section),'. Schedule 3. In Schedule 4, paragraphs 1, 2, 4, 5, 7, 9, 14, 20, 22, 25, 32, 38, 55 and 56. In Schedule 5, paragraphs 26, 43, 44 and 45.
Enduring Powers of Attorney Act 1985 (c. 29)	The whole Act.
Insolvency Act 1986 (c. 45)	In section 389A(3)— the 'or' immediately after paragraph (b), and in paragraph (c), the words 'Part VII of the Mental Health Act 1983 or'. In section 390(4)— the 'or' immediately after paragraph (b), and in paragraph (c), the words 'Part VII of the Mental Health Act 1983 or'.
Public Trustee and Administration of Funds Act 1986 (c. 57)	Section 2. Section 3(7).
Child Support Act 1991 (c. 48)	In section 50(8)— paragraphs (b) and (d), and the 'or' immediately after paragraph (c).
Social Security Administration Act 1992 (c. 5)	In section 123(10)— in paragraph (b), 'a receiver appointed under section 99 of the Mental Health Act 1983 or', in paragraph (d)(i), 'sub-paragraph (a) of rule 41(1) of the Court of Protection Rules Act 1984 or', in paragraph (d)(ii), 'a receiver ad interim appointed under sub-paragraph (b) of the said rule 41(1) or', and 'receiver,'.
Trustee Delegation Act 1999 (c. 15)	Section 4. Section 6. In section 7(3), the words 'in accordance with section 4 above'.

Short title and chapter	*Extent of repeal*
Care Standards Act 2000 (c. 14)	In Schedule 4, paragraph 8.
Licensing Act 2003 (c. 17)	In section 47(10), the definition of 'mentally incapable'.
Courts Act 2003 (c. 64)	In section 64(2), the words 'Master of the Court of Protection'.

Index

References are to Paragraph Numbers
References to the Appendix are in Italics